European Perspectives on Attrition in Sexual Offenses

European Perspectives on Attrition in Sexual Offenses

Edited by Rahime Erbaş

Foreword by Davor Derenčinović

LEXINGTON BOOKS
Lanham • Boulder • New York • London

Published by Lexington Books
An imprint of The Rowman & Littlefield Publishing Group, Inc.
4501 Forbes Boulevard, Suite 200, Lanham, Maryland 20706
www.rowman.com

86-90 Paul Street, London EC2A 4NE

British Library Cataloguing in Publication Information Available

Library of Congress Cataloging-in-Publication Data

Names: Erbaş, Rahime, editor.
Title: European perspectives on attrition in sexual offenses / [edited by] Rahime Erbaş.
Description: Lanham : Lexington Books, [2023] | Includes bibliographical references and index.
Identifiers: LCCN 2023021147 (print) | LCCN 2023021148 (ebook) | ISBN 9781666925135 (cloth) | ISBN 9781666925142 (ebook)
Subjects: LCSH: Sex crimes—European Union.
Classification: LCC HV6593.E85 .E856 2023 (print) | LCC HV6593.E85 (ebook) | DDC 362.883094—dc23/eng/20230621
LC record available at https://lccn.loc.gov/2023021147
LC ebook record available at https://lccn.loc.gov/2023021148

Contents

Cases

Anayasa Mahkemesi, Application of B.A., App no. 2016/9123, Date: 18.05.2021

Bundestagsdrucksache (Parliament Papers of the German Bundestag) of 4 October 1962 – IV/650.

Bundestagsdrucksache (Parliament Papers of the German Bundestag) VI/3521.

Bundestagsdrucksache (Parliament Papers of the German Bundestag) of 2 July 2014 – 18/1969.

Bundestagsdrucksache (Parliament Papers of the German Bundestag) of 6 July 2016 – 18/9097.

B.V. v Belgium App no 61030/08 (ECtHR, 2 May 2017)

Cassazione penale, Sez. III, 04/07/2000, n. 7772

Cassazione penale, Sez. III 11/11/1996, Rotella

Cassazione penale, Sez. III, 26/08/2016, n. 35473

Cassazione penale, Sez. III, 19/11/2019, n.2201

Cassazione penale, Sez. III, 29/05/2018, n.43553

Cassazione penale, Sez. III, 08/10/2019, n.1570

Cassazione penale, Sez. III, (ud. 19/11/2015), dep. 05/5/2016, n.18679

Cassazione penale, Sez. III, 14/04/1999, n.1636

Cassazione penale, Sez. III, 21/07/2008 n.30403

Corte Costituzionale, judgment of 11 January 2021, no. 1

DJ v Croatia App no 42418/10 (ECtHR, 24 July 2012)

I.G. v the Republic of Moldova App no 53519/07 (ECtHR, 15 May 2012)

I.P. v the Republic of Moldova App no 33708/12 (ECtHR, 28 April 2015)

Italian Criminal Court of Cassation, sec. II, judgment of 7 February 2004, no. 37395

Italian Criminal Court of Cassation, sec. I, judgment of 7 February 2008, no. 6072

Italian Criminal Court of Cassation, sec. III, judgment of 7 July 2008, no. 27469

Italian Criminal Court of Cassation, sec. VI, judgment of 20 January 2009, no. 9531

Italian Criminal Court of Cassation, sec. VI, judgment of 13 February 2009, no. 6490

Italian Criminal Court of Cassation, sec. V, judgment of 31 July 2009, no. 31758

Italian Criminal Court of Cassation, sec. III, judgment of 14 December 2011, no. 12464

Italian Criminal Court of Cassation, sec. III, judgment of 23 May 2013, no. 29725

Italian Criminal Court of Cassation, sec. II, judgment of 16 January 2014, no. 5768

Italian Criminal Court of Cassation, sec. III, judgment of 30 September 2014, no. 6168

Italian Criminal Court of Cassation, sec. III, judgment of 28 October 2014, no. 21020

Italian Criminal Court of Cassation, sec. III, judgment 18 September 2015, no. 40366

Italian Criminal Court of Cassation, sec. VI, judgment of 13 November 2015, no. 5258

Italian Criminal Court of Cassation, sec. III, judgment of 4 March 2017, no. 16543

Italian Criminal Court of Cassation, sec. III, judgment of 4 October 2017, no. 45589

Italian Criminal Court of Cassation, sec. I, judgment of 1 March 2018, no. 9427

Italian Criminal Court of Cassation, sec. V, judgment of 3 January 2018, no. 104

Italian Criminal Court of Cassation, sec. I, judgment of 14 March 2018, no. 11604

Italian Criminal Court of Cassation, sec. III, judgment of 2 July 2018, no. 29613

Italian Criminal Court of Cassation, sec. IV, judgment of 8 October 2018, no. 44890

Italian Criminal Court of Cassation, sec. V, judgment of 28 January 2019 no. 3989

Italian Criminal Court of Cassation, sec. VI, judgment of 9 May 2019, no. 19922

Italian Criminal Court of Cassation, sec. VI, judgment of 2 July 2019, no. 6126

Italian Criminal Court of Cassation, sec. VI, judgment of 22 July 2019, no. 32781

Italian Criminal Court of Cassation, sec. III, judgment of 21 August 2019, no. 36307

Italian Criminal Court of Cassation, sec. III, judgment of 29 August 2019, no. 36636

Italian Criminal Court of Cassation, sec. III, judgment of 13 September 2019, no. 38014

Italian Criminal Court of Cassation, sec. III, judgment of 18 September 2019, no. 38606

Italian Criminal Court of Cassation, sec. III, judgment of 15 October 2019, no. 42118

Italian Criminal Court of Cassation, sec. V, judgment of 6 November 2019, no. 45141

Italian Criminal Court of Cassation, sec. III, judgment of 17 December 2019, no. 12628

Italian Criminal Court of Cassation, judgment of 6 February 2020, no. 5092

Italian Criminal Court of Cassation, sec. III, judgment of 24 March 2020, no. 10596

Italian Criminal Court of Cassation, sec. V, judgment of 29 April 2020, no. 13273

Italian Criminal Court of Cassation, sec. III, judgment of 31 July 2020, no. 23419

Italian Criminal Court of Cassation, sez. III, judgment of 8 September 2020, no. 25266

Italian Criminal Court of Cassation, Un. Sec., judgment of 1 October 2020, no. 27326

Italian Criminal Court of Cassation, sec. III, judgment of 6 December 2020, no. 19987

Italian Criminal Court of Cassation, sec. III, judgment of 14 December 2020, no. 35700

Italian Criminal Court of Cassation, sec. V, judgment of 21 January 2021, no. 2496

Italian Criminal Court of Cassation, sec. III, judgment of 4 March 2021, no. 19611

Italian Criminal Court of Cassation, sec. III, judgment of 26 March 2021, no. 11631

Italian Criminal Court of Cassation, sez. III, ord. judgment of 22 April 2021, no. 25334

Italian Criminal Court of Cassation, Un. Sec., prel. hear., judgment of 15 July 2021

Italian Criminal Court of Cassation, sec. III, judgment of 19 November 2021, no. 1559

J.L. v Italy App no 5671/16 (ECtHR, 27 May 2021)

M. and Others v Italy and Bulgaria App no 40020/03 (ECtHR, 31 July 2012)

M.A. v Slovenia and N.D. v Slovenia App no *16605/09 (*ECtHR, *15 January 2015)*

M. C. v Bulgaria, App no 39272/98 (ECtHR, 4 December 2003)

Maslova and Nalbandov v Russia App no 839/02 (ECtHR, 24 January 2008)

NA v Moldova App no 13424/06 (ECtHR, 24 September 2013)

Norway (Supreme Court), Rt. 1974 s. 1121,

R. v Steele, [2021] ONCA 186

R. v Steele, [2019] ONSC 3207

R. v Ewanchuk, [1999] 1 S.C.R. 330

S.Z. v Bulgaria App no 29263/12 (ECtHR, 3 March 2015)

SAP de Navarra, Sección 2ª, núm. 38/2018, de 20 de marzo (Roj: 86/2018)

Smith v Lees 1997 JC 73

STS, Sala de lo Penal, Sección 1ª, núm. núm. 344/2019, de 4 de julio (Roj: 2200/2019)

STSJ de Navarra, Sala de lo Civil y Penal, núm. 7/2018, de 30 de noviembre (Roj: 473/2018)

Sweden (Supreme Court), NJA 1975 s. 594
Sweden (Supreme Court), NJA 1977 s. 630
Sweden (Supreme Court), NJA 1985 s.757
Sweden (Supreme Court), NJA 1990 s. 210
Sweden (Supreme Court), NJA 1996 s. 509
Sweden (Supreme Court), NJA 2004 s. 176
Sweden (Supreme Court), NJA 2008 s. 482 I and II
Sweden (Supreme Court), NJA 2015 s. 501
Sweden (Supreme Court), NJA 2019 s. 668
Sweden (Supreme Court), NJA 2021 s. 536
Sweden (Supreme Court), NJA 2022 s. 237
Tribunal Busto Arsizio, 26 January 2022
United Kingdom, R v R [1991] 3 WLR 767
W v Slovenia App no 24125/06 (ECtHR, 23 January 2014)
X and Y v the Netherlands App no 8978/80 (ECtHR, 26 March 1985)
Y v Bulgaria App no 41990/18 (ECtHR, 20 February 2020)
Y v Slovenia App no 41107/10) (ECtHR, 28 May 2015)
Yargıtay, CGK, Date: 29.06.2021, E. 2020/14-93, K. 2021/319
Yargıtay, CGK, Date: 01.06.2021, E. 2019/38, K. 2021/233
Yargıtay, CGK, Date: 30.3.2021.E. 2020/14-185, K. 2021/149
Yargıtay, CGK, Date: 23.03.2021, E. 2019/14-637, K. 2021/139
Yargıtay, CGK, Date: 01.12.2020, E. 2020/14-218, K. 2020/496
Yargıtay, CGK, Date: 23.06.2020, E. 2019/14-357, K. 2020/313
Yargıtay, CGK, Date: 22.11.2018, E. 2017/394, K. 2018/555
Yargıtay, CGK, Date: 30.06.2015, E. 2014/810, K. 2015/268
Yargıtay, CGK, Date: 19.11.2013, E. 2013/14-326, K. 2013/461
Yargıtay, CGK, Date: 26.5.2009, E. 2008/5-187, K. 2009/128
Yargıtay, CGK, Date: 25.03.2003, E. 2002/5-324, K. 2003/55
Yargıtay, 14. CD., Date: 13.04.2021, E. 2020/3852, K. 2021/2924
Yargıtay, 14. CD., Date: 25.3.2021, E. 2019/5092, K. 2021/2392
Yargıtay, 14. CD., Date: 02.06.2020, E. 2019/3764, K. 2020/2381
Yargıtay, 14. CD., Date: 14.01.2020, E. 2019/4645, K. 2020/381
Yargıtay, 14. CD., Date: 21.03.2016, E. 2016/2371, K. 2016/2708

Yargıtay, 14. CD., Date: 17.11.2014, E. 2014/7697, K. 2014/12784

Yargıtay, 14. CD., Date: 23.06.2014, E. 2012/8212, K. 2014/8562

Yargıtay, 14. CD., Date: 20.06.2012, E. 2012/6645, K. 2012/7000

Yargıtay, 12. CD., Date: 21.11.2018, E. 2018/1722, K. 2018/9484

Yargıtay, 9. CD., Date: 11.11.2021, E. 2021/1435, K. 2021/9173

Yargıtay, 9. CD., Date: 29.03.2021, E. 2021/3657, K. 2021/10428

Yargıtay, 2. CD., Date: 25.02.2013, E. 2012/16734, K. 2013/3690

65 0 K 189121 12 K, Verdict (Municipality Court of Sarajevo, dated from October 13, 2013)

65 0 K 128387 10 K, Verdict (Municipality Court of Sarajevo, dated from 08.07.2010)

65 0 Km 430959 14 Km Verdict (Municipality Court of Sarajevo, dated from 04/12/2014)

T04 0 KT 0047277 21, Indictment (Prosecutorial Office of Zenica, dated from 04/01/2022)

Legislation

Abusive Behaviour and Sexual Harm (Scotland) Act 2016

Act 316/1994 on Amendment to the Criminal Code of Finland ch 20

Act 723/2022 on Amendment to the Criminal Code of Finland

Bill C-127 (1983), An Act to Amend the Criminal Code in Relation to Sexual Offences and Other Offences Against the Person

Canadian Criminal Code (R.S.C.) 1985, c. C-46

CEDAW/C/82/D/148/2019, 18 July 2022

Code of Criminal Procedure Decreto del Presidente della Repubblica 22 settembre 1988, n. 447

Code of Criminal Procedure Regio Decreto 19 ottobre 1930, n. 1399

Contempt of Court Act 1981

Council Decision of 11 May 2017 (2017/865/EU)

Council Decision of 11 May 2017 (2017/866/EU)

Council of Europe Convention on preventing and combating violence against women and domestic violence (CETS No. 210), Istanbul, 11 May 2011

Criminal Code of Bosnia and Herzegovina [3/03, 32/03, 37/03, 54/04, 61/04, 30/05, 53/06, 55/06, 32/07, 8/10] 74

Criminal Code of Brčko District BH [6/05, 21/10, 9/13, 26/16, 13/17, 50/18, 19/20]

Criminal Code of Federation of Bosnia and Herzegovina [36/2003, 21/2004-corr.69/2004, 18/2005, 42/2010, 42/2011, 59/2014, 76/2014, 46/2016, 75/2017]

Criminal Code of Finland 39/1889

Criminal Code of Republika Srpska [64/2017, 104/2018, 15/21, 89/21]

Code of Republika Srpska on the Special Registry of Convicted Persons for Sexual Abuse and Exploitation of Children [31/18]

Criminal Justice Act 1988

Criminal Justice and Public Order Act 1994

Criminal Procedure (Scotland) Act 1995

D.P.R. no. 115 of 30 May 2022

Danish Penal Code of 15 April 1930

Dayton Peace Agreement, Annex IV - Constitution of Bosnia and Herzegovina 1995

Decreto Legislativo 28 Luglio 1989, n. 271

Directive 2011/92/UE of 13 December 2011

Directive 2011/93/UE of 13 December 2011

Directive 2012/29/UE of 25 October 2012

Draft law S. 2530, 3 December 2021

Draft law S. 2005, 27 April 2022

European Commission, Proposal for a Directive COM/2022/105 (final) of the Parliament and of the Council on combating violence against women and domestic violence now goes further in the same direction (SWD (2022) 62 final), Strasbourg, 8 March 2022

European Parliament Resolution, 16 September 2021

German Civil Code (BGB)

German Criminal Code (StGB)

Icelandic Penal Code 19/1940

Juries Act 1974

Law no. 4 of 11 January 2018

Law no. 7 of 1 September 2006

Law no. 38 of 6 February 2006

Law no. 38 of 23 April 2009

Law no. 53 of 5 May 2022

Law no. 66 of 15 February 1996

Law no. 69 of 19 July 2019

Law no. 75 of 20 February 1958

Law no. 77 of 27 June 2013

Law no. 119 of 15 October 2013

Law no. 154 of 5 April 2001

Law no. 172 of 1 October 2012

Law no. 205 of 25 June 1993

Law no. 238 of 23 December 2021

Law no. 269 of 3 August 1998

Law no. 654 of 13 October 1975

Legge 15 febbraio 1996, n. 66 Norme contro la violenza sessuale. (GU Serie Generale n.42 del 20-02-1996)

Legislative Decree no. 21 of 1 March 2018

Legislative Decree no. 39 of 4 March 2014

Legislative Decree no. 212 of 15 December 2015

Legislative Decree no. 286 of 1998

Ley Orgánica no. 1 of 28 December 2004

Ley Orgánica no. 10 of 6 September 2022

Megan's Law, California Megan's Law

Organic Law 10/1995, of November 23, of the Criminal Code (BOE num. 281, 24 November 1995)

Organic Law 10/2022, of September 6, on the comprehensive guarantee of sexual freedom (BOE num. 215, 7 September 2022)

Sexual Offences Act 2003

Sexual Offences (Northern Ireland) Order 2008

Sexual Offences (Scotland) Act 2009

Spanish Constitution (BOE num. 311, 29 December 1978)

Swedish Criminal Code (1962:700)

Presidential Decree no. 115 of 30 May 2002

R.D. no 1398 of 19 October 1930

The Hague Principles on Sexual Violence

Turkish Penal Code of 2005

Turkish Penal Procedure Code of 2005

Foreword

Davor Derenčinović

Sexual offenses refer to any criminal act that involves sexual conduct without the other person's consent or where the other person is unable to give consent. These offenses can vary from sexual assault to rape and may include a wide range of non-consensual sexual activity, including groping unwanted sexual touching, and sexual harassment. Sexual offenses can have severe and long-lasting consequences for the victim, including physical and emotional trauma. Therefore, it is essential to understand that sexual offenses are serious crimes, and everyone has the right to be safe from sexual violence and abuse.

According to data from the United Nations Office on Drugs and Crime (UNODC), globally, one in three women and one in six men have experienced some form of sexual violence in their lifetime. However, sexual crimes are often underreported, meaning the number of incidents may be significantly higher than reported statistics suggest. Furthermore, even when reported by victims or third persons (very seldom), sexual offenses often fall out in the inquiry or investigation stage for various reasons. In this regard, two major phenomena impact the effective investigation, prosecution, and adjudication of sexual offenses.

The first is known in criminology as a dark number (dark figure) of criminality. It refers to the criminal (including sexual) offenses committed but for various reasons not disclosed or not known to the criminal justice system. The other is the phenomenon known as attrition, that is, same as the dark figure, very typical for sexual offenses. Attrition refers to the process by which cases are lost or dropped out of the criminal justice system before reaching an outcome. Both phenomena contribute to the *de facto* filtering between the crime in reality and crime in adjudication, as Daly and Bouhours presented in their article on attrition in five jurisdictions (2010). According to their research covering 15 years period in Australia, Canada, England and Wales, Scotland, and the United States, only 14 percent of sexual violence incidents victims report to the police. Of these, 30 percent proceed to prosecution, 20 percent are adjudicated in court, 12.5 percent are convicted of any sexual offense, and 6.5 percent are convicted of the original offense charged. They found that, in the past 35 years, average conviction rates have declined from 18 percent to 12.5 percent.

Many factors contribute to attrition in sexual offense cases. These include the reluctance of victims to come forward due to fear of retaliation, stigma, and shame. The victims may not report the crime to law enforcement because they fear retaliation, shame, or disbelief. Even when victims report the crime, law enforcement may not investigate the case thoroughly, or prosecutors may not bring charges if they believe there is insufficient evidence. Another factor is the complexity of investigating and prosecuting sexual offenses, which can involve issues such as consent, coercion, and trauma, and systemic barriers within the justice system, such as lack of resources, biased attitudes, and legal and procedural hurdles. Other factors that can contribute to attrition include:

- The use of plea bargaining may result in lesser charges or sentences for the offender.
- The willingness of victims to participate in the criminal justice process.
- The ability of victims to testify effectively in court.

Efforts to address and reduce attrition in sexual offense cases have included:

- Improving police training and resources.
- Increasing victim support services.
- Implementing reforms to legal and procedural processes.

These efforts aim to ensure that victims feel more comfortable reporting sexual offenses and that cases are investigated and prosecuted more effectively, leading to more successful outcomes in the criminal justice system. These efforts also include increasing public awareness and using evidence-based practices to investigate and prosecute cases.

This book edited by an outstanding scholar, assistant professor Dr. Rahime Erbaş from the Istanbul University Faculty of Law significantly contributes to the comparative studies of attrition in sexual offenses covering seven countries—Bosnia and Herzegovina, Germany, Italy, Spain, Sweden, the UK, and Türkiye. The added value of this study is that the authors analyzed various jurisdictions and legal systems. Their research focused on how those systems' distinctive features impact attrition in sexual offenses. In this regard, they touched upon issues like trial by jury vs. trial by professional judges and investigation/adjudication of sexual crimes in inquisitorial and adversarial jurisdictions.

Some contributions in this thought-provoking book referred to the jurisprudence of the European Court of Human Rights in the domain of positive obligations of states. This concept relates to the idea that states are responsible not only to refrain from violating human rights but also for taking active steps to protect and promote them. Positive obligations refer to the duty of states to take proactive measures to ensure the effective enjoyment of human rights by individuals within their jurisdiction. These obligations require states to take measures to prevent human rights violations, investigate and prosecute human rights abuses, and provide remedies for victims of human rights violations.

Positive obligations under the European Convention on Human Rights (ECHR) can be challenging to implement, as they require states to take proactive steps to protect human rights rather than simply refrain from violating them. However, they are vital for ensuring that individuals can fully enjoy their fundamental human rights and freedoms. I believe this book very convincingly reinforces relevant aspects of states' positive obligations concerning sexual crimes and their positive impact to the reduction of attrition rates.

The contribution of this book to the field of criminal justice in general, but mainly to criminal law (substantive and procedural) as well as to criminology in the context of searching for the causes of high attrition in sexual offenses as well as the appropriate remedies, is remarkable. For the style that is friendly even to those potential readers who might not be the experts in the field as well as for the well-founded and verifiable conclusions of the research, I warmheartedly recommend this title to everyone, being scholar or practitioner, who come across the issue that is of common concern in most of the countries.

Strasbourg, March 2023.

Acknowledgments

I would like to express my profound thanks and gratitude to all contributors of the book. Further, I sincerely thank Prof. Dr. Liane Wörner, Prof. Dr. Valentina Bonini, Prof. Dr. Fiona Leverick, Dr. Büşra Demiral Bakırman, Dr. Chara Chioni-Chotouman and Anu Sivaganesan, for giving me constant support and encouragement during this book project. I appreciate the meaningful gift of having such brilliant colleagues.

I do thank you, my family, for your unconditional love and support.

I would also like to thank Becca Beurer, Emilia Rivera, and Samuel Withers for their guidance and precious help.

—Rahime

Introduction

Rahime Erbaş

The attrition phenomenon in sexual offenses lies at the heart of this book. As such, it aims to address the high attrition rate in sexual offenses among a set of European jurisdictions as follows: Bosnia and Herzegovina, Germany, Italy, Spain, Sweden, the UK, and Türkiye. Attritions, a loss of cases, may occur in any stage within the criminal justice system: at the police level, investigation stage by prosecutor or at trial stage, as Jehle elaborated.[1] The edited book demonstrates how the cases attrite through their journey from the scale between commencement to the finalization point of the case within the criminal justice system through the eyes of different jurisdictions in Europe. With that being said, this book focuses on the causes of the attrition problem stemming from both a substantive criminal law and criminal procedure law perspective by underpinning through sets of statistical data from various jurisdictions in Europe.

The common myths on sexual offenses, well known as *rape myths*, are considered one of these main causes of attrition as myths influence the judicial authorities as well as the victims. When the judicial actors are not professionals such as juries or lay judges, the attrition problematic may worsen even if the legal professionals are not immune from being influenced from these myths while delivering the justice. Chapter 1 by Fiona Leverick is a very representative picture of the main ideas and debate on rape myths' influence in criminal justice system through the jury involvement. As such, chapter 1 dismantles the problematic regarding the influence of these myths in terms of the jury decision-making process. The core points in reading the chapter that should be borne in mind is that reaching high conviction rates does not necessarily solve the problem of high attrition rate as long as it is the case on which a conviction is secured where the evidence shows that it is beyond reasonable doubt. After all, as Leverick emphasizes, what the correct conviction rate in sexual offenses is remains an ambiguous question due to many reasons, even bureaucratic ones. Accordingly, Leverick addresses this problem from the three UK jurisdictions; Northern Ireland, Scotland, and England and Wales that represent jurisdictions more close to the adversarial in adversarial- inquisitorial scale. She argues that extensive evidence shows that the jury decision-making process is prejudiced by false beliefs about rape and 'real' rape victims as well as showing that professional judges are not immune from these beliefs. In this regard, she stresses the pressing need to introduce measures. As such, it brings to the forth the reports of three reviews: *The Gillen Review* for Northern Ireland; *the Dorrian Review* for Scotland; *the End-to-End Rape Review* for England and Wales.

What's more remarkable in chapter 1 is that it conveys some proposals as to abolishing or limiting the use of the jury system for sexual cases. In so doing, a particular proposal by the Dorrian Review suggests designing a system from beginning and an idea that professional judges would be the most appropriate decision-makers, *albeit,* she highlights that juries have a centuries-long history among the three UK jurisdictions in penal matters as a way to inject democracy into justice affairs. However, according to Leverick, if the jury system continues to exist in sexual offense cases, some form of educational measures might serve an effective tool in avoiding the influence of rape myths.

Whether a jury, as a concept of randomly composed people without legal education, may be more prone to be influenced from myths inherited in a given society stands as a core debate in dealing with rape myths' influence within the criminal justice system. Regarding this significant point, chapter 2 by Armando Saponaro analyzes the Italian criminal procedure which historically served a source of Roman law and had an explicitly inquisitorial system until 1989. After 1989, Italy radically changed its approach toward an adversarial system in adversarial- inquisitorial scale by adopting a new criminal procedure code. Saponaro displays that Italy has deliberately excluded the jury' role from sexual offenses by considering any possible influence of society through the jury's involvement following the transformation process from inquisitorial to adversarial systems in 1989.

Another core debate in dealing with rape myths is that the attrition rate may vary on whether a jurisdiction is more close to the adversarial or inquisitorial system in adversarial- inquisitorial scale. Saponaro first provides a summary of studies that measure the attrition rate differences between adversarial and inquisitorial systems in Europe and concludes higher attrition rates are observed in adversarial jurisdictions than in inquisitorial ones. Then, he takes the opportunity to compare one jurisdiction- Italy- that has had both inquisitorial and adversarial experience. He notes how strong the principle of mandatory prosecution, which is significant to avoid loss of cases, is constitutionally ensured in Italy; however, the principle is *de facto* softened. Before reaching any conclusion relying upon the jurisdictions system models, he calls on prudency since many factors, including the given jurisdiction's sexual offenses definitions, may cause the loss of cases. Chapter 2 provides fruitful comparisons among European countries as well as the US criminal system on the matter from the adversarial-inquisitorial scale, while analyzing the Italian penal reforms in various years. What is more interesting to note, Saponaro draws an inference that the introduction of the adversarial model in Italy in 1989 has been a factor of decrease in the attrition rate at the trial stage, in contrast with the other adversarial model, for example, the UK, where the attrition at the trial stage is one of the highest rates in Europe for two main reasons: *the absence of the jury* and *the participation of the victim as a plaintiff with full trial powers.* It is, thus, observed that Italian reform in 1989 adopted the adversarial system by measuring the system's consequences in sexual offenses.

This choice made by Italian lawmakers was because rape myths' influence as a factor in attrition rates outside the legal framework, as chapter 3 by Elisa Simó Soler, Miguel Lorente Acosta, and Elena Martínez García brings to light in the example of Spain. They reveal that justice is not simply delivered through the legal frame by considering facts appeared as a reality. However, according to Simó, Lorente, and Martínez, reality does not exist as neutral or a simple description of the events. It is, however, the outcome of considering certain facts under a given meaning relying upon the values, myths and stereotypes that society inherited around these behaviors. Even if the terms rape myths and stereotype are interchangeably used in the literature and Lonsway and Fitzgerald said "rape myths are perhaps best conceptualized as stereotypes,"[2] the chapter considers both together as distorted beliefs inherited in society regarding sexual assault cases in order to comprehend the profound influence of these beliefs in justice for penal matters.

Spanish criminal law, in fact, appears among European jurisdictions that have just recently experienced a radical shift in its law on sexual offenses. In that regard, the centerpiece of chapter 3 is the way of envisaging a new roadmap against stereotyping by analyzing the Spanish Organic Law in 2022, which may serve as an example to generate ideas for other jurisdictions. It demonstrates that this new law determines a set of areas for the eradication of stereotyping. This new law in Spain, from 6 September, 2022, adopted the "only yes is yes" model in determining the consent in sexual assault cases. According to Simó, Lorente, and Martínez, this adaptation represents that this new law has *evident anti-stereotyping background.*

Regarding the contemporary developments in approaching consent in sexual offenses, which has two main models, "yes is yes" or "no means no," German law has been pioneer. That is to say, the German criminal law was the first jurisdiction to question the traditional interpretation of consent element in sexual offenses through a reform among European jurisdictions. On the other hand, the field of sexual offenses has been considered as one of the most controversial areas of German criminal law. Chapter 4 by Lena Gmelin and Hannah Wörner provides a comprehensive and critical analysis on the reform discussions and the current legal framework in German criminal law. Particularly, *Cologne sex attacks*[3] in 2016 and respectively the *#MeToo movement*, played a significant role in bringing this issue before the law maker's attention and a sharp increase in reported sexual offenses occurred in 2016. Gmelin and Wörner consider this development as an increase for the willingness to report; they showed that the conviction rate for sexual offenses is still relatively low in Germany. The authors provide a statistical data on the matter.

The reform movements on sexual offenses in 2016 was carried and as such adopted the so-called "no-means-no" model in determining the consent element of sexual offenses in Germany. Gmelin and Wörner analyze the German criminal law experience after this adaptation. They argue that the overall structure of the amended provisions in the Criminal Code are dogmatically unsuccessful and, *de lege lata*, fail to provide a comprehensive protection for the victim to ensure the sexual self-determination to the fullest extent. That being said, the authors consider this adaptation for an important step toward improved protection of sexual self-determination. Albeit, they call for the reform of sexual offenses toward the transition into a "yes-only-means-yes" model, as the consensus model by arguing that it is better suited to protect sexual self-determination.

In terms of the idea, eradication of rape myths and stereotypes through the adaptation of the "only yes is yes" model, we change to a Nordic lens in chapter 5 where Dennis Martinsson analyzes the Swedish provisions on rape particularly after the reform in 2018, on which the affirmative consent, "(only) yes means yes" model, just as in Spain, and more interestingly the offense of negligent rape, were introduced. He provides profound insights into the *travaux préparatoires* which refers to the documents regarding the judicial and political reasoning of a given legislation in Sweden. Further, Martinsson displays where are the areas of attrition present in the current Swedish provisions on the matter. He considers the legal framework regarding the consent element of sexual offenses as a way of correcting attrition and as such he provides valuable insights into the lessons learned from Sweden as well as referring to the ambiguities in the legal framework.

In chapter 5, Martinsson, indeed, opens a far reaching window toward Nordic countries such as Denmark, Finland, Norway and even Iceland as well as Sweden in terms of both rape legislations and recent reforms movements on sexual offenses. He expresses that attrition in sexual offenses is considered as an area in need for legislative revision in Nordic countries. As such, Iceland in 2018, Denmark in 2021, Finland in 2022, Sweden in 2018 and 2022 amended their law on sexual offenses, and Norway has launched a statutory reform, although no government bill has yet been presented. It is notable that a close and frequent interaction among Nordic countries exists, e.g., the introduction of negligent rape was partially inspired by Norway, as Martinsson remarks. It can, thus, be concluded that chapter 5 serves the very representative picture of Nordic law on sexual offenses.

Our previous book, *Global Problems in Sexual Offenses* (Lexington, 2022), drew attention to that the traditional coercive model that means sexual offenses can be committed only by force and, thus, the resistance of the victim must be sought, has begun to disappear and new models appears in some jurisdictions, such as Germany, Spain and Sweden. Chapters 3, 4, and 5 in this new book dive into details of this jurisdiction.

Attrition, from the perspective of criminal law, is not only caused by issues in criminal procedure, but is primarily linked to how to define sexual offenses, in particular the consent element. Saponaro showed us the criminal procedure aspects of attrition in chapter 2 as mentioned above. Now, Lucia Parlato and Marta Palmisano first dive into the regulatory changes in sexual offenses definitions. Italian law makers distinctly opted for the term "violence," consequently "sexual violence" in the legal framework, deliberately in order to cover all forms of human acts, although the term violence is a criminological term, not normative. This was the choice of Italian law makers as an objective and comprehensive term by virtue of the eradication of the outdated concepts such as "pudicity" or "honor" from the legal definitions during the transformations of sexual offenses from the crimes against public morality to an individual's sexual autonomy. We observe a constant change in legal framework from 1996 to 2022 in various years. This comprehensiveness, according to Parlato and Palmisano, is not free from certain critical points, in particular with aspects of violence against women and domestic violence, as they discuss in a detailed manner.

Considering the ECtHR case-law on prosecution of sexual offenses, i.e., its theoretical roots as positive obligation, Parlato and Palmisano focus on the Italian case-law to bring the actual evolution of the Italian system to light. They emphasize how much important language is used by judicial authorities for the satisfaction of sexual offense victims since they remark offensive language may be used in some judgments, especially in gang rape cases. This is, because, "gender" prejudices and stereotypes are still anchored within the socioeconomic and cultural context of Italy. In so doing, chapter 6 demonstrates the reasons why this type of offense significantly contributes to the dark figure of crime and respectively attrition.

Parlato and Palmisano show us that having comprehensive and well-equipped legislative instruments for a jurisdiction does not suffice to solve the problem of attrition in sexual offenses. Then, the problem is even worsened where no such unified criminal law provision in a jurisdiction exists, as chapter 7 for Bosnia and Herzegovina displays. Ena Kazić-Çakar analyzes three applicable positive Criminal Codes—Bosnia and Herzegovina, Brčko District and Republika Srpska—in the same country. Both similarities and differences on regulating sexual offenses among them are present, which leads to an unharmonized incrimination of sexual offenses. Kazić-Çakar offers critical assessments on the existing regulations as a core impediment to the efficient fight against sexual violence in Bosnia and Herzegovina and provides sets of statistics. As novelty in this jurisdiction, a sex offenders' registry, which is a controversial tool in dealing with sexual offenses, was established. However, apart from the controversies on such registry, the lack of harmonization is notable in the registry, as Kazić-Çakar remarks.

Difficulties in proving sexual offenses are among the main causes of attrition. The lack of evidence or the insufficiency in evidence may lead the sexual offense cases to attrite through the criminal justice system, from police investigation to the pre-trial and from pre-trial to trial stage. This time we seek the causes of high attrition in the application of criminal procedure. Especially, in "he said—she said" situations, where the core question—through its journey from the first instance to the last instance court—is, whether the sexual assault had occurred or not. Chapter 8 by Rahime Erbaş, Neslihan Can, Ahsen Akdemir, and Selen Çakırhan displays the Turkish law approach and solutions on difficulties of proving sexual offenses, particularly in situations where the sole evidence is the statement by the victim. In proving, rape myths come as an unspoken impediment. The chapter offers some recently collected data from judicial statistics, covering the period of the last five years, which shows that the attrition rate in Türkiye is high. In this context, the chapter critiques the traditional approach as seeking the necessity of resistance to prove the consent. Erbaş, Can, Akdemir, and Çakırhan highlight the significance of corroborating the evidence and, as such, provide four main examples applied together by the Turkish case-law.

This edited collection brings together analyses of scholars from criminal law and criminal procedure law across a number of European jurisdictions on the attrition phenomenon in sexual offenses, which is mostly known as criminological phenomenon. This can be considered as the novelty of the book because it acknowledges that the causes of high attrition in sexual offenses have various roots in defining sexual offenses in criminal codes and in investigating and prosecuting within the criminal procedure. That being said, covering a set of key areas, such as rape myths and stereotypes, having two main models, "only yes is yes" or "no means no" in approaching consent in sexual offense, poses difficulties in proving sexual offenses; the "he said—she said" situations. The book critically analyses the attrition phenomenon from criminal and criminal procedure law and, as such, completes the previous book, *Global Problems in Sexual Offenses* (Lexington, 2022) which called for a holistic approach and comprehensive protection for victims of sexual offenses in criminal procedure law.

I hope the readers enjoy the book.

Rahime Erbaş
Istanbul University, Türkiye
March 2023

NOTES

1. Jörg-Martin Jehle, 'Attrition and Conviction Rates of Sexual Offenses in Europe: Definitions and Criminal Justice Responses' (2012) 18 Eur J Crim Policy Res 145, 151.
2. Kimberly A. Lonsway and Louise F. Fitzgerald, 'Rape Myths: In Review' (1994) 18 (1) Psychology of Women Quarterly 133, 134.
3. <https://www.bbc.com/news/world-europe-35250903> accessed March 15, 2023.

1

Addressing the Problem of Rape Myths in Jury Decision-Making

Lessons from the UK Jurisdictions

Fiona Leverick

The[1] difficulties involved in prosecuting rape[2] have reached the agenda of reform bodies and governments worldwide. There are two broad issues: complainer[3] re-traumatization and the low conviction rate. Regarding the first, there is overwhelming evidence that those who engage with the criminal justice system after making an allegation of rape find the experience extremely distressing. Complainers report that they feel abandoned after reporting the offence to the police and that there is no-one who keeps them informed or prepares them for what will happen next. They often experience lengthy delays before the case comes to court and find the experience of being cross-examined about their account traumatizing.[4]

In terms of conviction rates, the picture is equally worrying. In Scotland, the conviction rate in prosecuted rape/attempted rape cases in 2019–20 was 51 percent, lower than for any other crime.[5] But focusing on convictions at trial understates the problem. There is evidence that only a minority of those who have experienced a sexual assault report it to the police.[6] Even if the incident is reported, that is no guarantee that it will be prosecuted. In Scotland in 2019–20, 2,343 rapes/attempted rapes were reported to the police,[7] but there were only 130 convictions,[8] just 5.5 per cent of reported cases.[9] These figures are similar in all three UK jurisdictions (England and Wales, Scotland, and Northern Ireland).

In this chapter, I focus on the measures that have been proposed to address these issues in the three UK jurisdictions: England and Wales, Scotland, and Northern Ireland. All three have separate legal systems, but all use juries in serious criminal cases. In these three UK jurisdictions there have been major reviews of the prosecution of rape. In Northern Ireland, the Gillen Review reported in 2019;[10] in Scotland the Dorrian Review reported in 2021[11] and in England and Wales the End-to-End Rape Review also reported in 2021.[12] There is some commonality between the recommendations of the three reviews, but also some differences.

In this chapter I will argue that the jury system as it presently operates in the UK jurisdictions is problematic, because of the body of evidence demonstrating that jurors are prejudiced by false beliefs about rape and rape victims (so called rape myths) when reaching decisions about guilt in rape cases. I will examine the recommendations made by the three UK reviews to address the problem of rape myths and evaluate their likely prospect of success.

BACKGROUND

Before proceeding, it is necessary to say a little about the prosecution of rape in the UK jurisdictions. All three UK jurisdictions are typical adversarial systems. Allegations are reported initially to the police, who will undertake an investigation. If the police consider there is sufficient evidence that a crime has been committed, they will pass the case on to the relevant prosecution authority (the Crown Prosecution Service in England and Wales, the Procurator Fiscal in Scotland, and the Public Prosecution Service in Northern Ireland). Prosecutors in all three jurisdictions operate under a principle of expediency—they have discretion over whether or not to prosecute. Cases will only be prosecuted if there is (a) sufficient evidence such that there is a realistic prospect of conviction[13] and (b) it is in the public interest to prosecute.[14]

If a case is prosecuted, and assuming that the accused does not plead guilty, in all three UK jurisdictions, the decision about whether the accused is guilty will be taken by a jury—a group of lay people selected at random from the local community. The trial will be presided over by a judge, but their role is to be a neutral umpire, making sure that the rules of evidence are followed, and directing the jury about the law which should be applied. There are some differences in the nature of the criminal jury between the jurisdictions. In England and Wales and in Northern Ireland, juries have 12 members, strive to reach a unanimous verdict (although if this is not possible, a 10/2 verdict can be accepted) and have two verdict choices (guilty and not guilty). In Scotland, the criminal jury has 15 members, can return a verdict by simple majority (i.e., if eight of the 15 members agree) and has three verdicts (guilty, not guilty, and not proven). The not proven verdict is a peculiarity of Scots law—it is a second acquittal verdict, which has exactly the same effect as a not guilty verdict—the accused is acquitted of all charges and cannot be reprosecuted.[15] The not proven verdict has been extensively discussed,[16] including its possible impact in rape cases,[17] but for the purposes of this chapter it is not a material consideration, so I will say no more about it. The pertinent point here is that the jury is the decision-making body. This will not be the case in all jurisdictions, some of which use professional judges or mixed tribunals of professional judges and lay members. I will say more about this—specifically the extent to which we might be more confident in the decisions of professional judges—towards the end of the chapter.

In the remainder of this chapter, I focus on the measures that have been proposed in England and Wales, Scotland, and Northern Ireland to address the low conviction rate in rape cases. Before doing so, however, it is necessary to examine why the conviction rate is so low.

THE INFLUENCE OF RAPE MYTHS IN THE COURTROOM

The Difficulties of Proving Rape?

Why, then, is the conviction rate for rape so low? Some commentators have suggested that this is because rape cases are inherently difficult to prove as there are rarely eyewitnesses to the event in question and ultimately the case comes down to the word of one person against another. It is also different to other crimes in terms of what the prosecution needs to prove. Rape in Scots law is defined as sexual intercourse without the consent of the complainer (or without any reasonable belief by the accused that the complainer consented).[18] In a typical rape case, the fact that sexual intercourse took place is rarely a contested issue. The difficulty lies in proving that the complainer did not consent to this and that the accused did not reasonably believe that there was consent. Contrast this to a case of, say, a non-sexual assault, where the prosecution merely has to prove that the accused intentionally or recklessly caused another person to suffer or apprehend immediate unlawful violence.[19] In this respect, one might expect a 'naturally' low conviction rate for rape—proving the absence of consent is a harder proposition than proving that the accused caused another person to apprehend violence.

We might also say that in this context, a 51 percent conviction rate at trial is not something that we should be unduly concerned about. This is, after all, around half of all cases that are prosecuted. But this would be to neglect the fact that so few cases *are* prosecuted. As I noted in the introduction, only a fraction of cases ever reach trial. These cases are the strongest ones, where the prosecutor considered there to be a reasonable prospect of conviction. Many rape cases fall at this hurdle because there is not a realistic prospect that a jury would return a guilty verdict. It is also an exaggeration to say that in most rape cases the only evidence is the word of the accused and the complainer. Indeed, that is *never* true in Scotland because corroboration is required in all criminal cases.[20] If there is no corroborating evidence, the case cannot proceed. Such corroboration might be found, for example, in physical evidence of injuries to the complainer, or from evidence of the complainer's distress shortly after the incident.

The Concept of Rape Myths

Why then are juries so reluctant to convict in rape cases? The answer seems likely to lie at least in part by jurors being unduly influenced by rape myths—false and prejudicial beliefs about how a genuine victim of rape would behave, both during and immediately after the incident and when giving evidence in the courtroom. Various scales exist to 'measure' the extent to which individuals believe in rape myths[21] (although as I will discuss below, these are not unproblematic). Such beliefs can be broadly divided into four categories:[22]

- Beliefs that blame the victim/survivor, such as the belief that people who get voluntarily intoxicated are at least partly responsible for their rape, or that if the complainer did not scream, fight or get injured, then it is not rape.
- Beliefs that cast doubt on allegations, such as the belief that false allegations due to revenge or regret are common or that any delay in reporting rape is suspicious.
- Beliefs that excuse the accused, such as the belief that male sexuality is uncontrollable once 'ignited,' or that women often send mixed signals about their willingness to engage in sexual activity.
- Beliefs about what 'real rape' looks like, such as the belief that rape only occurs between strangers in public places or that it is always accompanied by violence.

It has sometimes been disputed whether these beliefs are actually "false."[23] But I contend that they are. It may be that in individual cases they are sometimes true—it may be true, for example, that women occasionally make false allegations of rape. But the vast majority—if not all—of these beliefs *are* false if they are expressed as general statements applicable to all (or the majority of) rape cases.

It has also been suggested that there exists little evidence of widespread acceptance of these myths. Thomas has argued that "hardly any jurors believe what are often referred to as widespread myths and stereotypes about rape and sexual assault."[24] But my view is that the evidence on which Thomas bases this claim is flawed (and runs contrary to a substantial body of research to the contrary, as discussed below). Thomas's claim is based on the results of a study she conducted with jurors who had recently sat on real cases (some were sexual offence cases; some were for other types of crime). Jurors were presented with a list of 17 'rape myths' and were asked whether they agreed or disagreed with them. Even on the basis of her own study, there was evidence that jurors held prejudicial and false beliefs. For example, 27 percent of Thomas's participants reported that they either agreed, or were unsure whether they agreed, with the statement "it is difficult to believe rape allegations that were not reported immediately"; 15 percent agreed or were unsure whether "if a person doesn't physically fight back, you can't really say it was rape"; and 13 percent agreed or were unsure whether "a rape probably didn't happen if the victim has no bruises or marks."[25]

But this aside, Thomas's research suffers from methodological problems that means it under-estimates the problem of rape myths in jury decision-making.[26] One of the most pertinent problems lies with the use of a questionnaire administered by a court official, which is likely to be subject to social desirability bias.[27] Social desirability bias is the desire for survey respondents to provide 'socially acceptable' answers and there is evidence that this affects the extent to which people answer truthfully when asked about their belief in rape myths.[28] There is also evidence that people who score low on rape myth measurement questionnaires still express false and prejudicial beliefs during mock jury deliberations—often the very same beliefs that they professed not to hold.[29]

Rape Myths in Mock Jury Deliberations

Let us turn then to the evidence that rape myths arise in jury deliberations. The first point to note is that it is not permissible to watch or record the deliberations of real juries in rape cases (or indeed any criminal cases).[30] Such evidence as there is of rape myths influencing jury deliberations comes from mock jury studies—studies in which researchers attempt to re-create the conditions of a real trial and recruit members of the public to act as jurors. Mock jury studies vary in terms of the realism with which they reflect what would happen in a real trial. It is common for reasons of time and cost to use written stimuli (such as trial transcripts) or to conduct the experiment on an individual basis, asking jurors for their verdict decisions, but not including any deliberation with other jurors.

We do, however, have evidence from highly realistic mock jury studies of the influence of rape myths during deliberations. The study I discuss here is one that I was involved in as a researcher, but there is also evidence from similarly realistic studies undertaken elsewhere.[31] This study, known as the

Scottish Jury Research,[32] was not designed specifically to investigate rape myths. Rather it was designed to investigate the difference that the distinctive features of the Scottish jury make to jury decision-making. However, because it involved a rape trial, and because jury deliberations were recorded, it sheds considerable light on how juries deliberate in rape cases.

The study's research methods have been discussed in detail elsewhere.[33] In brief, jurors were recruited from the general (jury-eligible) public to reflect the characteristics of the local population. They watched a professionally prepared video of a rape trial, where the roles were played by an experienced trial judge and professional actors, and where the script was written in consultation with legal advisors. They were directed as they would have been in a real trial and retired to deliberate to a verdict. Deliberations lasted for up to 90 minutes and were audio and video recorded. Thirty-two juries of either 12 or 15 members watched the rape trial.[34]

What we found was considerable evidence of false and prejudicial beliefs being expressed during the deliberations.[35] These centered around three main areas: the belief that an absence of extensive injuries and/or a 'failure' to shout for help is evidence of consent; that women regularly make false rape allegations; and that even a short delay in reporting an incident is evidence that it is fabricated.

Lack of physical resistance as evidence of consent: In 28 of the 32 juries, the view was expressed that a failure to physically resist an attack is evidence of consent. The belief that a 'real' rape victim would always shout for assistance was expressed in 16 of the 32 juries.[36] Acquittal verdicts were often supported by reference to the absence of more extensive injuries to the complainer or the absence of any injuries to the accused.[37] Jurors commented, for example, that "if you're being attacked… then to me you would scratch, you would scream, you would try and do anything possible to get him off"[38] and "in spite of being weaker and smaller, she could have tried to defend herself; you can always defend."[39] This is despite the psychological literature indicating that individual reactions to traumatic events vary significantly and many individuals experience a 'freezing' or dissociative response.[40]

Delayed reporting as evidence of fabrication: In the trial scenario jurors watched, there was a delay of around 40 minutes between when the accused left the complainer's flat and when she telephoned the police to report the incident. Although this delay was very short, in 13 of the 32 juries the view was expressed that this cast doubt on the truth of the allegations. This was despite the fact that the jurors received a direction from the trial judge advising that there can be good reasons why a rape victim might delay reporting, and that this does not necessarily indicate that the allegation is false.[41] One juror stated, for example, that "the time delay factor . . . was a bit sketchy" and that this, together with the evidence that the complainer called her sister before calling the police, was the factor that led him to favor a not guilty verdict.[42]

The prevalence of false allegations: We may not be able to quantify the scale of false allegations of rape, but it is reasonable to assume that it is unlikely to be substantial.[43] Nonetheless, in 27 of 32 juries, jurors speculated that the complainer might have made a false allegation to get revenge against the accused, as she had hoped to resume their relationship and was disappointed he did not wish to. This claim was not very plausible. The complainer and accused had a brief relationship, ending two months prior to the events in question. According to the accused, the two of them had consensual sexual intercourse when he called round to her flat, but he then stated he did not want to continue their relationship and left. It was agreed in evidence that there had only been two short telephone calls between the complainer and accused since their relationship ended and there was no evidence presented that the complainer wished to resume it. Jurors made comments such as "it's a female thing of no hell like a woman scorned," "there [are] hundreds of cases coming out where women have lied about rape" and "it looks like a motive for her to actually want to set the guy up that this is not going to happen, we are never going to be, but I'm going to bring you down."[44] Jurors sometimes suggested that the complainer's injuries could have been self-inflicted, suggesting for example that "pressing yourself very hard to make yourself bruised, you can do it" or that it is "fairly easy to scratch yourself if you really want to."[45]

Further support for the proposition that rape myths affect jury deliberations comes from a study involving real jurors undertaken in Australia and New Zealand.[46] The researchers conducted post-verdict interviews with jurors who had sat on real sexual offence cases. They too identified considerable evidence that misconceptions about sexual violence were present in jurors' discussions. Jurors often drew on 'real rape' stereotypes, including the extent of a complainer's physical resistance, in determining credibility and—despite judicial warnings stressing there may be good reasons for delayed reporting—placed undue weight on this factor. In 10 of the 18 cases reviewed, there was evidence of jurors' endorsement of victim-blaming attitudes related to the complainant's clothing, flirtatious behavior, lifestyle, intoxication or sexual history.

As noted in the introduction, there have been three reviews of the prosecution of rape undertaken, one in each of England and Wales (the End-to-End Rape Review), Scotland (the Dorrian Review), and Northern Ireland (the Gillen Review). The reviews were all wide ranging and focused both on the problem of secondary victimization and on the problem of rape myths affecting jury decision-making. My main focus in this chapter is to examine the proposals (or lack of them) that have been made in relation to the second of these issues: addressing rape myths.

DID THE REVIEWS ACCEPT THAT RAPE MYTHS AFFECT JURY DECISION-MAKING?

The first thing to note is that while all three reviews accepted that rape myths might affect jury decision-making, there were differences in the thoroughness with which they considered this issue. The Gillen Review recognized that "[t]here really can be no doubt that rape myths exist in some parts of our society,"[47] although it did also point to a lack of "empirical evidence to say whether actual individual jurors or jury verdicts in serious sexual offences in Northern Ireland are or are not affected by misconceptions in light of judicial directions to ignore them, albeit there is substantial evidence of research with moot jurors."[48] The Gillen Review did not examine the large body of mock jury research pointing to the influence of rape myths in any detail,[49] although even without it, the Review recognized that rape myths were a problem that needed to be addressed.

The Dorrian Review took place a year or so later than the Gillen Review and was able to consider the preliminary findings of the Scottish Jury Research. The Review examined this evidence,[50] as well as other existing evidence of rape myths affecting jury deliberations and concluded that it was compelling.[51] This evidence, the review stated, "accorded with the view of many Review Group members that rape myths remain prevalent amongst jurors and are very difficult to displace."[52]

The End-to-End Rape Review was more disappointing in this respect. Although it did state that "only evidence about the victim that is pertinent to the case should be used at court and a victim's credibility should not be undermined by pre-conceptions or rape myths,"[53] it made no reference to the body of literature on mock jury studies demonstrating that rape myths arise in deliberations. The entirety of the Review's discussion of the supporting research was to note that "[t]he effect of rape myths on juries is, however, disputed"[54] and that while a "significant number of studies have found that juries are affected by rape myths, a recent study has questioned whether rape myths are as prevalent as others found."[55] The recent study is that of Thomas discussed earlier and it is unfortunate that the Review did not acknowledge the limitations of this work. The Review was accompanied by a research report, which conducted online surveys, focus groups, and interviews with criminal justice stakeholders,[56] but here too the existing academic research in this area was noted only in a single short paragraph, citing one study by Ellison and Munro, but giving this equal prominence with Thomas's research.[57]

Ultimately the Review made no recommendations relating to rape myths, other than to recommended that the Law Commission for England and Wales should "examine law, guidance and practice relating to the use of evidence in prosecutions of serious sexual offences and consider the need for reform in order to increase the understanding of consent and sexual harm."[58] The project, it was stated, "is likely to consider issues such as the way rape myths are tackled as part of the court process."[59] The Law Commission accepted the reference and, at the time of writing, a 12-month project was underway.[60] While this may well lead—ultimately—to changes in practice, it is disappointing that the End-to-End Review has delayed the process of addressing such a pressing problem. The Law Commission is an independent publicly funded body charged with keeping the law of England and Wales under review and recommending law reform where it is needed. It has no power to implement any reforms that it considers necessary. That requires action from Government (or other policy makers). In her annual report, the Victims' Commissioner for England and Wales describes the End-to-End Review proposals as "underwhelming, both in their scope and resourcing" and states that they "represent some real missed opportunities to bring speedy and effective change."[61]

Because of its lack of concrete recommendations to address rape myths, the End-to-End Review will not be considered further. It is worth briefly considering why the approaches of the reviews differed. A notable difference between the Dorrian Review/Gillen Review, on one hand, and the End-to-End Review, on the other, is the extent to which rape complainers were represented, both in the review group itself and in terms of who gave evidence to the reviews.

The Dorrian Review was led by the second most senior judge in Scotland, Lady Dorrian. The review group membership included other senior judicial figures, representatives from the Scottish Courts and Tribunals Service (the body that runs the court system in Scotland), the prosecution service, the police, and legal practitioners who have acted to defend rape cases. It included three representatives from third sector (charitable) organizations, who represented the interests of rape victims.[62] The Scottish Government had a single representative on the group (which comprised 22 members in total), but did not lead the review.

The Gillen Review was constituted slightly differently. It was, in effect, undertaken by Sir John Gillen himself, a former Lord Justice of Appeal (a senior judge). He was supported by an advisory panel of 12 members, including three legal practitioners, two academics, and two representatives of third sector victim support groups (Victim Support NI and Nexus NI).[63] It also took evidence from an enormous range of organizations and individuals, including academics, independent sexual violence advocates, and third sector organizations.[64]

Both of these can be contrasted to the End-to-End Review, which was undertaken by the Ministry of Justice, a department of the UK Government. It commissioned research with "criminal justice stakeholders," but it is unclear who was represented in these discussions and very little reference is made to them in the End-to-End Review document itself. It did also include Emily Hunt—a campaigner on sexual violence—as an Independent Advisor.[65] But the End-to-End Review is essentially a policy document—a document which "sets out the government's action plan for improving the Criminal Justice System's response to rape in England and Wales."[66] It comprises mostly of tables of actions, with target dates and responsibilities, but many of these "actions" have little substance. The only one relating to rape myths is, as noted above, to refer the issue to another body (the Law Commission). The Victims' Commissioner has lamented that the End-to-End Rape Review was "carried out by the very government departments and agencies responsible for the poor state of rape in the first place"[67] and contrasted it to the Gillen and Dorrian Reviews that were both undertaken by an independent and senior judge.

WHAT HAS BEEN PROPOSED TO ADDRESS THESE ISSUES?

A number of different measures might be considered to address the problem of rape myths influencing jury decision-making. These include jury directions (given by the trial judge), expert evidence (given by a neutral expert, unconnected with the court) or a pre-trial video. There are different options relating to who might present such a video—whether this be a judge, a psychologist or another expert. The focus of all these measures would be to educate jurors and try and change any false or prejudicial beliefs about rape that they might hold.

Another suggestion that has been made is that jurors are pre-screened so that biased jurors are excluded from decision making,[68] although this suffers from the difficulty of how biased jurors would be identified, especially as jurors who score low on rape myth measurement questionnaires can still express problematic beliefs during deliberations. It has also been suggested that jurors might be asked to give reasons for their verdicts,[69] although this too suffers from a number of difficulties, most obviously the practicalities of how this would work when there are 12 (or 15) jurors, not all of whom may be able to articulate their reasons for preferring conviction or acquittal (or who might be reluctant to reveal their real reasons due to social desirability bias).

These measures, of course, all pre-suppose that the jury is the appropriate body for making decisions in rape trials. A further possibility is that juries do not hear rape trials at all, and are replaced either by a professional judge, or by a mixed tribunal of lay people and professional judges, as already happens in many other jurisdictions.

The Gillen Review

The Gillen Review recommended that "strong consideration be given to the literature that extols the virtues of early invocation of the concept of dispelling rape myths at the commencement stage of such trials."[70] It considered a number of options for achieving this, including judicial directions, expert evidence, and a pre-trial video.[71] Expert evidence was rejected on the basis that it would "almost inevitably lead to demands by the defense to call competing evidence which in turn will be more costly, will delay and elongate the trial and introduce perhaps even more complexity into an already complex situation."[72]

Ultimately it recommended that its preferred approach was a short pre-trial video to be shown to jurors—a possible length of seven minutes was suggested. The video, the Review stated, should be presented by "an authoritative source such as a number of judges."[73] The benefit of such a video over individual judges giving directions would be "uniformity, in the sense that cases would not depend upon the capacity of individual judges to 'sell' the concept."[74] The idea that the video be presented by an expert such as a psychologist was considered but rejected because "there is a danger that the jury might react adversely to some experts rather than neutral judges and their presence might trigger applications for the calling of counter experts."[75]

The Dorrian Review

The Dorrian Review also reached the conclusion that it was necessary for "information on certain rape myths to be communicated to the jury in an objective and clear manner."[76] It was less clear about what the most appropriate way of doing this might be. While nothing was said about the possibility of expert evidence, a pre-trial video and jury directions were both discussed. In Scotland, it is already mandatory for trial judges to give directions to jurors aimed at combatting certain rape myths—those relating to delayed reporting and the use of force.[77] The Review stressed that these should continue to be utilized wherever appropriate and that consideration be given to providing them at the start of the trial, rather than after the conclusion of the evidence, as presently happens.[78] An expanded range of rape myths should also be targeted.[79]

There was also support for a pre-trial video, with the Review concluding that a "carefully worded video, debunking such myths, could have considerable value."[80] But there was caution over "recommending the immediate and universal introduction of what would be a yet untested video in Scotland."[81] It was therefore recommended that there should be further discussion of the best means of providing the information to a jury, with a view to introducing a pilot program in the first instance.[82]

One other measure proposed by the Dorrian Review was the creation of new specialist courts for the prosecution of rape and serious sexual offences.[83] The measures outlined above were recommended by the Dorian Review on the assumption that the new specialist court will involve juries making determinations of guilt. The most radical of the Review's recommendations, however, is that consideration "should be given to developing a time-limited pilot of single judge rape trials to ascertain their effectiveness."[84] The Review recognized this would be "controversial and unpopular with many people"[85] and indeed was unable to make a unanimous recommendation, with "views being fairly evenly split between retaining and dispensing with a jury."[86] But the Review did not reach its conclusion lightly—it gave full consideration to the arguments in favor of juries, such as their life experience and the "democratic benefit of community involvement."[87] Against this, however, the Review argued that the evidence that jurors are influenced by rape myths "cannot be left unexamined and ignored."[88]

WILL EDUCATIONAL APPROACHES BE EFFECTIVE?

The primary focus of both the Gillen and Dorrian Reviews, then, was on educational measures, either in the form of jury directions and/or a pre-trial video. The question then arises of whether these are likely to be effective in combatting false beliefs. The evidence is mixed, with some studies concluding that jury directions (or expert testimony) can be effective in addressing biases,[89] but others concluding that they have no effect.[90] The difficulty with most of these studies is that they have been undertaken in less than realistic settings, which limits the weight that can be placed on them.[91]

The most realistic of the relevant studies is that of Ellison and Munro,[92] who, in a mock trial context, tested the impact of 'myth-busting' jury directions on physical resistance, delayed reporting and the degree of distress exhibited by the complainer when giving evidence. They found that the directions on delayed reporting and complainer demeanor were relatively effective—jurors who had been exposed to them were less likely to make false statements on these issues during deliberations. The directions on the use of force did not, however, have any observable effect on deliberations.

This is perhaps not surprising. Even a cursory examination of the psychological literature on attitude and belief formation and change suggests that some beliefs can be very deep seated and resistant to efforts to change them.[93] It is unlikely that something as simple as telling jurors that their beliefs are 'wrong' is going to be effective. What it might do is make jurors more cautious in *expressing* those beliefs, as they realize it may be socially undesirable to do so. There is some evidence that points to ways of improving the effectiveness of jury directions, such as giving them in advance of the trial[94] and explaining to jurors why they are being given (perhaps pointing to, for example, contrary evidence that 'freeze' reactions are a natural response to traumatic situations).[95] But even so, it is difficult to be one hundred percent confident that educational efforts will be entirely effective in addressing false beliefs about rape. And there may be some rape myths where it is simply too difficult to formulate an appropriate direction—the belief that false allegations of rape are common, for example. Unlike directions relating to freeze reactions or to delayed reporting, there *is* no body of objective evidence that can be referenced in this context to challenge biased views.

ARE PROFESSIONAL JUDGES THE ANSWER?

The difficulties of addressing the false beliefs that jurors hold about rape might suggest that the answer is, in fact, to use professional judges to determine rape cases (or a mixed tribunal of professional judges and lay persons). Professional judges (called sheriffs) are already used in less serious cases in Scotland, some of which might include sexual offence cases. Indeed, there are many jurisdictions around the world, including those bound by the European Convention on Human Rights (ECHR), that do not have lay participation in criminal cases at all.[96]

But can we be confident that professional judges do not hold the same false beliefs as jurors? There is plenty of evidence to suggest that professional judges are not immune from the effect of bias on their decision-making.[97] This fear might be lessened by the fact that judges have to give reasons for their decisions and there is certainly some evidence that written judgments can reduce the effect of bias in judges.[98] That said, the effect of written judgments should not be over-stated. In Sweden, rape cases are determined by one professional judge assisted by three lay judges. A conviction requires three of the four to vote for conviction and the professional judge must write a judgment on the case. Researchers examined 12 of these judgments from the period 2018–2020 and found that they still showed evidence of rape myths influencing decision-making, in particular false assumptions about the level of emotion that would be shown by a 'real' victim of rape.[99]

This might suggest that judge only trials—even with reasons being given—are not the answer. But let us not dismiss that possibility too quickly. While judges and jurors might both hold false beliefs, these beliefs are more easily addressed in judges. Judges are a small and easily identified body who can be educated over time. Research has shown that the most effective methods of combatting false beliefs about rape are longitudinal interactive educational programs,[100] something which is not cost effective to do with jurors, but which is more feasible with judges. One of the other recommendations of the Dorrian Review was that the new specialist sexual offences court would be presided over by a small pool of judges, all of whom would be specially trained. Prosecutors and defense lawyers would also need training in order to be accredited to work in the specialist court. This approach makes the effective education of judges an even more feasible prospect. A similar project in New Zealand—where a pilot specialist sexual offences court has been in operation—has reported highly positive results.[101]

But whether it would be feasible—or appropriate—to introduce into the UK jurisdictions a system where rape cases are heard by judges sitting alone is doubtful. The UK jurisdictions have a long history of using juries in criminal cases and there are persuasive justifications for their use. They inject democracy into decision-making, provide a check against state power and open up the justice system to public scrutiny.[102] Jurors can also be more effective fact finders than judges. They can bring experience of everyday situations into their assessments that professional judges—who tend to be drawn from a very narrow segment of society—are unlikely to be able to do.[103]

In any case, it is one thing to design a system from scratch and conclude that professional judges would be the most appropriate decision makers. It is quite another to take a system where the use of a jury in serious criminal cases has been established for centuries and to abolish it (albeit only in a sub-set of cases). While the Scottish Government is consulting on the possibility of a pilot of judge only trials, as suggested by the Dorrian Review, the chances of this coming to fruition must be slim. If juries continue to be used, there are some grounds for optimism that educational measures—of some form—might be effective. They certainly should not be rejected yet.

CONCLUSION

In this chapter, I have demonstrated that the way that juries approach their task as the decision makers in rape trials is problematic, as there is extensive evidence that their decision-making is prejudiced by false beliefs about rape and 'real' rape victims. This is manifested in the extremely low conviction rates for rape and other sexual offences. There is a pressing need to introduce measures to address this problem.

There is often resistance to the idea that measures should be taken with a view to improving conviction rates. It is, admittedly, impossible to identify what the 'correct' conviction rate should be in rape cases. But improving the conviction rate is a legitimate aim when only around six per cent of reported rapes result in conviction and there is evidence that a substantial proportion of incidents go unreported. If the aim was solely to improve conviction rates, in some sort of bureaucratic sense, then that would clearly not be appropriate. But it is not. It is about securing convictions in cases where the evidence supports the conclusion that it is beyond reasonable doubt that the accused committed the offence.[104] But ultimately even arguments based on conviction rates are not accepted, there must surely be acceptance that decisions about conviction in rape cases should be based solely on the evidence and not influenced by false beliefs about what constitutes 'real' rape and how genuine rape victims behave. These biases undermine the legitimacy of the criminal justice system and are not conducive to public confidence in its outcomes.

Two reviews in the UK jurisdictions have made recommendations as to how the problem of biases in jury decision-making should be addressed—both have called for educational measures to combat false beliefs. The Dorrian Review in Scotland has suggested that if lesser measures do not work, a pilot of judge only trials should be undertaken. We lack the evidence at present to reach an informed view on which—if either—of these measures is likely to be most effective. But what is clear is that the present situation should not be allowed to continue.

POSTSCRIPT

On 26 April 2023, the Scottish Government published the Victims, Witnesses and Justice Reform (Scotland) Bill. Section 65(1) of that Bill states that there will be a time-limited pilot of trials without a jury for rape or attempted rape charges. This follows the recommendation made in the Dorrian Review. The pilot has been controversial with legal practitioners and, at the time of writing, still has yet to pass through the parliamentary process to become law.

NOTES

1. Much of the research reported here was undertaken as part of the Scottish Jury Research project. I was a member of the research team for that project and I am hugely grateful to my fellow team members: James Chalmers (University of Glasgow), Vanessa Munro (University of Warwick), Rachel Ormston and Lorraine Murray (both from Ipsos MORI Scotland).

2. The chapter focusses primarily on rape, but similar issues arise in terms of other serious sexual offences.

3. "Complainer" is the legal term in Scots law for an alleged victim.

4. See e.g., O Brooks-Hay, L Bradley and M Burman, Justice Journeys: Informing Policy and Practice Through Lived Experience of Victim-Survivors of Rape and Serious Sexual Assault (2019).

5. Scottish Government, *Criminal Proceedings in Scotland, 2021–22* (2022) 20.

6. See e.g., Rape Crisis Scotland, *Annual Report for 2020–21* (2021) 29 (only just over half of those seeking support from Rape Crisis Scotland reported their experience to the police); Scottish Government, Scottish Crime and Justice Survey 2019/20: Associated Data Tables, table 7.26a (only 22 per cent of those who had experienced forced sexual intercourse reported it to the police).

7. Scottish Government, *Recorded Crime in Scotland 2019–20* (2020) 27.

8. Scottish Government, *Criminal Proceedings in Scotland, 2019–20* (2021) table 4(b).

9. This calculation is indicative rather than exact, as figures relate to different years and not a single set of cases. That said, the number of convictions for rape/attempted rape across the last few years has not varied very much (at 125, 105, 99, 106 and 104 in the five years from 2014 to 2019–20). I have not used the most recent set of figures from 2020–21 because they will have been affected by court delays caused by the COVID pandemic.

10. Sir John Gillen, Report into the Law and Procedures in Serious Sexual Offences in Northern Ireland (2019).

11. Scottish Courts and Tribunals Service, Improving the Management of Sexual Offence Cases: Final Report from the Lord Justice Clerk's Review Group (2021). This review is known as the Dorrian Review, as it was led by Lady Dorrian, Scotland's second most senior judge.

12. HM Government, The end-to-end rape review report on findings and actions (CP 437, June 2021) <https://www.gov.uk/government/publications/end-to-end-rape-review-report-on-findings-and-actions>accessed 30 May, 2023.

13. This is the test in England and Wales: Code for Crown Prosecutors (2018). The precise wording of the test differs slightly between jurisdictions but is substantially similar in Scotland and Northern Ireland.

14. Code for Crown Prosecutors (2018). See similarly Prosecution Code (2022) (Scotland) and Code for Prosecutors (2016) (Northern Ireland).

15. Save in exceptional circumstances set out in the Double Jeopardy (Scotland) Act 2011. These apply equally to not guilty and not proven verdicts.

16. See e.g., J Chalmers, F Leverick and VE Munro, 'Beyond doubt: the case against 'not proven'' (2022) 85(4) Modern Law Review 847–878.

17. See e.g., J Chalmers, F Leverick and VE Munro, 'The provenance of what is proven exploring (mock) jury deliberation in Scottish rape trials' (2021) 48(2) Journal of Law and Society 226–249 at 248.

18. Sexual Offences (Scotland) Act 2009 s.1. The definition of rape is near identical in England and Wales and in Northern Ireland—see s.1 of the Sexual Offences Act 2003 (England and Wales); s.1 of the Sexual Offences (Northern Ireland) Order 2008.

19. The definition of 'common' assault in England and Wales—see s.39 of the Criminal Justice Act 1988.

20. There must be at least two sources of evidence in respect of each 'crucial fact' (the identity of the perpetrator and key elements of the offence): Smith v Lees 1997 JC 73.

21. See e.g., M Burt, 'Cultural myths and supports for rape' (1980) 38(2) Journal of Personality and Social Psychology 217–230; DL Payne, KA Lonsway and LF Fitzgerald, 'Rape myth acceptance: exploration of its structure and its measurement using the Illinois Rape Myth Acceptance Scale' (1999) 33 Journal of Research in Personality 27–69; H Gerger, H Kley, G Bohner and F Siebler, 'The acceptance of modern myths about sexual aggression scale: development and validation in German and English' (2007) 33(5) Aggressive Behaviour 422–440; S McMahon and GL Farmer, 'An updated measure for assessing subtle rape myths' (2011) 35(2) Social Work Research 71–81.

22. See F Leverick, 'What do we know about rape myths and juror decision making?' (2020) 24(3) International Journal of Evidence & Proof 255–279 at 257.

23. H Reece, 'Rape myths: is elite opinion right and popular opinion wrong?' (2013) 33(3) Oxford Journal of Legal Studies 445–473.

24. C Thomas, 'The 21st century jury: contempt, bias and the impact of jury service' [2020] Crim LR 987–1011 at 1001.

25. C Thomas, 'The 21st century jury: contempt, bias and the impact of jury service' [2020] Crim LR 987–1011 at 1002–1004.

26. For a more detailed discussion of these flaws, see J Chalmers, F Leverick and V Munro, 'Why the jury is, and should still be, out on rape deliberation' [2021] Criminal Law Review 753–771; E Daly et al, 'Myths about myths? A commentary on Thomas (2020) and the question of jury rape myth acceptance' (2023) 7(1) Journal of Gender-Based Violence 189–200.

27. RJ Fisher and JE Katz, 'Social-desirability bias and the validity of self-reported values' (2000) 17(2) Psychology and Marketing 105–120.

28. RM Venema, 'Police officers' rape myth acceptance: examining the role of officer characteristics, estimates of false reporting, and social desirability bias' (2018) 33(1) Violence and Victims 176–200 at 190.

29. L Ellison and V Munro, 'A stranger in the bushes or an elephant in the room? Critical reflections upon received rape myth wisdom in the context of a mock jury study' (2010) 13 New Criminal Law Review 781–801 at e.g., 790 (the view that a failure to fight back on the part of the complainer is evidence of consent) and 794–795 (the view that false rape accusations are common and often used as a way of 'getting

back at' men); AM Zidenberg, F Wielinga, B Sparks, K Margeotes and L Harkins, 'Lost in translation: a quantitative and qualitative comparison of rape myth acceptance' (2022) 28(2) Psychology, Crime & Law 179–197.

30. In Scotland and Northern Ireland, see s.8 of the Contempt of Court Act 1981. In England and Wales, see s.20D of the Juries Act 1974.

31. See e.g., L Ellison and V Munro, 'Of 'normal sex' and 'real rape': exploring the use of socio-sexual scripts in (mock) jury deliberation' (2009) 18 Social and Legal Studies 291–312; L Ellison and V Munro, 'Getting to not guilty: examining jurors' deliberative processes in and beyond the context of a rape trial' (2010) 30 Legal Studies 74–97; L Ellison and V Munro, 'Better the devil you know: real rape stereotypes and the relevance of a previous relationship in (mock) juror deliberations' (2013) 17 International Journal of Evidence & Proof 299–322.

32. R Ormston, J Chalmers, F Leverick, V Munro and L Murray, Scottish Jury Research: Findings from a Large-Scale Mock Jury Study (Edinburgh: Scottish Government 2019).

33. See R Ormston, J Chalmers, F Leverick, V Munro and L Murray, Scottish Jury Research: Findings from a Large-Scale Mock Jury Study (Edinburgh: Scottish Government 2019) chapter 2; J Chalmers, F Leverick and VE Munro, 'The provenance of what is proven: exploring (mock) jury deliberation in Scottish rape trials' (2021) 48(2) Journal of Law and Society 226–249 at 232–234.

34. There was a second trial involved in the study that was also watched by 32 juries, but this was an assault trial so need not concern us here. The number of jurors varied because an aim of the study was to test whether the number of jurors made any difference to the deliberations. There were no differences of relevance to our discussion.

35. These findings are reported more fully in J Chalmers, F Leverick and VE Munro, 'The provenance of what is proven: exploring (mock) jury deliberation in Scottish rape trials' (2021) 48(2) Journal of Law and Society 226–249.

36. 'The provenance of what is proven,' at 236 and 240.

37. 'The provenance of what is proven,' at 236–237.

38. 'The provenance of what is proven,' at 236.

39. 'The provenance of what is proven,' at 236.

40. M Schauer and T Elbert, 'Dissociation following traumatic stress: etiology and treatment' (2010) 218(2) Zeitschrift für Psychologie/Journal of Psychology 109–127; BP Marx et al., 'Tonic immobility as an evolved predator defense: implications for sexual assault survivors' (2008) 15(1) Clinical Psychology: Science and Practice 74–90.

41. See Criminal Procedure (Scotland) Act 1995, ss. 288DA and 288DB.

42. 'The provenance of what is proven,' at 243–244.

43. See e.g., L Kelly, 'The (in)credible words of women: false allegations in European rape research' (2010) 16(12) Violence Against Women 1345–1355; D Lisak et al, 'False allegations of sexual assault: an analysis of ten years of reported cases' (2010) 16(12) Violence Against Women 1318–1334; P Rumney, 'False allegations of rape' (2006) 65(1) Cambridge Law Journal 128–158.

44. 'The provenance of what is proven,' at 245; J Chalmers, F Leverick and VE Munro, 'Handle with care: jury deliberation and demeanour-based assessments of witness credibility' (2022) 26(4) International Journal of Evidence & Proof 381–406.

45. 'The provenance of what is proven,' at 245.

46. Y Tinsley, C Baylis and W Young, ''I think she's learnt her lesson': juror use of cultural misconceptions in sexual violence trials' (2022) 52(2) Victoria University of Wellington Law Review 463–486.

47. Gillen Review, para 6.81.

48. Gillen Review, para 6.82.

49. The review reported before the Scottish Jury Research—which showed extensive evidence of such myths—had concluded. Nonetheless there was other evidence that could have been referred to.

50. Dorrian Review, paras 5.18–5.20, 5.31–5.36 and 5.37–5.44.

51. Dorrian Review, para 5.54.

52. Dorrian Review, para 5.17.

53. End-to-End Rape Review, para 24.

54. End-to-End Rape Review, para 113.

55. End-to-End Rape Review, para 113.

56. R George and S Ferguson, Review into the Criminal Justice System Response to Adult Rape and Serious Sexual Offences across England and Wales: Research Report (2021).

57. Research Report, at 71.

58. End-to-End Rape Review, para 114.

59. End-to-End Rape Review, para 114.

60. See Law Commission, Terms of Reference (2021) <https://s3-eu-west-2.amazonaws.com/lawcom-prod-storage-11jsxou24uy7q/uploads/2021/12/Agreed-Terms-of-Reference-Evidence-in-Sexual-Offences.pdf> accessed 30 May, 2023.

Law Commission, Review of Evidence in Sexual Offences: A Background Paper (2021).

61. Victims' Commissioner Annual Report 2020/21 (CP463, 2021), at 12.

62. Dorrian Review, Annex 2. The organizations involved were Rape Crisis Scotland, Victim Support Scotland and Scottish Women's Aid.

63. Appendix F. Nexus NI is the Northern Ireland Rape Crisis Association.

64. Gillen Review, Appendix F.

65. End-to-End Rape Review, Foreword.

66. HM Government, The end-to-end rape review report on findings and actions (CP 437, June 2021).

67. Victims' Commissioner Annual Report 2020/21 (CP463, 2021), at 12.

68. D Willmott and D Boduszek, 'Rape on trial: The influence of jury bias on verdict outcome' (2016) The Justice Gap, 7 September 2016.

69. Law Society of Scotland, Improving Victims' Experiences of the Justice System: Consultation Response (2022), at 35.

70. Gillen Review, para 6.90.

71. It also considered—and recommended—education in schools: see paras 6.68 onwards. This will not be considered further here as while valuable, it is a measure that will only be effective in the very long term.

72. Gillen Review, para 6.106.

73. Gillen Review, para 6.99.

74. Ibid.

75. Gillen Review, para 6.100.

76. Dorrian Review, para 5.54.
77. See Criminal Procedure (Scotland) Act 1995, ss. 288DA and 288DB.
78. Dorrian Review, para 5.57.
79. Dorrian Review, para 5.57.
80. Dorrian Review, para 5.55.
81. Dorrian Review, para 5.56.
82. Dorrian Review, para 5.56.
83. Dorrian Review, chapter 3.
84. Dorrian Review, para 5.70.
85. Dorrian Review, para 5.1.
86. Dorrian Review, para 5.3.
87. Dorrian Review, para 5.2.
88. Dorrian Review, para 5.52.
89. See e.g., N Brekke and E Borgida, "Expert psychological testimony in rape trials: a social-cognitive analysis" (1988) 55(3) Journal of Personality and Social Psychology 372–86; NP Spanos, SC Dubreuil and MI Gwynn, "The effects of expert testimony concerning rape on the verdicts and beliefs of mock jurors" (1991) 11(1) Imagination, Cognition and Personality 37–51.
90. See e.g., KR Klement, BJ Sagarin and JJ Skowronski, "Accusers lie and other myths: rape myth acceptance predicts judgments made about accusers and accused perpetrators in a rape case" (2009) 81(1–2) Sex Roles 16–33; FT Nitschke BM McKimmie and EJ Vanman, "The effect of trauma education judicial instructions on decisions about complainant credibility in rape trials" (2023) 29(1) Psychology, Public Policy, and Law 69–92.
91. For further discussion of the research in this area, see F Leverick, "What do we know about rape myths and juror decision making?" (2020) 24(3) International Journal of Evidence and Proof 255–279 at 270–273.
92. L Ellison and V Munro, "Turning mirrors into windows: assessing the impact of (mock) juror education in rape trials" (2009) 49(3) British Journal of Criminology 363–383.
93. See e.g., ,WD Crano and A Gardikiotis, "Attitude formation and change," in JD Wright (ed), International Encyclopedia of the Social & Behavioral Sciences (2nd edn, 2015) 169–174; GR Maio, G Haddock and B Verplanken, The Psychology of Attitudes and Attitude Change (3rd edn, 2018).
94. See J Chalmers and F Leverick, Methods of Conveying Information to Jurors: An Evidence Review (Edinburgh: Scottish Government, 2018) 27–31.
95. F Leverick, "Jury instructions on eyewitness identification evidence: a re-evaluation" (2016) 49(3) Creighton Law Review 555–588 at 581.
96. E.g., Türkiye, the Netherlands and South Africa: see EJ Leib, "A comparison of criminal jury decision rules in democratic countries" (2008) 5(2) Ohio State Journal of Criminal Law 629–644 at 631–632.
97. See e.g., JF Irwin and DL Real, "Unconscious influences on judicial decision-making: the illusion of objectivity" (2010) 42(1) McGeorge Law Review 1–18; H Spamann and L Klöhn, "Justice is less blind, and less legalistic, than we thought:

evidence from an experiment with real judges" (2016) 45(2) The Journal of Legal Studies 255–280.

98. See e.g., Z Liu, "Does reason writing reduce decision bias? Experimental evidence from judges in China" (2018) 47(1) The Journal of Legal Studies 83–118; JZ Liu and X Li, "Legal techniques for rationalizing biased judicial decisions: evidence from experiments with real judges" (2019) 16(3) Journal of Empirical Legal Studies 630–670.

99. L Wallin, S Uhnoo, Å Wettergren and M Bladini, "Capricious credibility—legal assessments of voluntariness in Swedish negligent rape judgements" (2021) 22(1) Nordic Journal of Criminology 3–22. See similarly R Barn and V Kumari, "Understanding complainant credibility in rape appeals: a case study of high court judgments and judges' perspectives in India" (2015) 55(3) The British Journal of Criminology 435–453.

100. LF Hudspith, N Wager, D Willmott and B Gallagher, "Forty years of rape myth acceptance interventions: a systematic review of what works in naturalistic institutional settings and how this can be applied to educational guidance for jurors" (2023) 24(2) Trauma, Violence, & Abuse 981–1000.

101. Ministry of Justice, Evaluation of the Sexual Violence Court Pilot (2019).

102. M Redmayne, "Theorising jury reform," chapter 6 of L Farmer, S Marshall, A Duff and V Tadros (eds) The Trial on Trial Volume 2 (2006) 99–153.

103. See J Chalmers, F Leverick and VE Munro, "Handle with care: jury deliberation and demeanour-based assessments of witness credibility" (2022) 26(4) International Journal of Evidence & Proof 381–406.

104. F Leverick, "Improving the management of sexual offence cases in Scotland: the Dorrian Review" (2021) 25(3) Edinburgh Law Review 385–393 at 392.

BIBLIOGRAPHY

Barn, R. and Kumari, V. 'Understanding complainant credibility in rape appeals: a case study of High Court judgments and judges' perspectives in India' (2015) 55(3) The British Journal of Criminology 435–453.

Brekke, N. and Borgida, E. 'Expert psychological testimony in rape trials: a social-cognitive analysis' (1988) 55(3) Journal of Personality and Social Psychology 372–386.

Brooks-Hay, O., Bradley, L. and Burman, M. Justice Journeys: Informing Policy and Practice Through Lived Experience of Victim-Survivors of Rape and Serious Sexual Assault (2019).

Burt, M. 'Cultural myths and supports for rape' (1980) 38(2) Journal of Personality and Social Psychology 217–230.

Chalmers, J., Leverick, F. and Munro, V.E. 'Handle with care: Jury deliberation and demeanour-based assessments of witness credibility' (2022) 26(4) International Journal of Evidence & Proof 381–406.

Chalmers, J., Leverick, F. and Munro, V.E. 'The provenance of what is proven exploring (mock) jury deliberation in Scottish rape trials' (2021) 48(2) Journal of Law and Society 226–249.

Chalmers, J., Leverick, F. and Munro, V.E. 'Why the jury is, and should still be, out on rape deliberation' [2021] Criminal Law Review 753–771.

Chalmers, J., Leverick, F. and Munro, V.E. 'Beyond doubt: the case against 'not proven'' (2022) 85(4) Modern Law Review 847–878.

Chalmers, J., Leverick, F. and Munro, V.E. 'The provenance of what is proven: exploring (mock) jury deliberation in Scottish rape trials' (2021) 48(2) Journal of Law and Society 226–249.

Chalmers. J. and Leverick, F. Methods of Conveying Information to Jurors: An Evidence Review (Edinburgh: Scottish Government, 2018).

Crano, W.D. and Gardikiotis, A. 'Attitude formation and change' in JD Wright (ed), International Encyclopedia of the Social & Behavioral Sciences (2nd edn, 2015) 169–174.

Daly, E. et al. 'Myths about myths? A commentary on Thomas (2020) and the question of jury rape myth acceptance' (2023) 7(1) Journal of Gender-Based Violence 189–200.

Ellison, L. and Munro, V.E. 'A Stranger in the bushes or an elephant in the room? Critical reflections upon received rape myth wisdom in the context of a mock jury study' (2010) 13 New Criminal Law Review 781–801.

Ellison, L. and Munro, V.E. 'Better the devil you know: real rape stereotypes and the relevance of a previous relationship in (mock) juror deliberations' (2013) 17 International Journal of Evidence & Proof 299–322.

Ellison, L. and Munro, V.E. 'Getting to not guilty: examining jurors' deliberative processes in and beyond the context of a rape trial' (2010) 30 Legal Studies 74–97.

Ellison, L. and Munro, V.E. 'Of 'normal sex' and 'real rape': exploring the use of socio-sexual scripts in (mock) jury deliberation' (2009) 18 Social and Legal Studies 291–312.

Ellison, L. and Munro, V.E. 'Turning mirrors into windows: assessing the impact of (mock) juror education in rape trials' (2009) 49(3) British Journal of Criminology 363–383.

Fisher, R.J. and Katz, J.E. 'Social-desirability bias and the validity of self-reported values' (2000) 17(2) Psychology and Marketing 105–120.

George, R. and Ferguson, S. Review into the Criminal Justice System Response to Adult Rape and Serious Sexual Offences across England and Wales: Research Report (2021).

Gerger, H., Kley, H., Bohner H. and Siebler, F. 'The acceptance of modern myths about sexual aggression scale: development and validation in German and English' (2007) 33(5) Aggressive Behaviour 422–440.

Gillen, Sir John. Report into the Law and Procedures in Serious Sexual Offences in Northern Ireland (2019).

HM Government, The end-to-end rape review report on findings and actions (CP 437, June 2021) <https://www.gov.uk/government/publications/end-to-end-rape-review-report-on-findings-and-actions>accessed January 10, 2023.

Hudspith, L.F., Wager, N., Willmott, D. and Gallagher, B. 'Forty years of rape myth acceptance interventions: a systematic review of what works in naturalistic institutional settings and how this can be applied to educational guidance for jurors' (2023) 24(2) Trauma, Violence, & Abuse 981–1000.

Irwin, J.F. and Real, D.L. 'Unconscious influences on judicial decision-making: the illusion of objectivity' (2010) 42(1) McGeorge Law Review 1–18.

Kelly, L. 'The (in)credible words of women: false allegations in European rape research' (2010) 16(12) Violence Against Women 1345–1355.

Klement, K.R., Sagarin, B.J. and Skowronski, J.J. 'Accusers lie and other myths: rape myth acceptance predicts judgments made about accusers and accused perpetrators in a rape case' (2009) 81(1–2) Sex Roles 16–33.

Law Commission, Review of Evidence in Sexual Offences: A Background Paper (2021).

Law Commission, Terms of Reference (2021) <https://s3-eu-west-2.amazonaws.com/lawcom-prod-storage-11jsxou24uy7q/uploads/2021/12/Agreed-Terms-of-Reference-Evidence-in-Sexual-Offences.pdf> accessed January 10, 2023.

Law Society of Scotland, Improving Victims' Experiences of the Justice System: Consultation Response (2022).

Leib, E.J. 'A comparison of criminal jury decision rules in democratic countries' (2008) 5(2) Ohio State Journal of Criminal Law 629–644.

Leverick, F. 'Jury instructions on eyewitness identification evidence: a re-evaluation' (2016) 49(3) Creighton Law Review 555–588.

Leverick, F. 'What do we know about rape myths and juror decision making?' (2020) 24(3) International Journal of Evidence & Proof 255–279.

Leverick, F. 'Improving the management of sexual offence cases in Scotland: the Dorrian Review' (2021) 25(3) Edinburgh Law Review 385–393.

Lisak, D. et al. 'False allegations of sexual assault: an analysis of ten years of reported cases' (2010) 16(12) Violence Against Women 1318–1334.

Liu, J.Z. and Li, X. 'Legal techniques for rationalizing biased judicial decisions: evidence from experiments with real judges' (2019) 16(3) Journal of Empirical Legal Studies 630–670.

Liu, Z. 'Does reason writing reduce decision bias? Experimental evidence from judges in China' (2018) 47(1) The Journal of Legal Studies 83–118.

Maio, G.R., Haddock, G. and Verplanken, B. The Psychology of Attitudes and Attitude Change (3rd edn, 2018).

Marx, B.P. et al. 'Tonic immobility as an evolved predator defense: implications for sexual assault survivors' (2008) 15(1) Clinical Psychology: Science and Practice 74–90.

McMahon, S. and Farmer, G.L. 'An updated measure for assessing subtle rape myths' (2011) 35(2) Social Work Research 71–81.

Ministry of Justice, Evaluation of the Sexual Violence Court Pilot (2019).

Nitschke, F.T., McKimmie, B.M. and Vanman, E.J. 'The effect of trauma education judicial instructions on decisions about complainant credibility in rape trials' (2023) 29(1) Psychology, Public Policy, and Law 69–92.

Ormston, R., Chalmers, J., Leverick, F., Munro, V.E. and Murray, L. Scottish Jury Research: Findings from a Large-Scale Mock Jury Study (Edinburgh: Scottish Government 2019).

Payne, D.L., Lonsway, K.A. and Fitzgerald, L.F. 'Rape myth acceptance: exploration of its structure and its measurement using the Illinois Rape Myth Acceptance Scale' (1999) 33 Journal of Research in Personality 27–69.

Rape Crisis Scotland, *Annual Report for 2020–21* (2021).

Redmayne, M. 'Theorising jury reform', chapter 6 of Farmer, L., Marshall, S., Duff, A. and Tadros, V. (eds) The Trial on Trial Volume 2 (2006) 99–153.

Reece, H. 'Rape myths: is elite opinion right and popular opinion wrong?' (2013) 33(3) Oxford Journal of Legal Studies 445–473.

Rumney, P. 'False allegations of rape' (2006) 65(1) Cambridge Law Journal 128–158.

Schauer, M. and Elbert, T. 'Dissociation following traumatic stress: etiology and treatment' (2010) 218(2) Zeitschrift Für Psychologie/Journal of Psychology 109–127.

Scottish Courts and Tribunals Service, Improving the Management of Sexual Offence Cases: Final Report from the Lord Justice Clerk's Review Group (2021) (the Dorian Review).

Scottish Government, *Criminal Proceedings in Scotland, 2019–20* (2021).

Scottish Government, *Criminal Proceedings in Scotland, 2021–22* (2022).

Scottish Government, *Scottish Crime and Justice Survey 2019/20* (2021).

Spamann, H. and Klöhn, L. 'Justice is less blind, and less legalistic, than we thought: evidence from an experiment with real judges' (2016) 45(2) The Journal of Legal Studies 255–280.

Spanos, N.P., Dubreuil, S.C. and Gwynn, M.I. 'The effects of expert testimony concerning rape on the verdicts and beliefs of mock jurors' (1991) 11(1) Imagination, Cognition and Personality 37–51.

Thomas, C. 'The 21st century jury: contempt, bias and the impact of jury service' [2020] Crim LR 987–1011.

Tinsley, Y., Baylis C. and Young, W. ''I think she's learnt her lesson': juror use of cultural misconceptions in sexual violence trials' (2022) 52(2) Victoria University of Wellington Law Review 463–486.

Venema, R.M. 'Police officers' rape myth acceptance: examining the role of officer characteristics, estimates of false reporting, and social desirability bias' (2018) 33(1) Violence and Victims 176–200.

Victims' Commissioner. Annual Report 2020/21 (CP463, 2021).

Wallin, L., Uhnoo, S., Wettergren, Å. and Bladini, M. 'Capricious credibility—legal assessments of voluntariness in Swedish negligent rape judgements' (2021) 22(1) Nordic Journal of Criminology 3–22.

Willmott, D. and Boduszek, D. 'Rape on trial: The influence of jury bias on verdict outcome' (2016) The Justice Gap, 7 September 2016.

Zidenberg, A.M., Wielinga, F., Sparks, B., Margeotes, K. and Harkins, L. 'Lost in translation: a quantitative and qualitative comparison of rape myth acceptance' (2022) 28(2) Psychology, Crime & Law 179–197.

2

Attrition in Sexual Offenses and Legal Procedural Models

The Italian Case

Armando Saponaro

Sexual offenses pose a problem that many countries across both the globe and Europe face. Attrition in sexual offenses is often defined as the percentage of cases in which an individual is not prosecuted or convicted for a sexual offense.[1] Sometimes from a criminological point of view, attrition includes the "dark figure of crime" and so indicates as well the number of sexual offenses that go unreported not only unprosecuted.

From a strict procedural point of view, looking at the criminal justice system functioning, attrition could be defined as the "process by which rape cases fail to proceed through the justice system."[2] *Liz Kelly, Jo Lovett, and Linda Regan* correctly pointed out four key points in adversarial legal systems at which attrition occurs, comparing the UK patterns with an international research: "the decision to report itself; the police investigation stage; case referral to prosecutors; the court stage."[3] However, in many of the inquisitorial legal systems in Europe, there is not an intermediate stage between the police investigation and trial. Prosecution in some countries starts when a case is registered, and prosecutors take charge of the investigation and decisions about case disposal. "Prosecution," is shaped very differently among countries "in terms of the power of the prosecuting authority and their relationship with the police."[4] Looking at attrition in sexual offenses, following a general simplified structure of criminal justice systems that overcomes variations between different countries' legal procedural models, "four key phases can be pointed out: making a formal report; investigation; prosecution/charge; and trial."[5] In Italy "prosecution" still nowadays means the "commencement of penal action," to submit a formal charge against an identified suspect to a court and, it is not possible to discontinue the case and police must transfer all reported cases to the prosecuting authority as it happens in France and Germany.[6]

In 2009, it was emphasized as a "critical issue in several English-speaking countries with common-law systems," so following accusatorial/adversarial model of the criminal process, by one of the most extensive reports on attrition in Europe.[7] In this context emerged the case of the UK. A study conducted in 2005 stressed "an ongoing decline in the conviction rate for England and Wales" estimated based on Home Office figures on reported rape cases, falling at an all-time low of 5.6 percent.[8] After an international data confrontation with other European countries, it concluded that though some main problems, such as the "classical" attrition paradox, an increase in reporting linked to a decrease in conviction rate, cross-cut adversarial and inquisitorial legal systems, still several "European countries have higher prosecution and conviction rates than the UK."[9] Moreover, *Lovett and Kelly* underlined that in England and Wales, "the conviction rate dropped from the mid-1980s 24 percent to 5 percent in 2004, recovering to 6 percent by 2006."[10] *Daly and Bouhours* in 2010 confronting data about Australia, Canada, England and Wales, Scotland, and the United States in the previous 35 years found an overall decline in "average conviction rates, from 18 percent to 12,5 percent," and "that England and Wales show the highest degree of attrition over time."[11] Within this group of common law criminal justice system countries, they analyzed attrition at the court stage, emerging a surprising polarization between the United States on one side and England and Wales on the other side, about court data on rates regarding either conviction or trial, extrapolating convictions at trial. Variations anyway suggest that court processes vary by country, notwithstanding an accusatorial model trial. England and Wales had "a most unusual pattern of a high trial rate (69 percent) and a very low conviction rate at trial (29 percent)," while the United States showed the lowest trial rate (8 percent) but the highest conviction rate at trial (74 percent).[12] It is consequently possible to wonder whether attrition at the court stage is even partially correlated to the accusatorial or inquisitorial model of criminal justice and the same structure of the accusatorial process or specifically adversarial trial. Italy in 1989 has been characterized by a unique radical switch from an inquisitorial model of criminal process to an accusatorial one. Analyzing conviction rate before and after this procedural model discontinuity, the features of this reform, and their impact on its trend, could suggest an answer to this question.

THE 1989 ITALIAN REFORM OF CRIMINAL JUSTICE SYSTEM: ADVERSARIAL TRIAL AND ATTRITION

The new Code of Criminal Procedure, approved by *Decreto del Presidente della Repubblica 22 settembre 1988, n. 447*, has come into force on 24 October 1989. The Italian criminal justice reform was not simply a modification of some elements, but the introduction of a new code and thus the adoption of a completely different legal model. The shift from the inquisitorial to the accusatorial model was expressly one of the law reform goals. Regarding the stage of research and acquisition of evidence after reporting the crime, the typical figure of the investigating judge, an icon of inquisitorial tradition, was abolished. The trial was modeled on the adversarial structure with the introduction of cross-examination and exclusionary rules concerning evidence. The examination of the witness had been previously conducted by the judge in the 1930 Code of Criminal Procedure.[13] Thus, a distinguishing element of the reform and innovative break with the previous model was the defendant's counsel and the prosecutor questioning witnesses, under an equality-of-arms principle, with a merely regulating function assigned to the court, to avoid questions suggesting the answer in the direct examination, as well as "detrimental" ones during both direct and cross-examination. The peculiarities of the Italian "accusatory style" with respect to the Anglo-American model, emphasized by *Cordero*, on the other hand, are certainly the principle of mandatory prosecution, the possibility for the judge to acquit and to supplement the trial evidence ex officio.[14] The principle of mandatory prosecution is even embedded in the constitutional law, but many Italian scholars stressed that "penal action in Italy is *de facto* discretionary as in other countries, and perhaps more" because the resources available to public prosecutors' are chronically short despite the massive crime reporting.[15] The other peculiarities do not impact the adversarial main core of the trial because even when evidence is admitted by the judge without parties' motions the cross-examination scheme is maintained.

Regarding sexual offenses, the only element of difference between the common law model and the trial remodeled by the Italian criminal justice reform is the jury. In the common law system when sexual offenses cases go to trial are adjudicated by jury, while in Italy, still by a professional judge. The Italian jury, the Court of Assizes, even after the reform, has been reserved for particularly serious crimes such as murder. It is mixed up anyway with professional judges. The 1989 new Criminal Procedure Code constitutes a unique example in Europe of a shift from a criminal justice system characterized by the inquisitorial model to a system more oriented toward the accusatory model. It should be emphasized that this is not a transition between two pure models. Although the previous 1930 Code of Criminal Procedure had the figure of the investigating judge, that is, a judge who gathered evidence and supported the prosecution, simultaneously had a trial stage with limited adversarial features, such as the possibility for the accused to challenge the evidence and confront witnesses even if with the mediation and interposition of the trial judge. Questions to the witness were asked by the trial judge at the request of the defense counsel.

The clear discontinuity anyway between the two models when the 1989 Code of Criminal Procedure came into force, allows testing the hypothesis that the form of the inquisitorial or accusatory legal model of criminal justice may have an impact on attrition and particularly whether the accusatory model is correlated with a lower or higher conviction rate than previous inquisitorial model, especially at trial. According to the data exposed in the introduction, setting aside the case of the United States, and in Europe looking at England and Wales lower and declining conviction rate and ratio, a negative effect should be expected, that is from 1990 onwards a lower conviction rate.

Setting the period to check has a limit. In 1996 the Italian legal definitions of sexual offenses changed, thus it is not possible to compare conviction rates along a temporal line totally before and after the procedural cleavage traced by the 1989 reform, testing a hypothetical impact of the accusatorial legal model of criminal justice on attrition. The unification of actual rape i.e., "carnal conjunction," with different offense of violent "libidinal" acts, substantially other sexual acts unlike penetration and characterized by concupiscence into a single type of offense, was enacted.[16] In the pre-1996 period, ISTAT[17] criminal justice statistics referred to actual rape i.e., carnal conjunction separately from other acts of violent lechery.[18] Even when, e.g., the European Sourcebook of Crime and Criminal Justice Statistics utilized infra, the conviction rate figure for sexual offenses is calculated by considering the sum of convictions for both criminal offenses, the problem is the change in terminology used and its exegetical interpretation by case law according to the unified legal definition. Some behaviors previously criminalized and falling under the two definitions prior to the 1996 reform may be excluded from the unified formulation and vice versa. *Erbaş* has underlined that attrition, from the perspective of criminal law, could not only relate to criminal procedural system models and structures but link with how to define sexual offenses as well.[19] Like the 1996 Italian reform, for example, the Turkish Penal Code of 2005 regulated sexual offenses according to a paradigm shift, leading to a transition regarding legal interest for sexual offenses from public morality to sexual integrity as such, becoming crimes against individual liberty. Consequently, "the legal language considerably changed, and as such, the outdated concepts derived from public morality were removed."[20] In this respect, a controversy has emerged in the Italian context about the interpretation of sexual acts other than carnal conjunction formerly called violent acts of libidinousness by Art. 521 of the Criminal Code of 1930, and later included by Law No. 66 of 1996,[21] Art. 609 bis in the unified legal definition of violent "sexual acts."[22]

One of the earliest Italian Supreme Court rulings on the topic compared the two laws to see whether the reform had decriminalized some minor conduct such as groping, lewd touching, and so on. It is a paradigmatic example. If the new 1996 wording was found to be more restrictive, decriminalizing certain conduct, according to the "more favorable to the offender" clause, it would also apply to acts that occurred before its enactment, resulting in acquittal due to the intervening decriminalization. Although upholding the sentence imposed by the judges of the previous degrees, the Supreme Court observed as follows:

> The more restrictive notion of "sexual acts" than that of acts of lechery assumes relevance in some controversial hypotheses such as kissing that is not deep and not directed to an erogenous zone, some fleeting touches in non-erogenous zones, and exhibitionist acts not involving any inter-corporal intercourse, which, if they cannot be qualified" "as other than sexual crimes" end up being criminally irrelevant. [23]

The difficulties of establishing the continuity or conversely the interpretative discontinuity between acts of lechery and sexual acts is well expressed by the contrast found in the Court's words, later echoed by other decisions. On the one hand, the Court ruled that "constitutes 'act of libidinousness' any act of tampering with another's body, not merely in the intimate parts, other than carnal conjunction and liable to excite sexual concupiscence." On the other hand, the Court ruled as follows:

> [T]he adjective sexual pertains to sex from the anatomical, physiological or functional point of view, but does not limit its value to the purely genital aspects of the interpersonal relationship since the notion of sexual acts must include all those that are capable of compromising the free determination of the sexuality of the passive subject and entering his sexual sphere in a manner connoted by coercion.[24]

The reform of sexual offenses of the Turkish Penal Code in 2005 analyzed by *Erbaş*[25] that resulted in removing the outdated concepts derived from public morality has many similarities with the 1996 Italian reform. Another ruling of the Italian Supreme Court pointed out precisely that "the intervening equalization of rape and violent libidinous acts is consequential to the assertion that sexual violence is an offense against the person, and expressly stated that the new expression 'sexual acts' takes on different connotations in the sense that, first and foremost, any moralistic reference contained in the term libidinous is removed."[26]

In short, the sexual act included the objectively erogenous zones deemed by science not only medical, but also psychological and anthropological-sociological, and was detached from the investigation of its impact in the social and cultural context in which it took place implied by the moralizing dimension of the concupiscence.[27] Injury to the victim's free determination, such as by coercion or inability to express consent, was sufficient in the Court's opinion. The exegetical issue concerns the identification of decriminalized area due to the greater restrictiveness of the notion of sexual acts covering behaviors not uniquely pertaining to the sexual sphere. Some examples are kissing not deep and not directed to an erogenous zone, being able to express affectivity as well, or because the touching was fleeting and directed to non-erogenous zones beyond the concupiscence of the offender in the situational context.[28] In this vein, the Supreme Court's interpretation of the notion of an act constituting sexual assault includes anyway e.g., a pat on the butt,[29] but then specifying if it should last an appreciable time lapse to discriminate the unlawful area of conduct.[30] The lack of comparability of data related to conviction rates before and after the 1996 reform becomes even more clear when considering the still controversial example of the "kiss."[31] Recently, several Supreme Court rulings have confirmed the inclusion as a "sexual act" even of kissing on the mouth that is limited to mere lip contact unless justified by particular social, cultural or family contexts in which the act appears to lack erotic value,[32] if it is a "stolen kiss,"[33] or a surprise kissing[34] but excluding the simple and fleeting kiss on the cheek to the victim, if no act capable of interfering with the victim's sexual sphere can be deemed to have been accomplished thereby.[35]

Due to the reasons just examined, it would be a prudent approach to consider from a methodological point of view a 1990–1996 window period for testing the impact of the change in the procedural legal model on convictions for crimes of sexual violence. This will purge the influence of the 1996 change in the legal discipline of sexual offenses and peculiarly their definitions. Furthermore, it will avoid the effect of the time gap between the commission of the crime and the trial stage and conviction, considering the partial continued application of the former Code of Criminal Procedure for some cases under the transitional rule in the initial years 1990–1991.[36] Although it is no longer possible to carry out a sophisticated statistical analysis, since the data are dated, the trend could never have been incremental, if the introduction of a trial with accusatory features negatively influenced the outcome with reference to conviction rather than an acquittal.

THE 1989 CRIMINAL PROCEDURE CODE SHIFT TO ADVERSARIAL TRIAL AND THE CONVICTION RATE 1990–1996

In contrast, the figure as the conviction rate per hundred thousand population shows a virtually exponential upward progression. According to the European Sourcebook of Crime and Criminal Justice Statistics the rate of convictions for sexual violence per 100,000 population increases in Italy, in fact, from 0.8 in 1990 to 2.2 in 1996, with a change in the 1990–1996 period as much as 174 percent.[37] The European Sourcebook of Crime and Criminal Justice Statistics was chosen as the data source because it uses ISTAT data in relation to population, allowing a comparison of the trend with other nations. It also adopts a standard definition of rape that does not correspond to the formal legal definition. This for Italy implies that the standard definition unifies in a single figure the convictions related to both the rape of Art. 519 and the violent libidinous acts of Art. 521, the 1930 Italian Penal Code, consistent with the wording before the 1996 reform. This allows comparison with the post-1996 figure referring to the all-encompassing case of sexual assault in Art. 609 bis Penal Code, subject to the problem of the greater or lesser span of the new legal definition and its impact on the trend of convictions.[38] Since 1997, on the other hand, after the reform of the Criminal Code regarding sexual offenses, the conviction rate per hundred thousand inhabitants first stabilized being 2.2 in both 1997 and 1998, and then began to decline slightly in 1999 to 2.1,[39] in 2000 to 2, then having a rise in 2001 to 2.3, and continuing in subsequent years with limited variations around that rate.[40] In the same years 1990–1996 the rate of crimes reported by the Police to the judicial authorities[41] per hundred thousand inhabitants is basically stable around the value of 3 until 1996, except for a modest increase from 3.1 in 1989 to 3.9 in 1991.[42] It is possible to exclude that the increase in conviction rate can depend on variations in reporting. Lastly, the conviction rate incremental variation could be derived from an increase in the number of suspected persons and particularly from a different attitude to prosecution by public prosecutors. The 1989 criminal procedure reform indeed gave the direction of the investigation stage in the hands of public prosecutors, diminishing the role and the weight of the police regarding the decision to charge a suspected person and to refer a case to trial.[43] Considering the period from 1988 to 1996 the prosecution rate per 100,000 inhabitants has increased just mildly.

Data exposed in the table were compiled on the basis of the tables attached to the corresponding "Reports on the Administration of Justice for the Judicial Year" of the Attorney General's Office at the Supreme Court of Cassation. From the methodological point of view, it should first be noted that the indicated rate, because of the typology of data collection, includes

Table 2.1. Prosecution rate sexual violence per 100,000 inhabitants 1988–1996—Italy

1988	*1989*	*1990*	*1991*	*1992*	*1993*	*1994*	*1995*	*1996*
4.0	4.0	3.9	4.4	5.7	5.8	5.9	6.5	5.8

Source: Table 2.1 was created by the Author, with the data from "Reports on the Administration of Justice for the Judicial Year" of the Attorney General's Office at the Supreme Court of Cassation 1988-1996

also the registration of proceedings for which the offender was unknown. The proportion, however, between proceedings for which there was a formal charge against an identified offender and that of proceedings for which he or she remained unknown, from the same tables attached to the corresponding "Reports on the Administration of Justice for the Judicial Year" of the Attorney General's Office at the Supreme Court of Cassation, shows that it has remained substantially unchanged since 1990, although not referring specifically to sexual offenses. It is, on average for the registration of proceedings with unknown offenders 80 percent for all crimes overall, while on average 50 percent for all other crimes excluding theft.

From these points of view, the increase in convictions for crimes of sexual violence from 0.8 in 1990 to 2.2 in 1996, with a change in the 1990–1996 period of as much as 174 percent cannot be explained except by the 1989 reform of the Code of Criminal Procedure.

The introduction of the accusatory model would appear to be correlated with a significative increase rather than a decrease in the conviction rate. The introduction of the new Italian Code of Criminal Procedure in 1989 has confirmed a unique opportunity to test the possible correlation between procedural models of justice, particularly at the Court stage attrition point. It is worth noting that the Italian reform, at the trial stage, with respect to attrition, excludes the spurious variable of plea bargaining as far as the dispersal of cases is concerned. Plea bargaining, although provided by Art. 444 of the Code of Criminal Procedure of 1989, can only concern the measure of punishment but not the charge. Therefore, acceptance by the defendant of a lesser charge and thus conviction for a less serious crime or even excluding the sexual nature of the act is not possible. Therefore, the problem of the correspondence of the conviction with the original charge, that is, the act committed as qualified in light of the legal definition, does not arise. There is no difference between the alternative rite of plea bargaining and trial, for conviction in terms of the crime committed, having relevance only to the measure of the penalty. In the countries like England and Wales in Europe, where plea bargaining can regard even charges, the attrition attributed to a lesser conviction rate for rape itself is an object of public discussion and concern due to rape charge drop after a defendant offers to plead guilty to a lesser sexual offense. Even alternative convictions could also include rarely "non-sexual crimes such as a violent attack that was part of the incident."[44] In Italy bargains not only are limited to the qualitative and quantitative aspects of sentencing but are even quite marginal because most processes proceed to trial. A Eurispes (Institute of Political, Economic and Social Studies) research carried out in 2008 in cooperation with the Union of Criminal Lawyers Chambers examined at the national level the trials held in the first-degree trial phase at the Sections in the collegiate and monocratic composition of the Courts belonging to the statistical sample of the 27 territorial Criminal Lawyers Chambers, including detached Sections of significant statistical importance. The results have shown that plea bargaining was still quite marginal, notwithstanding ten years passed since the reform was enacted. Quite the totality of the cases continues to trial without bargaining, 90.6 percent, while overall only 4 percent are defined by plea bargaining.[45]

Although the figure refers to the totality of proceedings it can reasonably be assumed that it is also reproduced for proceedings involving crimes of sexual violence. Moreover, the survey took place more than a decade after the introduction of plea bargaining in 1989, which suggests that in the immediacy of its implementation, the percentage of trials settled utilizing the alternative to trial procedure was even lower. So, the conviction rate for sexual offenses regards quite only the outcome of the trial. The significant increase in the period under consideration 1990–1996, as much as 174 percent, previously highlighted can conclusively be attributed almost exclusively to the introduction of the adversarial model of trial.

In the introduction to this chapter, it has been underlined that in the common law context, there is a strong polarization between countries such as the United States that have a low rate of trials that go on to trial but then a high rate of trial convictions and countries such as England and Wales whose pattern displays a high trial rate compared to a very low conviction rate at trial. *Daly and Bouhours* attributed this difference to the United States standard organizational custom of plea bargaining because of early significative implementation and so the development of habitual practice, jointly with "greater emphasis in British court culture on adjudication and conviction by trial."[46] The efficiency in terms of increase of conviction rate at trial could stem from peculiar features of the accusatorial model implemented with the reform in 1989.

ITALIAN ACCUSATORIAL MODEL OF TRIAL AND ATTRITION: THE JURY AND THE VICTIM

A significant difference from the common law paradigm in the implementation of the accusatory model in Italy with the reform of the Code of Criminal Procedure is the absence of a jury for sexual offenses. The verdict delivered to a professionally trained judge could mitigate the effects of the adversarial trial structure and in particular cross-examination. In the common law system, there are numerous empirical studies on the influenceability of juries about stereotypes and prejudices that can be amplified or emphasized during the trial examination of the victim or other witnesses if not even instrumentally used by the defendant's defense. Exposure to rape myths by ordinary people who are members of juries is naturally greater than by a professionally trained judge.[47] This could have great importance in proceedings involving sexual offenses where very often the testimony of the victim, in the absence of other significant evidence, can be decisive. The judgment of the reliability of the victim's testimony can be influenced by cognitive biases or by victim-blaming processes, especially in certain socio-cultural contexts. The process of jury selection ideally tends in the common law system precisely to ensure the exclusion of people who have a prejudiced and preconceived view of what happened based on socio-cultural or biased elements, but of course, it has limitations. Awareness on the part of the police or prosecutors of such jurors stereotyping and prejudicial views of the crime based on certain elements such as the relationship between the offender and the victim, or the intake of alcohol or more generally the victim's e.g., seductive behavior prior to the commission of the violence, ethnicity, or even the context of the violence, invitation of the offender at the place where the rape occurred, also leads to the premature dismissal of cases because even if technically rape there is a reduced likelihood of obtaining a conviction. As observed by Estrich, the problem is "real rape" juxtaposed to "technical rape."[48]

The jury element could thus be the key to the negative correlation between the accusatory model and conviction rate at trial rather than other characteristics such as cross-examination in a highly polarized adversarial arena. Another profile is that when the jury is given two alternative charges it could convict on the lesser one, acquitting the defendant of rape. Of course, even professionally trained judges can be misled by gender stereotyping or other biases. In Italy, there is a famous ruling even of the Italian Supreme Court that upheld the acquittal of the defendant because *the very tight jeans pants* worn by the victim could have been removed and folded without the victim's cooperation, thus excluding the coercive element of violence or threat.[49] The Italian Supreme Court has then changed this precedent asserting a contrary principle.[50] There is, however, a fundamental difference between the jury and the professional judge that tempers the latter's adherence to rape myths. Apart from the consideration that it gives no account of reasons for decision and thus even if an appeal were allowed, it would be difficult to censure, the jury verdict of acquittal is not appealable in common law jurisdictions.

The Fifth Amendment to the US Constitution prohibits anyone from being tried twice for substantially the same crime, the Double Jeopardy Clause, thus appeals by the prosecution after an acquittal verdict are not normally allowed. It is the same in England and Wales setting aside the retrial that can be applied by the prosecutor according to provisions Part 10 of the Criminal Justice Act 2003, but only in respect of serious offenses listed in Part 1 of Schedule 5 of the 2003 Act that reformed the law relating to double jeopardy. Rape and other sexual offenses are among them. The provisions enable the prosecuting authorities, with the consent of the DPP, if in the public interest, "to apply to the Court of Appeal for an order quashing the original acquittal and directing a retrial," but very restrictively "where new and compelling evidence has come to light. The law in Scotland has not been changed so that these provisions do not apply to acquittals that take place in Scotland."[51] The retrial is allowed on the condition of new and compelling evidence and it does not permit a real appeal stressing stereotyped reasoning or rape myths expressions, and in fact, the verdict lacks even an account of reasons for the decision, as remarked before, being expressed just in the binary form, guilty vs. not guilty. When the trial is without jury, and the verdict is expressed by a judge as it happens in Italy and is possible in some other common law countries like Canada, there is control over the reasons for the decision. In this hypothesis, an appeal against acquittal can address victim-blaming stereotypes and rape myths affecting the decision-making process and then up to Supreme courts or High Courts, etc., depending on the jurisdiction involved. A paradigmatic case was the Court of Appeal for Ontario decision in *R. v. Steele*,[52] which debunked the usage of rape myths in credibility assessments by the trial judge, EJ Koke J,[53] in the decision appealed by the Crown.[54] The Court stressed that the law has been seeking to eradicate myths about the appropriate behavior of victims of sexual assault for decades, citing *R. v. Ewanchuk*:[55]

> Complainants should be able to rely on a system free from myths and stereotypes, and on a judiciary whose impartiality is not compromised by these biased assumptions (. . .) It is part of the role of this Court to denounce this kind of language, unfortunately still used today, which not only perpetuates archaic myths and stereotypes about the nature of sexual assaults but also ignores the law.[56]

The issue was the trial judge victim credibility assessment and inference about consent derived from the testimony of the complainant who could not provide a reason or explanation for her decision to enter the abandoned trailer where the sexual assault occurred without being "talked into" or in any way coerced into entering.[57] Another issue was the victim's conversation with her father just after the rape telling him that she was coming back home shortly. In the view of the trial judge response to her father was not congruent with the situation of someone who has just been sexually assaulted and has been kept involuntarily in the trailer, where the violence occurred, but would be more "consistent with the response of someone who is attempting to conceal her activities and whereabouts from her parents."[58] Judge Benotto J.A., concurring van Rensburg J.A., clearly stated that the trial judge applied irrelevant stereotypical views 'about the behavior of sexual assault victims "under the guise of a common-sense approach to credibility assessment" twice: either considering A.V.'s testimony about why the trailer or when examining her call with her parents.[59]

In Italy, Italian Supreme Court rulings on the subject of voluntary consumption by the victim of alcohol and drugs are in parallel paradigmatic about the internal control that can be implemented in the jurisdiction over a not guilty verdict when ruled by a professionally trained judge at the outcome of the trial with reference to stereotypes about the victim and rape myths. Victim blaming in sexual assault cases for the voluntary intake of alcoholic and narcotic substances is repeatedly disavowed by the Italian Supreme Court, which has always ruled out valid consent due to the presence of the "condition of mental or physical inferiority" taken advantage of by the agent, regardless of whether the intake is voluntary or induced. Voluntary intake of alcohol by the victim affects the person's power of self-determination. As a condition of vulnerability considered by Article 609 bis of the Criminal Code, it can be exploited by the agent for his own sexual gratification. The Court stated repeatedly that voluntariness does not preclude exploitation, and it is not necessary that the agent be the one to administer the psychotropic substances, behavior which, is essential just for aggravation of punishment.[60]

Another difference is certainly the presence of the victim within the trial with its own legal counsel and equal trial powers as those of the defendant and the prosecutor. In Italy the victim participating in the criminal process is called the "civil party"; it has its roots even in some legislative acts before Code Napoleon.[61] The victim can participate in the criminal trial, *albeit*, to make a civil claim for damages. Although the civil party has the purpose of achieving restitution or compensation for damages and therefore advances civil claims it cannot conclude on, for example, the amount of punishment, but the victim participates in the trial, presents and cross-examine witnesses presented by the defendant, file motions, so on. Unfortunately, there are no empirical studies on the possible influence of the civil plaintiff on the final verdict by the judge in the criminal process.

Judicial cases from the past, such as that of *the Circeo massacre* in the 1970s, suggest that the presence of the victim with her/his own legal counsel can sometimes even be decisive in countering, prejudices and stereotyping, the assumption of rape myths by the prosecutor and the judge. The case has been considered a clear example of victim blaming because the offenders' legal counsel and Italian media placed the responsibility for the crime on the personal and socio-economic characteristics of the victims, as depicted in Italian newspaper articles, stressing their lack of compliance with social standards of moral virtue.[62] It was even reported that one of the offenders defense lawyers declared to the media: "if the girls had stayed by the hearth, where they belonged if they had not gone out at night, if they had not agreed to go to those boys' houses, nothing would have happened."[63] *Donatella Colasanti*, the survivor victim, while the other girl *Rosaria Lopez* was murdered, participated in the trial as a civil party, and the secured convictions are attributed mainly to the battle of her defense attorney *Tina Lagostena Bassi*. The victim can effectively contrast socio-cultural assumptions that may undermine his or her credibility and trustworthiness, especially in cases where material evidence such as DNA is lacking and only circumstantial evidence or even the victim's own statements alone exist to support the accusatory hypothesis. The Victim civil party or in-courtroom European continental model especially in the actual Italian criminal process shows the compatibility of the trial adversarial structure introduced by the 1989 reform with victim active participation with qualified rights as a party. The visibility of the victim in the courtroom with a legal representative and all rights granted equally to the defendant, as in the emblematic case of Circeo Massacre, "give the victim a spectrum of opportunities to contrast and fight 'societal invisibility,' beliefs, attitudes, prejudices, and stereotypes, which oppose the acknowledgment of their victimization on the judicial terrain."[64] The adoption of a full-party victim-oriented model, or at least independent legal representation in adversarial common law criminal proceedings, is at the center of a great debate and the provision of independent legal representation for victims of intimate partner violence within dedicated family violence court divisions has been recently suggested by recommendation 60 of Victoria state Royal Commission into Family Violence in Australia.[65]

The absence of the jury and together with victim participation in a criminal trial could explain the sharp increase in convictions upon the introduction of the accusatory model of trial in Italy, boosting its features in favor of convicting the offender. The introduction of the right to cross-examine the witness has empowered even more the victim who participates in the trial with a legal patron as civil party as it habitually happens. This consents to efficiently counterbalance attacks on victim's credibility for example mentioning promiscuous sex habits. In addition, the judgment of the reliability of the victim's testimony is less influenced by cognitive biases or by victim-blaming processes, due to professional judge adjudication instead of a jury verdict, emphasizing the effect.

CONCLUSION

Attrition in sexual offenses is a complex issue. Comparing sexual violence prevalence with reporting clearly shows a wide gap and an under-representation of the phenomenon at the input level of criminal justice systems worldwide. The problem is that after reporting, along the criminal proceedings from the police stage to conviction, the dispersion of cases continues, and the pyramid becomes even narrower at the top. From the point of view of the criminal justice system, attrition undoubtedly could be attributed to different legal definitions of sexual offenses, at least partially. Anyway, a good question is whether legal procedural models of the criminal process can influence attrition. In Europe, continental countries have higher prosecution and conviction rates than the UK, even if some core problems are common to adversarial and inquisitorial legal systems. To trace a clear-cut distinction between accusatorial and inquisitorial models of criminal justice is difficult, due to post-modern hybridizations, but the adversarial structure of trial based on parity of "weapons," and on cross-examination of witnesses, together with the separation between prosecution and judge, are still distinctive features.

The 1989 reform of the criminal procedure code in Italy has given an interesting retrospective opportunity to verify whether the model of criminal justice has an impact on attrition at the court stage. It represents a unique switch between the previous inquisitorial model to an accusatorial one, other conditions being equal, at least until the reform of legal definitions of sexual offenses in 1996. Data has shown an impressive increase in convictions, the rate more than doubled from 1990 to 1996, despite the stability of reporting and referral of cases to trial, so it is possible to argue that the introduction of the accusatorial model led to a diminution of attrition at the court stage. The contrast with the UK where the attrition at the court stage is one of the highest in Europe, even compared with other countries sharing the common law jurisdiction model worldwide, nevertheless the accusatorial trial, can be explained by trial additional features of the Italian model: firstly the absence of the jury, more prone than a professional judge to blaming and stereotyping the victim, due to rape myths, without the counterbalancing control of a superior court, given the substantial exclusion of appealability of the jury verdict; secondly the participation of the victim as a plaintiff with full trial powers that through the possibility to present evidence and cross-examine the witnesses, allows to contrast stereotyping views and defense based on rape myths. The sharp conviction rate increment shown in the period 1990–1996 just after the introduction of the accusatorial trial is well explained by these elements, accusatorial trial, professional judge, victim's participation, and legal counsel, whose convergence was uniquely realized in Italy in 1989.

NOTES

1. Larry J Siegel, *Criminology: The core* (4th ed Wadsworth 2012) 56.
2. Jo Lovett and Liz Kelly, *Different systems, similar outcomes? Tracking attrition in reported rape cases across Europe* (CWASU 2009) 5.
3. Liz Kelly, Jo Lovett and Linda Regan, *Home Office Research Study 293 A gap or a chasm? Attrition in reported rape cases* (Home Office Research, Development and Statistics Directorate 2005) 30.
4. Jo Lovett and Liz Kelly, *Different systems, similar outcomes? Tracking attrition in reported rape cases across Europe* (CWASU 2009) 20.
5. *Ibid.* 10.
6. *Ibid.* 20.
7. *Ibid.* 5.
8. Liz Kelly, Jo Lovett and Linda Regan, *Home Office Research Study 293 A gap or a chasm? Attrition in reported rape cases* (Home Office Research, Development and Statistics Directorate 2005) 1.
9. *Ibid.* 29.
10. Jo Lovett and Liz Kelly, *Different systems, similar outcomes? Tracking attrition in reported rape cases across Europe* (CWASU 2009) 5; Research Development and Statistics – Office for Criminal Justice Reform, *Notifiable Offences and Numbers of Persons Prosecuted, Tried and Convicted for Rape Offences, England and Wales 2006* (Home Office 2008).
11. Kathleen Daly and Brigitte Bouhours, 'Rape and Attrition in the Legal Process: A Comparative Analysis of Five Countries Crime and Justice' (2010) 39 (1) Crime and Justice 565, 619.
12. *Ibid.* 583.
13. Regio Decreto 19 ottobre 1930, n. 1399.
14. Franco Cordero, *Procedura Penale* (Giuffrè 2012) 101.
15. Ermes Antonucci, 'The evolution of the principle of mandatory prosecution in Italy. A problematic case of gradual institutional change' (2021) 66 International Journal of Law, Crime and Justice 1, quoting Giuseppe Di Federico, 'Prosecutorial Independence and the Democratic Requirement of Accountability in Italy. Analysis

of a Deviant Case in a Comparative Perspective' (1998) 38 (3) British Journal of Criminology 371, 378.

16. Giovanni Fiandaca, Violenza sessuale, *Enciclopedia del diritto XLVI* (update IV 2000) 1153; Giangiulio Ambrosini, Violenza sessuale, *Digesto delle discipline penalistiche XV* (1999) 290.

17. Italian National Institute of Statistics.

18. ISTAT, 'L'Italia In 150 Anni. Sommario di Statistiche Storiche 1861–2010,' Istat 2011.

19. Rahime Erbaş, 'Challenges in Regulating Sexual Offences in Turkey' in Rahime Erbaş (ed), *Global Problems in Sexual Offenses* (Lexington Books, 2022) 3.

20. *Ibid.* 3–4.

21. Legge 15 febbraio 1996, n. 66 Norme contro la violenza sessuale. (GU Serie Generale n. 42 del 20-02-1996).

22. Vincenzo Musacchio, *Il delitto di violenza sessuale (art. 609 bis del Codice penale)* (Cedam 1999).

23. Cassazione penale, Sez. III, 04/07/2000, n. 7772.

24. Cassazione penale, Sez. III, 04/07/2000, n. 7772.

25. Erbaş (n 19) 5–6.

26. Cassazione Penale, Sez. III 11/11/1996, Rotella.

27. For a critical analysis see Alberto Cadoppi, *Commentario delle norme contro la violenza sessuale e contro la pedofilia* (CEDAM 2006) 449; Giuliano Marini, *Delitti contro la persona* (Giappichelli 1996) 261.

28. Giuseppe Amato, 'Se è chiara la direzione sessuale dell'atto anche il bacio sulla guancia è reato. Sussiste il delitto anche se la vittima reagisce e l'approccio «cade» su una zona non erogena' (1998) 25 Guida al Diritto 13.

29. Alessia Cavallo, 'Nuovo indirizzo della Cassazione in materia di "manomorta" (nota a Sez. III, 2/07/04, dep. 23/09/04, n.37395, Annunziata)' (2005) 45 (4) Cassazione Penale 1171; Annalisa Stile, 'Anche la "pacca" sul sedere costituisce violenza sessuale. L'interpretazione della Cassazione sulla nozione di atto sessuale (nota a Sez. III, 2/07/04 N. 37395, Annunziata)' (2005) 45 (4) Cassazione Penale 1182.

30. Cassazione penale, Sez. III, 26/08/2016, n. 35473.

31. Alberto Cadoppi, '"Un bacio è solo un bacio." Alla ricerca di una più appropriata tipizzazione dei reati sessuali' (2012) 1 L'Indice Penale 31; Rocco Lotierzo, 'Sulla configurabilità del reato di violenza sessuale nel caso di un bacio sulla bocca limitato al semplice contatto delle labbra (nota a Cass. sez. III pen. 13 febbraio 2007, n. 25112)' (2008) 48 (3) Cassazione Penale 1041; Matteo Vizzardi, 'Bacio sulle labbra e diritto penale: ancora sulla nozione di "atto sessuale"' (2008) 48 (2) Cassazione Penale 755; Andrea Fanelli, 'Sulla rilevanza penale del bacio' (1998) 6 Rivista Giuridica di Polizia Locale 749; Giovanni Fiandaca, 'La rilevanza penale del bacio tra anatomia e cultura, nota a Sent. Cass. Pen. 27/04/1998' (1998) 2 Foro Italiano 507; Stefania Tabarelli De Fatis, 'Sulla rilevanza penale del «bacio» come atto di libidine prima e dopo la riforma dei reati sessuali' (1997) 3 Rivista Italiana di Diritto Processuale Penale 1997 965.

32. Cassazione penale, Sez. III, 19/11/2019, n.2201; Cassazione penale, Sez. III, 29/05/2018, n.43553.

33. The simple kiss on the cheek or on the mouth by the minimal coercion needed to give it. Cassazione penale, Sez. III, 19/01/2018, n.20712.

34. Cassazione penale, Sez. III, 08/10/2019, n.1570.

35. Cassazione penale, Sez. III, (ud. 19/11/2015), dep. 05/5/2016, n.18679. The decision is critically examined by Michele Cappai, 'La qualificazione delle "violenze" prive di un contatto *corpore corpori* alla prova della recente giurisprudenza in tema di atti sessuali Nota a Cass., Sez. III, sent. 19 novembre 2015 (dep. 5 maggio 2016)' (2017) 2 Diritto Penale Contemporaneo 43.

36. The rule by Art. 241 Implementing, coordinating and transitional rules of the Code of Criminal Procedure, annexed to Decreto Legislativo 28 July 1989, n. 271, provided that the previous rules of the Code of Criminal Procedure of 1930 would continue to apply if the proceedings had reached the prodromic pre-trial stage or the trial stage itself. A limited number of cases would follow old rules at trial and resulting convictions in the years 1990–1991.

37. Council of Europe, *European sourcebook of crime and criminal justice statistics*, 1st edition Council of Europe, (1999) 60.

38. The European Sourcebook also includes data for the last year included in the previous edition. Comparison of successive editions of the European sourcebook reveals variations as noted by Aebi and Linde [Marcelo Aebi and Antonia Linde, 'Conviction Statistics as an Indicator of Crime Trends in Europe from 1990 to 2006' (2012) 18 (1) European Journal on Criminal Policy and Research, 103]. Each edition is an updated version of the previous one, consequently the figures included in the latest edition are supposed to be more reliable. Anyway, for Italy they are minor and not significant. For example, for the period under consideration the first edition of the European Sourcebook indicates the rate of persons convicted for 1996 as 2.2, the second edition indicates a value of 2.1, while for 1995 it is 1.7 according to both editions. However, the author verified the indicated rates with ISTAT (Italian National Institute of Statistics) data of persons convicted of sexual violence as well as updated population data (Reconstructed Resident Population - Years 1991–2001), finding minimal and insignificant variations from those indicated by the European Sourcebook.

39. Council of Europe, *European sourcebook of crime and criminal justice statistics*, 2nd edition Council of Europe, (2003).

40. Council of Europe, *European sourcebook of crime and criminal justice statistics*, 3rd edition Council of Europe, (2006).

41. The set of crime reports that law enforcement agencies transmit to the judicial authority, i.e., all those crimes of which law enforcement agencies have become aware of by means of their investigative activities or through citizen complaints: L'Italia In 150 Anni. Sommario di Statistiche Storiche 1861–2010, Istat 2011, p.265.

42. ISTAT, 'L'Italia In 150 Anni. Sommario di Statistiche Storiche 1861–2010,' Istat 2011 322.

43. Michele Morello, *Il nuovo processo penale. Parte generale* (Cedam 2000) 414.

44. Fewer rape convictions because plea bargains prevail, report suggests <https://www.theguardian.com/society/ 2010/mar/20/rape-convictions-lady-stern-cps> accessed October 3, 2022.

45. Eurispes—Unione Camere Penali, 'Rapporto sul processo penale,' Eurispes, 2008 25.

46. Kathleen Daly and Brigitte Bouhours, 'Rape and Attrition in the Legal Process: A Comparative Analysis of Five Countries Crime and Justice' (2010) 39 (1) Crime and Justice 565, 622.

47. Still very recently: Shannon M. Stuart, Blake M. McKimmie, and Barbara M.Masser, 'Rape Perpetrators on Trial: The Effect of Sexual Assault-Related Schemas on Attributions of Blame' (2019) 34 (2) J Interpers Violence 310; Fiona Leverick, 'What do we know about rape myths and juror decision making?' (2020) 24 (3) The International Journal of Evidence & Proof 255; Shannon Sommer, Joshua J Reynolds and Andre Kehn, 'Mock Juror Perceptions of Rape Victims: Impact of Case Characteristics and Individual Differences' (2016) 17 J Interpers Violence 2847; Grace Cowel, 'Attrition and rape law reform in the United Kingdom: The urgent need for reform to mitigate rape myth bias' (2020) 2 (2) International Review of Contemporary Laws 11.

48. Susan Estrich, *Real rape* (Harvard University Press 1987).

49. Cassazione Penale, Sez. III, 14/04/1999, n.1636.

50. Cassazione penale, Sez. III, 21/07/2008 n.30403.

51. The Crown Prosecution Service, Retrial of Serious Offences—Legal Guidance <https://www.cps.gov.uk/legal-guidance/retrial-serious-offences#:~:text=The%20retrial%20will%20take%20account,to%20proceed%20with%20a%20retrial> accessed October 5, 2022.

52. [2021] ONCA 186.

53. Fahamida Zahan, 'Assessing Credibility of Survivors: The ONCA Debunking Rape Myths and Stereotypes in R v Steele,' *The Court*. Ca (April 9, 2021) <http://www.thecourt.ca/assessing-credibility-of-survivors-the-onca-debunking-rape-myths-and-stereotypes-in -r-v-steele/> accessed October 5, 2022.

54. [2019] ONSC 3207.

55. [1999] 1 S.C.R. 330 95.

56. [2021] ONCA 186 18.

57. [2021] ONCA 186 21.

58. [2021] ONCA 186 29.

59. [2021] ONCA 186 20.

60. Nunzia Pentangelo, Marianna Pollio and Augusta Rapuano, Violenza sessuale e assunzione di alcol: la differenza tra "uso" e "abuso," Nota a sentenza Cassazione Penale n. 32462 del 16 luglio 2018 (ud. 19 gennaio 2018), Sez. III, Dott. ROSI Elisabetta—Presidente, Dott. SOCCI Angelo Matteo—rel. Consigliere. Pentangelo, N., Pollio, M. and Rapuano, A., 'Violenza sessuale e assunzione di alcol: la differenza tra "uso" e "abuso"'- Nota a sentenza Cassazione Penale n. 32462 del 16 luglio 2018 (ud. 19 gennaio 2018), Sez. III, Dott. ROSI Elisabetta – Presidente, Dott. SOCCI (Ius in itinere, July 29, 2019) <iusinitinere.it/violenza-sessuale-e-assunzione-di-alcol-la-differenza-tra-uso-e-abuso-22773> accessed October 6, 2022.

61. Armando Saponaro, '"Visible" and "Invisible" Victims in the Criminal Justice System: Victim-Oriented Paradigms and Models' In Raleigh Blasdell, Laura Krieger-Sample, and Michelle Kilburn (Eds.), *Invisible Victims and the Pursuit of*

Justice: Analyzing Frequently Victimized Yet Rarely Discussed Populations, (IGI Global 2021) 10.

62. Maria Giuseppina Pacilli, Federica Spaccatini, Chiara Ballone, Eleonora Gentile, and Ilaria Giovannelli, 'Moral virtue, victim blaming and helping intentions towards a rape victim. The role of victim's personality from (past) media narrative to present social perception' (2022) 2 Psicologia sociale, Social Psychology Theory & Research 183.

63. Niccolò Brighella, 'Il Massacro Del Circeo Ci Ricorda Che Dopo 46 Anni Continuiamo Col Victim Blaming' *vdnews* (September 29, 2021) <https://vdnews.tv/article/massacro-circeo-ricorda-dopo-quarantasei-anni-continuiamo-colpevolizzare-vittime> accessed October 4, 2022.

64. Armando Saponaro, '"Visible" and "Invisible" Victims in the Criminal Justice System: Victim-Oriented Paradigms and Models' in Raleigh Blasdell, Laura Krieger-Sample, and Michelle Kilburn (Eds.), *Invisible Victims and the Pursuit of Justice: Analyzing Frequently Victimized Yet Rarely Discussed Populations*, (IGI Global 2021) 14. In this paper the Author examines this issue more extensively.

65. Mary Iliadis, Kate Fitz-Gibbon, and Sandra Walklate, 'Improving justice responses for victims of intimate partner violence: Examining the merits of the provision of independent legal representation' (2019) 45 (1) International Journal of Comparative and Applied Criminal Justice 105.

BIBLIOGRAPHY

Aebi, M and Linde, A, 'Conviction Statistics as an Indicator of Crime Trends in Europe from 1990 to 2006' (2012) 18 (1) European Journal on Criminal Policy and Research 103.

Amato, G, 'Se è chiara la direzione sessuale dell'atto anche il bacio sulla guancia è reato. Sussiste il delitto anche se la vittima reagisce e l'approccio «cade» su una zona non erogena' (1998) 25 Guida al Diritto 13.

Ambrosini, G, Violenza sessuale, *Digesto delle discipline penalistiche XV* (1999) 290.

Antonucci, E, 'The evolution of the principle of mandatory prosecution in Italy. A problematic case of gradual institutional change' (2021) 66 International Journal of Law, Crime and Justice 1.

Brighella, N, 'Il Massacro Del Circeo Ci Ricorda Che Dopo 46 Anni Continuiamo Col Victim Blaming' *vdnews* (September 29, 2021) <https://vdnews.tv/article/massacro-circeo-ricorda-dopo-quarantasei-anni-continuiamo-colpevolizzare-vittime> accessed October 4, 2022.

Cadoppi A, *Commentario delle norme contro la violenza sessuale e contro la pedofilia*, (CEDAM 2006).

Cadoppi A, '"Un bacio è solo un bacio." Alla ricerca di una più appropriata tipizzazione dei reati sessuali' (2012) 1 L'Indice Penale 31.

Cappai, M, 'La qualificazione delle "violenze" prive di un contatto corpore corpori alla prova della recente giurisprudenza in tema di atti sessuali Nota a Cass., Sez.

III, sent. 19 novembre 2015 (dep. 5 maggio 2016)' (2017) 2 Diritto Penale Contemporaneo 43.
Cavallo, A, 'Nuovo indirizzo della Cassazione in materia di "manomorta" (nota a Sez. III, 2/07/04, dep. 23/09/04, n.37395, Annunziata)' (2005) 45 (4) Cassazione Penale 1171.
Cordero, F, Procedura Penale (GIUFFRÈ 2012).
Council of Europe, *European sourcebook of crime and criminal justice statistics*, 1st edition Council of Europe, (1999).
Council of Europe, *European sourcebook of crime and criminal justice statistics*, 2nd edition Council of Europe, (2003).
Council of Europe, *European sourcebook of crime and criminal justice statistics*, 3rd edition Council of Europe, (2006).
Cowel, G, 'Attrition and rape law reform in the United Kingdom: The urgent need for reform to mitigate rape myth bias' (2020) 2 (2) International Review of Contemporary Laws 11.
Daly, K and Bouhours, B, 'Rape and Attrition in the Legal Process: A Comparative Analysis of Five Countries Crime and Justice' (2010) 39 (1) *Crime and Justice* 565
Di Federico, G, 'Prosecutorial Independence and the Democratic Requirement of Accountability in Italy. Analysis of a Deviant Case in a Comparative Perspective' (1998) 38 (3) British Journal of Criminology 371.
Erbaş, R, 'Challenges in Regulating Sexual Offences in Turkey' in Erbaş R (ed), *Global Problems in Sexual Offenses* (Lexington Books, 2022) 3–24.
Estrich, S, *Real rape* (Harvard University Press 1987).
Eurispes – Unione Camere Penali, 'Rapporto sul processo penale,' Eurispes, 2008.
Fanelli, A, 'Sulla rilevanza penale del bacio' (1998) 6 Rivista Giuridica di Polizia Locale 749; Giovanni Fiandaca, 'La rilevanza penale del bacio tra anatomia e cultura, nota a Sent. Cass. Pen. 27/04/1998' (1998) 2 Foro Italiano 507.
Fewer rape convictions because plea bargains prevail, report suggests, <https://www.theguardian.com/society/2010/mar/20/rape-convictions-lady-stern-cps> accessed 3 October 2022.
Fiandaca, G, Violenza sessuale, *Enciclopedia del diritto XLVI* (update IV 2000) 1153
Iliadis, M, Fitz-Gibbon, K, and Walklate, S, 'Improving justice responses for victims of intimate partner violence: Examining the merits of the provision of independent legal representation (2019) 45 (1) International Journal of Comparative and Applied Criminal Justice 105.
ISTAT, 'L'Italia In 150 Anni. Sommario di Statistiche Storiche 1861–2010,' Istat 2011.
Kelly, L, Lovett, J and Regan, L, *Home Office Research Study 293 A gap or a chasm? Attrition in reported rape cases* (Home Office Research, Development and Statistics Directorate 2005) 30.
Leverick, F, "What do we know about rape myths and juror decision making?' (2020) 24 (3) The International Journal of Evidence & Proof 255.
Lotierzo, R, 'Sulla configurabilità del reato di violenza sessuale nel caso di un bacio sulla bocca limitato al semplice contatto delle labbra (nota a Cass. sez. III pen. 13 febbraio 2007, n. 25112)' (2008) 48 (3) Cassazione Penale 1041.

Lovett, J and Kelly, L, *Different systems, similar outcomes? Tracking attrition in reported rape cases across Europe* (CWASU 2009).

Marini, G, *Delitti contro la persona* (Giappichelli 1996).

Musacchio, V, *Il delitto di violenza sessuale (art. 609 bis del Codice penale)* (CEDAM 1999).

Pacilli, M G, Spaccatini, F, Ballone, C, Gentile, E, and Giovannelli, I, 'Moral virtue, victim blaming and helping intentions towards a rape victim. The role of victim's personality from (past) media narrative to present social perception' (2022) 2 Psicologia sociale, Social Psychology Theory & Research 183.

Pentangelo, N, Pollio, M and Rapuano, A, 'Violenza sessuale e assunzione di alcol: la differenza tra "uso" e "abuso"' Nota a sentenza Cassazione Penale n. 32462 del 16 luglio 2018 (ud. 19 gennaio 2018), Sez. III, Dott. ROSI Elisabetta—Presidente, Dott. SOCCI (Ius in itinere, July 29, 2019) <iusinitinere.it/violenza-sessuale-e-assunzione-di-alcol-la-differenza-tra-uso-e-abuso-22773> accessed October 6, 2022

Research Development and Statistics—Office for Criminal Justice Reform, *Notifiable Offences and Numbers of Persons Prosecuted, Tried and Convicted for Rape Offences, England and Wales 2006* (Home Office 2008).

Saponaro, A, '"Visible" and "Invisible" Victims in the Criminal Justice System: Victim-Oriented Paradigms and Models' in Raleigh Blasdell, Laura Krieger-Sample, and Michelle Kilburn (Eds.), *Invisible Victims and the Pursuit of Justice: Analyzing Frequently Victimized Yet Rarely Discussed Populations*, (IGI Global 2021)

Siegel, L J, *Criminology: The core* (4th ed Wadsworth 2012).

Sommer, S, Reynolds, J. J. and Kehn, A., 'Mock Juror Perceptions of Rape Victims: Impact of Case Characteristics and Individual Differences' (2016) 17 J Interpers Violence 2847.

Stile, A, 'Anche la "pacca" sul sedere costituisce violenza sessuale. L'interpretazione della Cassazione sulla nozione di atto sessuale (nota a Sez. III, 2/07/04 N. 37395, Annunziata)' (2005) 45 (4) Cassazione Penale 1182.

Stuart, S M, McKimmie, B M, and Masser, B M, 'Rape Perpetrators on Trial: The Effect of Sexual Assault-Related Schemas on Attributions of Blame' (2019) 34 (2) J Interpers Violence 310.

Tabarelli De Fatis S, 'Sulla rilevanza penale del «bacio» come atto di libidine prima e dopo la riforma dei reati sessuali' (1997) 3 Rivista Italiana di Diritto Processuale Penale 1997 965.

The Crown Prosecution Service, *Retrial of Serious Offences—Legal Guidance* <https://www.cps.gov.uk/legal-guidance/retrial-serious-offences#:~:text=The%20retrial%20will%20take%20account,to%20proceed%20with%20a%20retrial> accessed October 5, 2022.

Vizzardi, M, 'Bacio sulle labbra e diritto penale: ancora sulla nozione di "atto sessuale"' (2008) 48 (2) Cassazione Penale 755.

Zahan, F, 'Assessing Credibility of Survivors: The ONCA Debunking Rape Myths and Stereotypes in R v Steele,' *The Court. Ca* (April 9, 2021) <http://www.thecourt.ca/assessing-credibility-of-survivors-the-onca-debunking-rape-myths-and-stereotypes-in-r -v-steele/> accessed October 5, 2022.

3

Outside the Legal Framework

Myths and Stereotypes in Spanish Sexual Assault Cases

Elisa Simó Soler, Miguel Lorente Acosta, and Elena Martínez García

From an analytical perspective, we could explain justice as the result of a judgment of facts according to reality through the legal framework. Some limits established by the law that define which part of reality is legal and which one is illegal to exist. However, reality is neither neutral nor a simple description of events, it is rather the result of considering certain facts under a given meaning according to the values, myths, and stereotypes that society establishes around these behaviors.

Lippmann defined stereotypes for the first time in 1922 as a "distorted picture or image in a person's mind about people, things, places, situations . . . not based on personal experience, but derived culturally, that is interposed between the cognitive capacity of the person and his or her perceptions of the world."[1] What this statement entails is that the meaning of facts provided by myths and stereotypes can also play a key role in justice when the system must put them within the criminal legal framework as a crime or when it should leave them outside where the meaning defines them as part of normality or under the influence of some specific circumstances. The more facts are closer to structural social references, the more myths and stereotypes play a role in their meaning and the result of Justice.

Different studies disclosure the existence of several myths and stereotypes regarding sexual violence victims, aggressors, and circumstances. Some of these elements are part of the social imaginary that sexual assaults are committed by unknown men, at parties or in a leisure context, that injuries are always caused and the delay in reporting cases is considered to be evidence of lying. These references change the meaning of facts influencing the application of the legal framework and the result of Justice. If the intention is to guarantee the right of equal access to justice and a fair trial for women, disproving gender stereotypes is a positive State obligation arising from international treaties and conventions. In determining actions to achieve real equality, the field "outside the legal framework" becomes a priority scope of action.

OUTSIDE THE LEGAL FRAMEWORK

It would be difficult to accept for a given society a healthcare system in which most ill or sick individuals do not go to hospitals due to lack of trust in the system, its professionals and the fear of the treatment they would receive, and in which a significant number of patients suffer from the negative health consequences produced by the system's own response. This situation that we observe in this scenario is far from reality and unacceptable. However, it describes what is happening nowadays with sexual violence and the criminal justice system's response.

No distance between what lies outside and what lies within the legal framework exists. This lack of distance or overlap exists because the same references apply to both spaces. Both areas are part of the same culture, which determines reality and what is normal in that reality, as well as the way in which people live and establish social relationships under a legal framework based on the values, ideas, principles, and beliefs that people share as a society within a cultural reference.

Outside the Legal Frame Is Culture, and Inside the Legal Frame Is Culture

Culture is at the origin of everything, and culture means knowledge. Most people consider culture to be literature, art, or music, but these are cultural expressions. *Ridley* defines culture as the "capacity to accumulate ideas and inventions through generations, to transmit them to the rest of people and, this way, unify cognitive resources of individuals."[2] The essence of culture is knowledge, those cognitive elements that society shares in a continuous manner as a result of having shared references built from common ideas, values, beliefs and principles. These communal components are the ones that shape identities and organize the lives of people and social relationships considering the cultural elements.

The legal framework is the result of what elements (goods, rights, interests, and principles) society considers should be protected from certain behaviors, how to develop this protection to keep order, and what are the consequences of breaking it. This way, the legal framework maintains and protects the established order given by culture in a particular social organization.

The law operates within the legal framework while the moral and ethical elements inspired by the same referents that write the law operate outside said framework, where we can also find what society learns from the application of the law through the criminal justice system, which feeds these values with the judicial conclusions taken from the interaction between the legal frame and social conflicts.

The key to understanding how society organizes to obtain a "social order" and what are the acceptable limits for the social and individual relationships is to realize that they are based on cultural references. For example, as we mentioned at the beginning, the answer to why the criminal justice system's response to sexual violence is so poor lies in the knowledge (cognitive elements) that defines culture and establishes what is normal or not, good, or bad, correct, or incorrect, admissible or inadmissible. This knowledge results from the fact that people who have occupied positions of power throughout history have determined which "ideas and inventions" should be preserved by society and which should be discarded and the people who have made these decisions from their own viewpoint but affecting the whole population, have been mostly heteronormative, white, wealthy men.

Therefore, what is perceived as neutral or normal from the social point of view is not from the perspective of critical analysis because this "neutrality" and "normality" given by the "common knowledge" of culture have been determined by men under their own perspective and consideration about what is beneficial or necessary from their standpoint, without women's participation in this common knowledge. The result is that the references that define reality are androcentric.

The practical consequences of this androcentric determination of culture are two:

1. Reality is the result of what is supposed to be under the circumstances and elements that make things happen that way.
2. The meaning of reality, or the facts that make it up, is built on the cultural references that try to integrate these facts within the social framework.

Violence, Society, and Culture

The result of the androcentric determination is that all integrations have meaning. That meaning can be positive, when facts are coincident with the cultural references or negative if facts are contrary to the set social benchmarks. In any case, being positive or negative meaning (and how) depends on the sense provided by the androcentric references of culture, and the causes and consequences involved in the case considered from this viewpoint.

The social perception and position of some facts and behaviors depend on how close or far these facts are from the cultural ideas and values. Regarding violence, two general references exist to define violent behaviors based on this distance to cultural elements. These categories are "external violence" and "structural violence."

"External violence" is based on motivations far from cultural elements, being perceived as threatening to society and most cases are reported. This type of violence corresponds with people's general idea, and most criminal behaviors fall into this category. "Structural violence" was described by *Galtung* as referring to violent behaviors rooted in elements related to or close to the cultural reference.[3] This violence is not thought of as threatening because among its motivations is the idea of reestablishing the order that has been broken through someone's behavior, usually a person who is considered to be in an inferior position according to the androcentric model. These characteristics consolidate that this violence is not serious and occurs as part of "normality," causing most of this violence to go unreported.

Violence against women with its different expressions (intimate partner violence, sexual violence, harassment, genital mutilation . . .) is part of the "structural violence," and behind the aggressions are motivations related to the meaning that the androcentric culture provides to these acts. There are two main arguments in this sense: one is the idea of "normality," which is used especially when the result of the attack is not physically severe; and the other is "justification," which refers to the idea that there are reasons, causes and factors that explain violence against women as a consequence of their behavior or based on circumstantial elements that affect the man who exercises violence or the interpretation of the situation.

The cultural basis of "structural violence," in other words, the cultural basis of sexual violence, creates the necessary elements to use it as part of "normality" through all the arguments provided by androcentric culture, sometimes focused on women's behavior, some others on men's problems, and sometimes on the circumstances that surround the facts. The consequences of these cultural elements are explained at the beginning of the chapter but related to sexual violence. Most women that suffer sexual violence do not report the aggression,[4] a significant number of reported cases are not convicted,[5] and after the judicial process many victims suffer negative consequences, called "secondary victimization."[6] We, thus, become aware of the existence of elements that harm against women at all levels and stages, as they are both inside and outside the legal framework. They are part of a culture which, as a whole, comprises everything that lies in and outside the legal system.

In the end, we can draw a set of inferences from the analysis of social circumstances that all the elements play for the androcentric system:

1. There is a lack of confidence in the system.
2. The normalization or justification of facts through myths and stereotypes leads to greater impunity.
3. These elements and the way in which cases are approached produce damage to victims (secondary victimization).
4. This mistrust leads to women not reporting cases.
5. Society thinks that sexual violence is not so serious because it doesn't know its real dimensions and features.
6. This general situation of sexual violence is historical, but it does not produce a response by the system to change it:
   a. There is no answer to the poor response of the criminal justice service.
   b. There is no answer to the health impact produced on the victims.
7. The system has changed the law many times and has even changed the crime's meaning, from an attempt on the victim's honour to an attempt against sexual liberty, but it hasn't changed the way to respond nor the way to interpret reality and its facts.

The Role of Myths and Stereotypes

The system's response allows continuous feedback of myths and stereotypes, which strengthen them and amplify their use in different contexts and new circumstances. This is what is called "re-actualization of myths."

Everything counts in a game of lights and shadows to keep reality in the shade, and to perceive it as the story says, not as it is. These elements play a role in creating a strategy that keeps ideas and meanings within the references given by the system. The result is not the consequence of a particular decision, but what culture establishes through "cognitive resources" considered valid in organizing society. To achieve this result, the "help" of invisible and anonymous elements, such as myths and stereotypes, is needed to overcome all obstacles and resolve all the issues and conflicts that arise.

Following the idea of *Lévi-Strauss* about myths as a cognitive frame providing models that offer logical solutions to face contradictions,[7] when we analyze what happens with sexual violence, we see how myths and stereotypes act in this sense. Society establishes that "sexual violence does not exist under normal circumstances"[8], but then we see how sexual violence is committed as part of our social relationships. Therefore, there is a contradiction between what cultural and social references establish and what then happens as part of reality. This contradiction is double: first, sexual violence occurs; second, sexual violence occurs under "normal circumstances."

When reality shows society that things are different than expected, the way to resolve this contradiction is to deny the facts that create the conflict, and the procedure to solve it easily and immediately is to use the arguments that culture provides to explain its reality. These arguments follow two lines: The first one provides references that are not true, and this way it hides what culture does not want to be part of reality. Myths used to attain this goal are underrepresented in society: they hide what is part of sexual violence and make people think that, if these elements are part of an event, the aggression is not credible. For example, this happens when the main damage in a victim is psychological, when the woman did not report the attack or did so several days later, when the aggression is in the home and when the perpetrator is known by the victim and close to her, among other circumstances. The second presents references that are not part of what actually occurs in sexual violence but are presented as if they were true. When these elements are part of sexual violence people think that the aggression happened, although these features are not common. These myths are overrepresented in society and present sexual violence as something that it really is not. Among these myths, we find the idea that victims suffer important physical injuries, that the attacks occur in leisure places, parties, or isolated spaces, that perpetrators are strangers to the victim or that the victim or aggressor is drunk . . .[9]

In the end, there is a double argument that makes society (i.e., people, professionals as part of this people, and the system as a response provided by these professionals) interpret sexual violence based on elements and features that are not common when it does actually take place, and the real features and elements of sexual violence are used to negate it.

The criminal justice system's response to sexual violence reinforces the social and cultural ideas about sexual violence,[10] and thus emphasizes its expected features: it is not common, that its features are limited to the ones presented in the reported cases, that there are many false allegations, or that perpetrators are a "special kind of bad men." Hence, there is a continuity between what culture says about sexual violence and what society proves through the response provided by the criminal justice system response, and this idea is reinforced and preserved through all the myths and stereotypes that its own cultural references create around it, as we explain in the following pages.

INSIDE THE LEGAL FRAMEWORK

It is generally accepted that victims are widely neglected in the criminal justice system.[11] How each woman deals with her emotions after the crime may not combine well with the linearity of the criminal procedure, which follows a legally established set of phases and continues regardless of her circumstances. This can create tension between the criminal process and women's psychological process. The criminal procedure can be an impersonal and dehumanising experience if it fails to consider how victims can become invisible and instrumentalised, and the professionals appointed to protect them can fail to treat victims appropriately, compounding their maltreatment.

Although women are not a unified and homogeneous group,[12] the widespread assumption that all women are in a particular emotional state when they attend court positions them as mere subjects in need of protection and/or guardianship. The paternalistic view sees women's capacity for agency as limited to the moment of reporting, delegating further decisions to the professionals as it is considered that they are not able to make proper decisions.[13] The Spanish criminal justice system has adopted this image of helpless women for its functionality, with two aims: to avoid frustrating the expectations of the members of the legal professions involved in the administration of justice (namely, judges, prosecutors, lawyers, experts, polices, court clerk) used to a punitive model,[14] and in line with the criminal legislative policy that has renounced the structural-vindictive component of violence against women, understanding gender-based violence as individual acts rather than as the result of the patriarchy.[15]

The criminal justice system in Spain has been critiqued for poor quality research on sexual violence in comparison with other types of gender-based violence, and for the prevalence of institutional gender bias.[16] The *Group of Experts on Combating Violence against Women and Domestic Violence* regrets "that many judicial decisions seem to reproduce stereotypes or apply overly formalistic interpretations that diminish the criminal responsibility of the perpetrator or even blame the victim."[17]

Sexual Violence Victim's Prototype in Courts

Sexual violence myths are widely held, but these represent false beliefs about rape, its nature, and the circumstances surrounding it.[18] In particular, the image of the female victim of sexual violence is one of an injured, upset woman who has been assaulted by a stranger in a public place and has suffered extreme violence.[19] The specialized literature has summarised the archetype of the "ideal" victim following a series of features related to the violence exercised by the man and the woman's reaction, emotional development, previous sexual experience, the characteristics of the event and the delay in reporting.

Firstly, the requirement of getting hurt and fighting back lies in the fact that any act of sexual violence consists of a violent and forced penetration. When she is attacked, the victim is expected to do everything possible to escape.[20]

Secondly, regarding the woman's emotional state, according to *Randall*, the clearest example of this concept of an "ideal" victim is the expectation that "real" or "credible" victims of sexual assault will display their trauma in visible and stereotypical ways, including being shaky, crying, and expressing distress in other recognizable and gendered ways such as social isolation after having suffered the crime.[21] Moreover, it is thought that women often lie about sexual assault, make false allegations, and report crimes for money.[22]

Thirdly, the existence of a previous relationship harms the assessment of sexual violence, since, as *Temkin et al.* point out, "marital rape, rape by a former partner, or rape by someone with whom [the woman] has previously had consensual sex is not really rape"[23] since that consent is given for eternity, to all or any sexual activity. Fourthly, concerning crime circumstances, it is assumed to be a sudden attack, late at night, by a stranger in a public and remote place.[24]

What's more, some other preconceptions about the ways women dress, behave, and the previous use of drugs and alcohol, insinuating that women were "asking" to be sexually assaulted appear.[25] These conditions surrounding the crime and shaping its degree of credibility are highly exclusive and place the responsibility for the attacks on women "if they are out of their homes late at night or in solitary places or dress in a certain way."[26]

Finally, it is often claimed that the "real" victims are the ones who immediately report the facts to the police.[27] Time taken to report is understood as an element of suspicion regarding the authenticity of the reported facts, but that point of view, ignores that reporting is a right, not a duty as well as that the only legal time limit for reporting is the statutory limitation period.[28]

The power of the "real sexual violence victim" template affects how sexual aggression is defined and understood by the experts involved in the judicial process.[29] The employment of sexual violence myths in courts influences the decision-making process, reinforcing the beliefs of those who use those myths, whilst also raising suspicion in the minds of those who generally do not, potentially decreasing the victims' possibilities to be believed.[30]

However, the analysis of data from official Spanish governmental statistics reveals a completely different picture. Only 25.0 percent of women who have been raped present injuries.[31] Since each woman has a unique experience and reaction to sexual assault, her gestures and physical/emotional appearance cannot be taken as conclusive factors, whether the reality matches the stereotype or not. Of all women aged 16 years or older living in Spain, 13.7 percent have suffered sexual violence in their lifetime from any person (current partner, past partners, or people with whom they have not been in a relationship). Regarding sexual violence outside the couple, 21.6 percent of women report that the aggressor was a male relative, 49.0 percent a male friend or acquaintance, and 39.1 percent say that the aggressor was an unknown man.[32] In 59.1 percent of rape cases, the sexual aggression took place at the home of the victim, the perpetrator, or a third person.[33]

Until the recently enacted Organic Law 10/2022, of September 6, on the comprehensive guarantee of sexual freedom, the Criminal Code established that to be tried for sexual assault there must be violence or intimidation otherwise the facts would constitute a sexual abuse offense. The requirement of violence conditioned the interpretation of the facts, and the lack of psychological training excludes understanding of responses to sexual aggression such as dissociation and tonic immobility.[34] Nowadays, the distinction between sexual assault and sexual abuse has been eliminated in the Criminal Code and sexual assault any id considered to constitute any infringement of the sexual freedom of another person without his or her consent.[35] According to the new wording of Article 178, consent will only be understood to exist when it has been freely expressed through acts that, given the circumstances of the case, clearly show the will of the person.

This stereotype of the victim affects the administration of justice with negative effects on women, particularly those who do not fit into this victim model, as *Hohl and Stanko* state "[t]he greater the extent to which a complaint of rape conforms to ideas of 'real rape,' they show, the higher the chances that the case successfully navigates the challenges of the criminal justice system. The less the case—and the complainant herself– conforms to an ideal of femininity and its sexual violation, the lower the chances are that she is believed, and the case is considered a 'real rape.'"[36] Gender stereotyping in the courts is a manifestation of institutional violence that causes secondary victimisation.[37] It occurs when the State and its officials fail to act according to their obligations in cases of gender-based violence and, by action or omission, delay, obstruct or impede women's enjoyment and exercise of their human rights including their access to public policies aimed at preventing, protecting, investigating, and punishing acts of violence against women. For some researchers this dimension of institutional violence is closely linked to gender stereotyping in court.[38] Myths about women prevent them from exercising their rights, and when the criminal justice system does not trust their word, they suffer a second experience of violence. Paradoxically, when the system tries to turn victims into survivors the re-victimising dynamic of courts returns and confirms women in their status as victims.[39]

"La Manada" Spanish Case: An Example of Judicial Stereotyping

A paradigmatic case that marked a turning point in the treatment of sexual violence in Spain was the "Manada de Pamplona," in which an alleged rape by a group of five men (including a military officer and a civil guard) of an eighteen-year-old girl in a doorway was prosecuted. This procedure had high a significant degree of social and media repercussion that led to the preparation of a report by the Criminal Law section of the General Codification Commission at the request of the Ministry of Justice, as well as to the enactment of the Organic Law of comprehensive guarantee of sexual freedom. Not only was the legal qualification criticized, but also the content of the separate opinion in the Judgment of the Provincial Court of Navarra and several of the pieces of evidence provided by the prosecution, which questioned doubt on the credibility of the victim's version and the conformity of her conduct to that of a "real" victim of sexual aggression.

After the first conviction for sexual abuse in the Provincial Court of Navarra,[40] which had a dissenting vote, and a judgment confirming the verdict for sexual abuse with prevalence of the Superior Court of Justice of Navarra[41] with two separate opinions, the Supreme Court ruled that the proven facts were constitutive of a continuous crime of rape of Articles 178 and 179 of the Criminal Code, with the specific aggravations of Art. 180.1. 1ª and 2ª,[42] amending the qualification of the previous resolutions. The reporting judge warns of the possible existence of stereotypes in crimes against sexual freedom since "they have been a clear exponent of the function of legal norms in the recreation of stereotypes and social roles that have defined for centuries the unequal distribution of rights and obligations, discriminating the possibilities of women."[43] Such preconceived ideas affect the evaluation of the evidence and the construction of the proven facts.

The Supreme Court ruled on the importance of the factual account to criticize as inexplicable the absence of certain fundamental elements in the proven facts of the appealed judgment. The woman had consumed alcoholic beverages and was under the influence of alcohol at the time of the assault. The videos recorded by the defendants show that "the complainant was crouched, cornered against the wall by two of the defendants and screaming"[44] with "absent rictus, closed eyes, absence, dulling of her higher faculties, passivity, subjection, submission, absence of strength and vigour, cornered, crouched, screaming."[45] To legally argue the acquittal, the Magistrate maintains that it is "the undeniable relaxed expression, without a hint of rigidity or tension, of her face that prevents her from sustaining any feeling of fear, disgust, repugnance, rejection, refusal, uneasiness, discomfort . . . , and which is incompatible with the situation she claims to be living and which, according to her, left her paralyzed."[46]

The discrepancy refers to whether the sexual relations were consensual or not. The defence of the defendants argues that there was a prior agreement, and the sexual acts were conducted with the victim's consent. They rely on the absence of injuries as exculpatory evidence. The Provincial Court rejects this position and, despite considering that they did not act in an intimidating manner, holds that: "the defendants voluntarily created a situation of pre-eminence over the complainant, objectively appreciable, which gave them a privileged position over her, taking advantage of the superiority thus created, to sexually abuse the complainant, who in this way did not give her consent freely, but rather was vitiated, coerced or pressured by such situation."[47]

They maintain the victim's voluntariness argument on the appeal heard by the Superior Court of Justice, claiming the unconditional consent of the woman in the following terms: "[t]he defendants also had their cognitive faculties inhibited by alcohol, and in a state of euphoria they could have legitimately believed in the unconditional consent and active participation of the complainant."[48] Similarly, the magistrate pronounces himself in a separate opinion for which the non-externalization of an explicit or implicit refusal constitutes an invitation to accept sexual relations.[49]

Such approaches lead the Supreme Court to differentiate between consent and submission and recover the legislative framework set in the Istanbul Convention. According to the Supreme Court: "The intimidation caused the victim to adopt an attitude of submission, not consent, which according to the account of proven facts the defendants were aware of, and also took advantage of the situation of the complainant in the mentioned cubicle to which she had been taken to perform various acts of a sexual nature with her, with libidinous intent and acting in common accord."[50] Based on the reference in Article 36.2 of the Istanbul Convention to consent—which "must be given voluntarily as a manifestation of the free will of the person considered in the context of the surrounding conditions"—the Supreme Court concludes that it is impossible to understand as will the absence of physical resistance.

How they interpret the proven facts allows recognizing in them the concurrence of violence or intimidation that delimits the borderline between a crime of sexual aggression or sexual abuse. Neither the Provincial Court nor the Superior Court of Justice of Navarra found the concurrence of violence or intimidation (nor environmental intimidation). However, two magistrates of the Superior Court of Justice and of the Supreme Court considered that the five defendants intimidated the victim. They recovered fragments of the sentence of the Provincial Court of Navarra to describe the intimidating environment: "[i]t is undeniable that the complainant suddenly found herself in the hidden and narrow place described, with only one exit, surrounded by five men of much older ages with a strong physique; upon perceiving this atmosphere, she felt impressed and unable to react. [. . .] She felt intense anxiety and uneasiness, which caused her stupor and made her adopt an attitude of submission and passivity, determining her to do what the defendants told her to, keeping her eyes closed most of the time."[51]

THE STATES' DUE DILIGENCE RELATED TO GENDER STEREOTYPES AND THEIR POSSIBLE LIABILITY UNDER THE INTERNATIONAL FRAMEWORK: THE ISTANBUL CONVENTION

Given the existence of stereotypes in the previous lines we should now briefly analyse the set of positive and negative obligations that States have within the international framework of the Istanbul Convention (11 May 2011), which creates a duty of diligence for States and, in the event of non-compliance, liability for the latter.[52] This international treaty is directly applicable to the signatory States.

The Right to a Life Free of Gender Violence

First, we must recognize the creation of the right to a life free of violence for women, as a right of multilevel interpretation in the States that are part of the Treaty. Article 4 of the Istanbul Convention affirms this by establishing that "Parties shall take the necessary legislative or other measures to promote and protect the right of everyone, in particular women, to live free from violence in both the public and the private sphere" obliging them to condemn "all forms of discrimination against women" and to "take, without delay, the legislative measures and, where appropriate, the normative framework to remove any obstacle that impedes material equality, based in particular on sex, gender, race, colour, language, religion, political or any other opinion, national or social origin, membership of a national minority, property, birth, sexual orientation, gender identity, age, health status, disability, marital status, migrant or refugee status, or any other status."[53]

In no case, adds Article 4, are the necessary gender-specific and positive measures considered discriminatory. The Proposal for a Directive COM/2022/105 (final) of the Parliament and of the Council on combating violence against women and domestic violence now goes further in the same direction.[54]

In the Spanish case, through Article 10.5 of the Spanish Constitution, a multilevel interpretation leads us to integrate this fundamental right within our own legal framework of the fundamental right to equality (Art. 14 SC) and the fundamental right to life (Art. 15 SC).

State Obligations and Due Diligence

Article 5 of the Istanbul Convention establishes the existence of State obligations to comply with a level of due diligence. It provides for a threefold differentiated mandate: States undertake the measures to ensure that State authorities, officials, agents, and institutions, as well as other actors acting on behalf of the State, conduct themselves in accordance with this obligation.

On the other hand, to this end, states must clearly legislate on such "due diligence standards to prevent, investigate, punish and provide reparation for acts of violence covered by the scope of this Convention." Thirdly, "provide compensation for acts of violence falling within the scope of this Convention committed by non-state actors."

This entails the recognition of the creation of a double dimension of the duty of due diligence of States: a systemic dimension and an individual dimension. "The first, more generic, calls for State intervention aimed at guaranteeing a model of comprehensive and sustained regulation of violence against women that, in addition, pursues a global transformation of society that overcomes structural gender inequality."[55]

In this sense, patriarchy is the tool of control for perpetuating an unjust, unequal economic model—in a multiple and transversal manner—and oppressive of women. To this purpose, the measures to be articulated by the State must tend to "subvert the pre-existing patterns of structural subordination, gender hierarchies, systemic marginalization and structural inequalities, which are at the root of the violence suffered by women."[56]

For its part, the individual dimension of liability requires the existence of state obligations aimed at providing specific victims who suffer violence with effective measures of protection, punishment, and reparation, which requires a high degree of accommodation and flexibility.

Protection Actions Against the Obligation of Systemic and Individual Due Diligence

In line with this is the regulation of civil actions contained in the Istanbul Convention. According to Article 29, "Parties shall take the necessary legislative or other measures to provide victims with adequate civil remedies against the perpetrator of the crime," and it also adds, "adequate civil remedies against State authorities who have failed in their duty to take the necessary preventive or protective measures within the limits of their powers." The meaning of this double content attends to the double conception of due diligence in its individual and systemic level. Liability, therefore, is for both.

In addition to civil, criminal, or administrative actions, these remedies include a request for compensation to the victim to hold the perpetrators of the crime accountable. In the event of not being able to respond directly with their assets to such compensation, it then makes the State subsidiarily liable in the event of non-payment to the victim, without prejudice to the reimbursement that may then be claimed; all within a reasonable period of time. Once again, the individual and systemic levels reappear.

Contents of This Duty of Diligence, Especially from a Systemic Perspective

We have seen casuistry related to sexual violence. It has become evident that stereotypes are present in our culture and, therefore, also in the judicial context. If stereotypes are not detected, the result is impunity in the specific case but also in the eyes of society. For this reason, there is a clear *systemic* responsibility in this "deconstruction," which leads to *individual* responsibility. From the collective to the individual.

To this end, article 6 of the Istanbul Convention requires a gender perspective in implementation and impact assessment. Moreover, the right to civil, criminal, administrative and labour legislation lays the foundations for the transformation of our society and ensures women dignified and safe protection. In this dimension, the meaning of gender, inequality, and power discrimination –as a social-relational structure, but also as an inter-subjective one– must be understood. In this sense, the specialization of the legislator becomes unavoidable to comprehend the complex specificities that gender entails.

The right for legislation to be created with a gender impact assessment and under mainstreaming policies, stimulate a transformation of the current social pattern based on androcentric power relations and the subjugation of women. Gender stereotypes affect the credibility of women in court and compromise the judge's impartiality and the justice system's integrity. This entails, once again, the necessary (and rigorous) training and sensitization of judicial operators. As a result, the gender perspective should permeate in different stages to get a holistic transformation:[57]

1. Right to the regulation of preventive and treatment programs that are effective and implemented as specialized victim support systems (Arts. 16, 20, 56 of the Istanbul Convention). The risk assessment system requires positive action on the part of the State to be effective and consistent with the situation of the victims (Art. 51 of the Istanbul Convention), without placing a greater burden on them based on stereotypes.
2. Right to an effective judicial remedy in the face of gender-based violence through proper investigation and collection of evidence, protec-

tion, reparation, and specialization of the judge both in the investigation and prosecution phase, as well as adequate civil and criminal remedies (Arts. 29, 44 and 54 of the Istanbul Convention). In other words, there is a right to a fair trial without undue delay; not only the right to know what happened, but also the right to find out the circumstances or "context" in which it occurred. These two levels are necessary to understand and punish gender-based violence, as well as to prevent new aggressions. This requires a high level of training for legal operators through specific rules that address the gender impact and ensure the various aspects of the right to a fair trial and access to justice for women victims (Arts. 8, 11, 15 of the Istanbul Convention).

3. Right to due process, which includes a specific right to the evaluation of evidence, to judicial conviction, and to have these reflected in the reasoning of the sentence so that, if applicable, it can be determined, whether there has been a gender stereotypes underlie the judgement. That means, if the judge makes unjustified leaps into the void, with special emphasis on the circumstances expressed by the victim's statement and the way in which this has been taken into consideration by the judge. This requires a specific analysis. The reference to the "particular context in which the act occurred" will provide more data for the evidentiary assessment as a whole and so that the presumption of innocence can be raised through certainties and prosecution evidence that allows a rational and convincing explanation of what happened, without prejudices or evaluations in a certain sense being derived in the plenary session practised with contradiction and hearing (Art. 54 of the Istanbul Convention).
4. Right to compensation in the event of a system failure. The possibility of recognising the State's liability for not regulating the legal framework for effective police and jurisdictional protection, as well as for coordination between public institutions that could cause secondary victimization should be studied (Art. 30 of the Istanbul Convention).

THE NEW ROADMAP AGAINST STEREOTYPING: CONCLUSION

There is a feedback flow between society and justice that (re)constructs collective imaginaries. In this case, the figure of a victim of sexual assault is shaped from a set of stereotypes that condition the perception of an event and of a woman as a real act and victim of sexual violence. The study of the continuity that operates between society and the justice system is of the utmost relevance because the permeation of gender stereotypes in the Courts entails a deficient application of the rules (with the consequent generation of secondary victimization) and a positive reinforcement of social stereotypes due to the symbolic and material power that a sentence represents. There is some form of harmony between the elements that produce sexual violence and the elements that judge it. Its existence means that the relationship is dynamic and adaptive and that the system has a role to play in this process.

The panoply of national and international norms creates the objective and subjective content of women's right to a life free of violence and its correlative right of access to justice which directly points towards the absence of gender stereotypes. The duty of due diligence of States, which adopts a double dimension of liability, stipulates a high degree of enforceability on the State: the work of empowering victims so that they cease to be victims beyond the criminal process.

To fulfil this commitment, the Spanish Organic Law 10/2022, of September 6, on the comprehensive guarantee of sexual freedom, known as the "only yes is yes" Law, shows an evident anti-stereotyping background, at least in its wording. The use of gender stereotypes that sustain sexual violence appears in the Explanatory Memorandum as a reality to be corrected by Spain. Based on this commitment, the gender approach is established as one of the guiding principles of the law. According to it, "public administrations will include a gender approach based on the understanding of stereotypes and gender relations, their roots and their consequences in the application and evaluation of the impact of the provisions of the organic law" (Art. 2c). Thus, the normative deployment of the law must contemplate stereotypes' identification and prevention related to sexual violence, which entails its conceptualization as one of the conditioning factors of the exercise of sexual violence and the institutional response.

In addition, the Spanish Organic Law 10/2022 is focused on the prevention formula for the eradication of stereotyping in three areas. Firstly, by promoting general awareness campaigns to combat gender stereotypes and beliefs that sustain sexual violence, and specific campaigns aimed at men, teenagers, and children to eradicate prejudices based on stereotyped gender roles (Art. 9.1). Secondly, by ensuring that the digital and communication sphere provides information on sexual violence with objectivity, without gender stereotypes. To this end, the training of its staff (both on the job and during the university degree) on gender stereotypes is essential (Art. 10). Moreover, advertising that uses gender stereotypes that promote or normalize sexual violence against women, girls, boys, and teenagers will be illegal (Art. 11). Thirdly, training the entire team of professionals who interact with victims on gender stereotypes (Art. 23).

Eradicating gender stereotypes in sexual violence requires that awareness in an intersectional gender perspective permeates both citizens and professionals who interact with victims in the different phases of the judicial process for two crucial reasons: first, to recognize the multiple realities that make up women's lives, moving away from rigid models and interpreting reality adjusted to the context and circumstances of each woman. Second, to ensure

NOTES

1. Michaël Oustinoff, 'La evolución del estereotipo desde Walter Lippmann' (2019) 83 (1) Hermès La Revue 48.
2. Matt Ridley *Qué nos hace humanos* (Taurus 2004) 229, 260.
3. Johan Galtung 'Violence, peace and peace research' (1969) 6(3) Journal of Peace Research 167.
4. Physical violence and/or sexual violence by the current partner is reported in 12.5 percent of cases, rising to 34.3 percent if it is past partners and 8 percent when sexual violence is exercised outside the partner. Government Delegation against Gender Violence, 'Macro-survey on Violence against Women 2019' (2019 Madrid). <https://violenciagenero.igualdad.gob.es/violenciaEnCifras/macroencuesta2015/pdf/Macroencuesta_2019_estudio_investigacion.pdf> accessed November 14, 2022.
5. Elisa Simó Soler's doctoral thesis analysis in which 500 judgments of the Provincial Court of Valencia were analysed includes a ratio of convictions in cases of sexual violence of 64.5 percent. Similar results are obtained in the study carried out by the research group SEXVIOL. In a review of 178 judgments of the Provincial Court of Madrid, the percentage of conviction is 65.2 percent. SEXVIOL, 'Desmontando mitos a acerca de la Agresión Sexual. Un estudio de caso sobre la Audiencia Provincial de Madrid' (2022, Madrid). <https://www.ucm.es/sexviol/file/informe-sexviol-25-febrero-2022> accessed November 14, 2022.
6. The Spanish state does not collect data on secondary victimization, but it has been conceptualized by the Group of Experts on domestic and gender violence of the governing body of judges in Spain, being defined as "the negative psychological, social, legal and economic consequences left by the victim's relations with the criminal justice system. It supposes a frustrating clash between the legitimate expectations of the victim and the institutional reality, involving a loss of understanding about the psychological and physical suffering that the criminal act has caused, leaving them desolate and insecure and generating a loss of faith in the ability of the victim. community, professionals, and institutions to respond to their needs." Consejo General del Poder Judicial, Grupo de Expertos en Violencia Doméstica y de Género. 'Guía de buenas prácticas para la toma de declaración de víctimas de violencia de género' (2018 Madrid). <https://www.poderjudicial.es/cgpj/es/Temas/Violencia-domestica-y-de-genero/Grupos-de-expertos/Guia-de-buenas-practicas-para-la-toma-de-declaracion-de-victimas-de-violencia-de-genero> accessed November 14, 2022.

7. Claude Lévi-Strauss, *La estructura de los mitos. En Antropología estructural* (Paidós 1958).

8. El Ministerio de la Presidencia, Relaciones con las Cortes e Igualdad, Delegación del Gobierno para la Violencia de Géner, *Percepción Social De La Violencia Sexual* (Ministerio De Sanidad, Consumo Y Bienestar Social Centro De Publicaciones no: 25, Madrid 2018) 3, 59-80 <https://violenciagenero.igualdad.gob.es/violenciaEnCifras/estudios/colecciones/pdf/Libro_25_Violencia_Sexual.pdf> accessed November 14, 2022. <https://violenciagenero.igualdad.gob.es/violenciaEnCifras/estudios/colecciones/pdf/Libro_25_Violencia_Sexual.pdf> accessed November 14, 2022.

9. Janice Du Mont, Karen-Lee Miller and Terri L. Myhr, 'The Role of "Real Rape" and "Real Victim" Stereotypes in the Police Reporting Practices of Sexually Assaulted Women' (2003) 94 Violence Against Women 466, 469.

10. Katrin Hohl and Elisabeth A. Stanko, 'Complaints of rape and the criminal justice system: Fresh evidence on the attrition problem in England and Wales' (2015) 12(3) European Journal of Criminology 324, 325.

11. Raquel Castillejo Manzanares, Cristina Torrado Tarrío and Cristina Alonso Salgado, 'Mediación en violencia de género' (2011) 7 Revista de mediación 38, 40.

12. Du Mont, Miller and Myhr (n 9) 481.

13. David Casado-Neira and María Martínez González, 'La víctima simulada. Identidades forzadas en la violencia de género' (2016) 533 Política y sociedad 879, 882.

14. Encarna Bodelón González, 'La violencia contra las mujeres y el derecho no-androcéntrico: perdidas en la tradición jurídica del feminismo' in Patricia Laurenzo Copello, M. Luisa Maqueda Abreu and Ana Rubio Castro (coords), *Género, violencia y derecho* (Tirant lo Blanch 2008), 279, 288-289; Myriam Herrera Moreno, '¿Quién teme a la victimidad? El debate identitario en victimología' (2014) 2 Revista de Derecho Penal y Criminología 343, 363; Casado-Neira and González (n 13) 892.

15. Patricia Laurenzo Copello, 'La Tutela Específica de las Mujeres en el Sistema Penal: Una Decisión Controvertida' (2016) 1972 EMERJ 41, 63-64.

16. Committee on the Elimination of Discrimination Against Women, 'Observaciones finales sobre los informes periódicos séptimo y octavo combinados de España' (2015) CEDAW/C/ESP/CO/7-8, 1, 6–7. <https://www.refworld.org.es/country,,,,ESP,,564591b34,0.html> accessed November 14, 2022.

17. Group of Experts on Combating Violence against Women and Domestic Violence, 'Primer Informe de evaluación de GREVIO sobre las medidas legislativas y de otra índole que dan efecto a las disposiciones del Convenio del Consejo de Europa sobre Prevención y Lucha contra la violencia contra las Mujeres y la Violencia Doméstica Convenio de Estambul: España' (2020) GREVIO/Inf202019, 1, 75. <https://violenciagenero.igualdad.gob.es/marcoInternacional/informesGREVIO/docs/InformeGrevioEspana.pdf> accessed November 14, 2022.

18. Jennifer Temkin, Jacqueline M. Gray and Jastine Barrett, 'Different functions of rape myth use in court: findings from a trial observation study' (2016) 13(2) Feminist Criminology 1, 2.

19. Rights of Women, *From Report to Court. A handbook for adult survivors of sexual violence* (6th edn 2018, London) 9-10. <https://rightsofwomen.org.uk/wp-content/uploads/2019/03/From-Report-to-Court-2018.pdf> accessed November 14, 2022.

20. Du Mont, Miller and Myhr (n 9) 469; Temkin, Gray and Barrett (n 18) 11.

21. Melanie Randall, 'Sexual assault law, credibility, and "ideal victims": Consent, resistance, and victim blaming' (2010) 222 Canadian Journal of Women and the Law 397, 427.

22. Gabriela Knaul, 'Informe provisional de la Relatora Especial sobre la independencia de los magistrados y abogados,' A/66/289 10 august 2011, 1, par. 48. <https://undocs.org/pdf?symbol=es/A/66/289> accessed November 14, 2022.

23. Temkin, Gray and Barrett (n 18) 10.

24. Du Mont, Miller and Myhr (n 9) 469.

25. Juan Ramón Martínez Vargas, Giovanni Andrés Vega Barbosa, 'La obligación estatal de prevención a la luz del corpus iuris internacional de protección de la mujer contra la violencia de género' (2013) 19(2) Revista Ius et Praxis 335, 348; Marcela Paz Araya Novoa, 'Género y verdad. Valoración racional de la prueba en los delitos de violencia patriarcal' (2020) 32 Revista de estudios de la justicia 35, 48-50.

26. Knaul (n 22) par. 48.

27. Temkin, Gray and Barrett (n 18) 2.

28. Ignacio José Subijana Zunzunegui, 'La perspectiva de género en el enjuiciamiento de los delitos de violencia del hombre sobre la mujer' (2018) 1 Juezas y Jueces para la Democracia 27, 34.

29. For a complete study see: Liz Kelly, Jo Lovett and Linda Regan, *A gap or a chasm? Attrition in reported rape cases* (Home Office Research 293, London 2004). <https://webarchive.nationalarchives.gov.uk/ukgwa/20110218135832/rds.homeoffice.gov.uk/rds/pdfs05/hors293.pdf> accessed November 14, 2022.

30. Temkin, Gray and Barrett (n 18) 3.

31. Government Delegation against Gender Violence (n 4) 163.

32. Ibid, 159 and 311.

33. Ibid, 162.

34. Randall (n 21) 419.

35. Rahime Erbaş, 'Challenges in Regulating Sexual Offences in Turkey' in Rahime Erbaş (ed), *Global Problems in Sexual Offenses* (Lexington Books 2004) 3, 11.

36. Hohl and Stanko (n 10) 328.

37. José Manuel Bezanilla, M. Amparo Miranda and Jorge Humberto González Fabiani, 'Violaciones graves a derechos humanos: violencia institucional y revictimización' (2016) 2(15) Cuadernos de crisis y emergencias 21; Encarna Bodelón González, 'Violencia institucional y violencia de género' (2014) 48 Anales de la Cátedra Francisco Suárez 131, 132–133.

38. Sordo Ruz Tania, 'Violencia institucional por razón de género contra las mujeres: Casos paradigmáticos en el Estado mexicano' (2018) 76149 Miscelánea Comillas 421, 424, 427-428; González (n 37) 141; Saida Mantilla Ojeda and Bertha Lucía Avendaño Prieto, 'Diseño y análisis psicométrico de un instrumento para

evaluar victimización judicial en víctimas durante la etapa de denuncia' (2020) 17(2) Jurídicas 106, 110.

39. Olivia Smith and Tina Skinner, 'Observing Court Responses to Victims of Rape and Sexual Assault' (2012) 7(4) Feminist Criminology 298, 299.

40. SAP de Navarra, núm. 38/2018, de 20 de marzo (Roj: 86/2018).

41. STSJ de Navarra, Sala de lo Civil y Penal, núm. 7/2018, de 30 de noviembre (Roj: 473/2018).

42. STS, Sala de lo Penal, núm. 344/2019, de 4 de julio (Roj: 2200/2019).

43. ibid, FJ 5º-3.

44. SAP Navarra, núm. 38/2018, de 20 de marzo, FJ 3, letra a) p. 25.

45. Ibid, FJ 3, letra a) p. 22.

46. Separate opinion. SAP Navarra, núm. 38/2018, de 20 de marzo, FJ 2, letra e) p. 86.

47. SAP Navarra, núm. 38/2018, de 20 de marzo, FJ 3, letra c) p. 42.

48. STSJ Navarra, Sala de lo Civil y Penal, núm. 7/2018, de 30 de noviembre, FJ 9 pp. 31–32.

49. SAP Navarra, núm. 38/2018, de 20 de marzo, FJ 2º, letra e) p. 86.

50. STS, núm. 344/2019, de 4 de julio, FJ 5º 7.

51. SAP Navarra, núm. 38/2018, de 20 de marzo, FJ 3, letra b) p. 56.

52. The Istanbul Convention is an international treaty, signed within the Council of Europe, to which all countries that wish to join can adhere. The European Union is currently in the process of accession.

53. Concerning the Istanbul Convention, see Valentina Bonini and Rahime Erbaş (ed), *The 10th Anniversary of Istambul Convention, Italian Turkish Conference, Pisa 18 June 2021* (Pisa University Press 2021).

54. It is anchored in the Fundamental Charter of Rights of the European Union, CEDAW, Jurisprudence of the Court of Human Rights and national Jurisprudence, etc.

55. Elena Martínez García 'Los deberes del Estado en la protección de los derechos de las víctimas de violencia de género y la garantía de acceso a la justicia' (2017) 22 Teoría y Derecho 92, 109; Şeyma Kuş, 'The due diligence standard and combating violence against woman' in Valentina Bonini and Rahime Erbaş (ed), *The 10th Anniversary of Istanbul Convention, Italian Turkish Conference, Pisa 18 June 2021* (Pisa University Press 2021) 205.

56. García (n 55) 109.

57. It is also cited in the Proposal for a Directive of the European Parliament and of the Council on combating violence against women and domestic violence (COM/2022/105 final). This is a proposal, but we are on the right track in the European Union by having content that is directly binding for all member states.

the effectiveness of the measures adopted and avoid the generation of secondary victimization due to social and judicial disrepute.

BIBLIOGRAPHY

Araya Novoa, MP, 'Género y verdad. Valoración racional de la prueba en los delitos de violencia patriarcal' (2020) 32 Revista de estudios de la justicia 35–69.

Bezanilla JM, Miranda MaA and González Fabiani JH, 'Violaciones graves a derechos humanos: violencia institucional y revictimización' (2016) 2(15) Cuadernos de crisis y emergencias 21–33.

Bodelón González E, 'La violencia contra las mujeres y el derecho no-androcéntrico: perdidas en la tradición jurídica del feminismo' in Patricia Laurenzo Copello, Mª Luisa Maqueda Abreu, and Ana Rubio Castro (coords), *Género, violencia y derecho* (Tirant lo Blanch 2008).

Bodelón González E, 'Violencia institucional y violencia de género' (2014) 48 Anales de la Cátedra Francisco Suárez 131–155.

Bonini V and Rahime E, (ed), *The 10th Anniversary of Istanbul Convention, Italian Turkish Conference, Pisa 18 June 2021* (Pisa University Press 2021).

Casado Neira D, Martínez González M, 'La víctima simulada. Identidades forzadas en la violencia de género' (2016) 533 Política y sociedad 879–896. <https://doi.org/10.5209/rev_>

Castillejo Manzanares R, Torrado Tarrío C and Alonso Salgado C, 'Mediación en violencia de género' (2011) 7 Revista de mediación 38–44.

Committee on the Elimination of Discrimination Against Women, 'Observaciones finales sobre los informes periódicos séptimo y octavo combinados de España' (2015) CEDAW/C/ESP/CO/7–8. <https://www.refworld.org.es/country,,,,ESP,,564591b34,0.html> accessed November 14, 2022.

Consejo General del Poder Judicial, Grupo de Expertos en Violencia Doméstica y de Género. 'Guía de buenas prácticas para la toma de declaración de víctimas de violencia de género' (2018 Madrid). <https://www.poderjudicial.es/cgpj/es/Temas/Violencia-domestica-y-de-genero/Grupos-de-expertos/Guia-de-buenas-practicas-para-la-toma-de-declaracion-de-victimas-de-violencia-de-genero> accessed November 14, 2022.

Du Mont J, Miller K.L, Myhr T.L, 'The Role of "Real Rape" and "Real Victim" Stereotypes in the Police Reporting Practices of Sexually Assaulted Women' (2003) 94 Violence Against Women 466–486. <https://doi.org/10.1177/1077801202250960>

Erbaş R, 'Challenges in Regulating Sexual Offences in Turkey' in Rahime Erbaş (ed), *Global Problems in Sexual Offenses* (Lexington Books 2004) 3–24.

Galtung J, 'Violence, peace and peace research' (1969) 6(3) Journal of Peace Research 167–191.

El Ministerio de la Presidencia, Relaciones con las Cortes e Igualdad, Delegación del Gobierno para la Violencia de Géner, *Percepción Social De La Violencia Sexual* (Ministerio De Sanidad, Consumo Y Bienestar Social Centro De Publicaciones no: 25, Madrid 2018) <https://violenciagenero.igualdad.gob.es/violenciaEnCifras/estudios/colecciones/pdf/Libro_25_Violencia_Sexual.pdf> accessed November 14, 2022.

Ministerio De Igualdad, Delegación del Gobierno contra la Violencia de Género, *Macroencuesta De Violencia Contra La Mujer* (Madrid 2019 <https://violencia

genero.igualdad.gob.es/violenciaEnCifras/macroencuesta2015/pdf/Macroencuesta_2019_estudio_investigacion.pdf> accessed November 14, 2022.

Group of Experts on Combating Violence against Women and Domestic Violence, 'Primer Informe de evaluación de GREVIO sobre las medidas legislativas y de otra índole que dan efecto a las disposiciones del Convenio del Consejo de Europa sobre Prevención y Lucha contra la violencia contra las Mujeres y la Violencia Doméstica Convenio de Estambul: España' (2020) GREVIO/Inf202019. <https://violenciagenero.igualdad.gob.es/marcoInternacional/informesGREVIO/docs/InformeGrevioEspana.pdf> accessed November 14, 2022.

Herrera Moreno M, '¿Quién teme a la victimidad? El debate identitario en victimología' (2014) 2 Revista de Derecho Penal y Criminología 343–404.

Hohl K and Stanko EA, 'Complaints of rape and the criminal justice system: Fresh evidence on the attrition problem in England and Wales' (2015) 12(3) European Journal of Criminology 324–341.

Kelly L, Lovett J and Regan L, *A gap or a chasm? Attrition in reported rape cases* (Home Office Research 293, London 2004). <https://webarchive.nationalarchives.gov.uk/ukgwa/20110218135832/rds.homeoffice.gov.uk/rds/pdfs05/hors293.pdf> accessed November 14, 2022.

Knaul G, 'Informe provisional de la Relatora Especial sobre la independencia de los magistrados y abogados,' A/66/289 10 august 2011. <https://undocs.org/pdf?symbol=es/A/66/289> accessed November 14, 2022.

Laurenzo Copello, P, 'La Tutela Específica de las Mujeres en el Sistema Penal: Una Decisión Controvertida' (2016) 1972 EMERJ 41–65.

Lévi-Strauss C, *La estructura de los mitos. En Antropología estructural* (Paidós 1958).

Mantilla Ojeda S and Avendaño Prieto BL, 'Diseño y análisis psicométrico de un instrumento para evaluar victimización judicial en víctimas durante la etapa de denuncia' (2020) 17(2) Jurídicas 106–125.

Martínez García E, 'Los deberes del Estado en la protección de los derechos de las víctimas de violencia de género y la garantía de acceso a la justicia' (2017) 22 Teoría y Derecho 92–118.

Martínez Vargas JR, Vega Barbosa G, 'La obligación estatal de prevención a la luz del corpus iuris internacional de protección de la mujer contra la violencia de género' (2013) 19(2) Revista Ius et Praxis 335–368.

Oustinoff M, 'La evolución del estereotipo desde Walter Lippmann,' (2019) 83(1) Hermès La Revue 48–53.

Randall M, 'Sexual assault law, credibility, and "ideal victims": Consent, resistance, and victim blaming' (2010) 222 Canadian Journal of Women and the Law 397–433.

Ridley M, *Qué nos hace humanos* (Taurus 2004).

Rights of Women, *From Report to Court. A handbook for adult survivors of sexual violence* (6th edn 2018, London). <https://rightsofwomen.org.uk/wp-content/uploads/2019/03/From-Report-to-Court-2018.pdf> accessed November 14, 2022.

Şeyma Kuş, 'The due diligence standard and combating violence against woman' in Valentina Bonini and Rahime Erbaş (ed), *The 10th Anniversary of Istanbul*

Convention, Italian Turkish Conference, Pisa 18 June 2021 (Pisa University Press 2021) 205–220.

SEXVIOL, 'Desmontando mitos a acerca de la Agresión Sexual. Un estudio de caso sobre la Audiencia Provincial de Madrid' (2022, Madrid). <https://www.ucm.es/sexviol/file/informe-sexviol-25-febrero-2022> accessed November 14, 2022.

Smith O and Skinner T, 'Observing Court Responses to Victims of Rape and Sexual Assault' (2012) 7(4) Feminist Criminology 298–326.

Sordo Ruz T, 'Violencia institucional por razón de género contra las mujeres: Casos paradigmáticos en el Estado mexicano' (2018) 76149 Miscelánea Comillas 421–440.

Subijana Zunzunegui IJ, 'La perspectiva de género en el enjuiciamiento de los delitos de violencia del hombre sobre la mujer' (2018) 1 Juezas y Jueces para la Democracia 27–39.

Temkin J, Gray JM and Barrett J, 'Different functions of rape myth use in court: findings from a trial observation study' (2016) 13(2) Feminist Criminology 1–20.

4

Reform Needs in German Criminal Law on Sexual Offenses

The Non-Compromise of "No-Means-No"

Lena Gmelin and Hannah Wörner

Sexual offenses law[1] is one of the most controversial areas of (criminal) law in Germany. In recent years, events in the media,[2] social movements and empirically observable phenomena[3] as well as the ratification of the Council of Europe Convention on Preventing and Combating Violence against Women and Domestic Violence[4] have prompted a critical review of national law governing sexual offenses and various reforms. Both the so-called "no-means-no" solution currently implemented in the central norm of law governing sexual offenses (§ 177 StGB[5]) and the overall structure of the division on sexual crimes are dogmatically unsuccessful and, *de lege lata*, do not achieve comprehensive protection of the legal right of sexual self-determination. For this reason, we argue *de lege ferenda* for a consensus-oriented law governing sexual offenses based on the "yes-means-yes" solution.

In 2021, police crime statistics in Germany recorded a total of around 106,700 crimes against sexual self-determination.[6] The number has risen steadily in recent years:

Table 4.1. Development of offences against sexual self-determination registered in the PKS

Reporting year	*2014*	*2015*	*2016*	*2017*	*2018*	*2019*	*2020*	*2021*
No. of registered cases	46.982	46.081	47.401	56.047	63.782	69.881	81.630	106.656
Change from previous year	+ 0.4 %	− 1.9 %	+ 2.9 %	**+ 18.2 %**[1]	+ 13.8 %	+ 9.6 %	+ 16.8 %	+ 30.7 %

Source: Table 4.1 was created by the Authors, with the data from Cf. BKA, PCS 2013–2021—Tables, Cases—Basic Table, key 100000, (<https://www.bka.de/EN/CurrentInformation/Statistics/PoliceCrimeStatistics/policecrimestatistics_node.html> accessed March 10, 2023).

1. The PCS itself does not show the development of case numbers in comparison between 2016 and 2017 due to the changes in the law.

The comparatively sharp increase in registered criminal offenses in 2017 is striking. In particular, the significant reform of law governing sexual offenses, the provisions of which came into force at the end of 2016,[7] is likely to have had an influence on the increase in registered cases—also in the context of the extensive public debate and the awareness campaigns accompanying the reform.[8] Although this development (especially the willingness to report) can generally be seen as positive,[9] it must be noted that the willingness of victims of crimes against sexual self-determination to report the offense is relatively low. Only around 12–18 percent of victims report the crime to the police.[10] The conviction rate among reported offenses is also low: prosecution statistics for 2019 show that of the nearly 70,000 reported acts against sexual self-determination, only about 11,500 resulted in a conviction;[11] this corresponds to a rate of 16.52 percent. These prosecution rates are a direct consequence not only of the difficult prosecution practice and its procedural and socio-psychological peculiarities, but also of the substantive legal situation. The so-called "no-means-no" solution currently implemented by German law (in the Criminal Code) has been met with considerable criticism. For some it goes too far, whereas for others it does not go far enough. Against this background, the following chapter asks whether the current legal solution in Germany is another viable German middle way[12] or to what extent German (substantive) law governing sexual offenses is in need of further reform with regard to the relevance of the victim's consent.

When dealing with dogmatic questions concerning the punishability of sexual contacts between adults[13] and persons generally capable of consenting[14] under German criminal law, firstly the prerequisites for punishability on one hand and the prerequisites of consent in the national criminal law system on the other must be clarified in general. An introduction to the specific development of law governing sexual offenses with its reforms up to the current regulations shows the dogmatic problems of the current legal situation and enables its critical analysis. Against the background of the significance of sexual self-determination in relation to the incriminated act, the unresolved questions of a "no-means-no" solution thereby emerge and make the examination of the viability of an "only-yes-means-yes" solution for German law governing sexual offenses necessary and ultimately viable.

REQUIREMENTS OF PUNISHABILITY IN GERMAN LAW GOVERNING SEXUAL OFFENSES

The sexual offenses of German criminal law (§§ 174–1841 StGB) know a multiplicity of offense characteristics, which describe different sexual actions. The *"(only) yes-means-yes" solution* is also referred to as the "consent principle" or "consent solution." According to this, sexual acts are punishable if not all involved persons have consented to the sexual act.[15] In contrast, according to the *"no-means-no" solution,* a sexual act is punishable (only) if a person involved in the sexual contact makes their contrary will known.[16] With regard to consent to the performance of an act (potentially) violating legal interests by the (potentially) violated person, a distinction must be made in German criminal law between the concepts of "consent" and "assent."[17] This differentiation is peculiar to the German criminal law system. To understand this, it is necessary to provide an overview of the prerequisites for criminal liability in German criminal law in general.

Principles of Punishability in German Criminal Law

In German criminal law, a crime is considered to be punishable if it meets several conditions. In order to provide a foundation for the following deliberations, a short overview of these conditions will be focused on completed crimes, not considering (punishable) attempts. Naturally, the act must be prohibited by criminal law. This means that the act must be defined as a criminal offense in the German Criminal Code or in another applicable law. According to the prevailing view, there are three main conditions for an act to then be punishable under said law.[18] *Firstly,* the act has to coincide with the substantive elements of the crime that are stated in the according law, i.e., the perpetrator must have performed the actions described in the criminal offense. These actions must have been committed intentionally.[19] *Secondly,* the action must have been unlawful, i.e., no grounds of justification must be on hand. The fulfillment of the substantive elements of the crime generally implies the unlawfulness of the act; however, if the act is justified (e.g., due to self-defense),[20] the action is no longer considered unlawful. *Thirdly*, the culpability of the perpetrator is to be examined. The perpetrator is considered culpable when they:

- have reached the age of criminal responsibility (generally 14 years), [21]
- are capable of appreciating the unlawfulness of their actions and able to act in accordance with any such appreciation (being of sound mind and not suffering from a pathological mental disorder, a profound disturbance of consciousness, an intellectual disability or any other serious mental disorder that affected their ability to understand what they were doing)[22]
- and aware of the wrongfulness of their actions (knowing that their action was prohibited by law),[23]
- and there are no lawful excuses on hand.[24]

(Only) when all three of these conditions are met, the action is considered punishable under German criminal law.

Differentiating Between Assent and Consent

If the victim or person whose legally protected rights are affected agrees to the performance of the action, their consent can influence the punishability of the crime. At this point, a distinction must be made between assent (*tatbestandsausschließendes Einverständnis*) and consent (*rechtfertigende Einwilligung*).[25]

Assent (tatbestandsausschließendes Einverständnis)

Certain offenses require an action without or against the will of the person entitled and can therefore not be realized if the entitled person *agrees to the action*. Some offenses expressly require an action *against the will of the entitled person*[26]—if that person agrees, this element of the offense is not fulfilled and criminal liability is excluded. In other offenses, the lack of or contrary will of the entitled person is implied: for example, §§ 123, 239, 242, 266 StGB contain elements of the offense that can only be realized without or against the will of the person entitled. To illustrate: § 242 para 1 StGB, which criminalizes theft, presupposes in the objective elements of the crime the *taking away of* another's property. This is understood to be the breaking of another's custody and the establishment of new custody *without or against the will of the entitled person.*[27] If there is effective consent on the part of the entitled person, this element of the crime can no longer be realized.[28] Notably, the explicit refusal or resistance by the entitled person is not required: according to general opinion, theft is not a "secret offense" (i.e., even if the entitled person witnesses the taking away, the element is fulfilled—the lack of reaction by the entitled person does not constitute approval of the removal of custody)[29] and does not require any special resistance by the entitled person. The existence of consent can therefore mean that the legal (objective) elements of the offense are not realized;[30] the existence of justification or excuses is then no longer relevant for the elimination of criminal liability.

For consent to be effective, the declarant must have a natural capacity of will;[31] there must at least be conscious internal consent.[32] Mere tolerance is not sufficient.[33] Consent must be voluntary.[34] However, failure of intent is irrelevant as long as it does not impair voluntariness.[35] The consent must factually be present at the beginning of and during the act. It is not necessary that the consent is declared (to the offender or otherwise).[36] The perpetrator does not have to be aware of the consent for it to preclude the offense. If the offender does not know about the consent, a punishable attempt may be considered. If the perpetrator is mistaken about the existence of consent, this is a mistake of fact according to § 16 StGB.[37]

Consent (rechtfertigende Einwilligung)

If the facts of the case do not require action against the will of the injured party, but the consent of the injured party exists, this can have a justifying effect. The so-called *justifying consent* (*rechtfertigende Einwilligung*) therefore has no effect on the realization of the objective elements of the offense. However, an effective consent can have the consequence that the respective behavior is exceptionally permitted—i.e., justified—due to this consent, because the entitled person waives legal protection.[38] Justifiable consent is expressly articled, for example, in § 228 StGB. According to this, bodily injury that has been inflicted with the consent of the injured person is only unlawful if the act, despite the consent, is contrary to "good morals." Thus, if a person consents to the performance of an act that physically abuses them or damages their health, the perpetrator is justified (barring a violation of morality) and is not liable to prosecution for the bodily injury under §§ 223 StGB.

The effectiveness of the consent presupposes that the injured person can generally dispose of the protected legal interest.[39] This is not possible in the case of public legal rights[40] and is restricted in the case of some offenses.[41] The person giving consent must be entitled to dispose of it, i.e., the sole holder of the protected legal interest.[42] Consent must also still exist at the time of the commission of the offense. Subsequent consent has no justifying effect.[43] Besides their effect, consent and assent also differ in some of their conditions for effectiveness. Whereas in the case of assent, actual existence is sufficient—i.e., an external declaration is not required—consent must be declared expressly or conclusively before the act is committed.[44] Furthermore, the person giving consent must be capable of consenting (not only of willing), i.e., as a result of their mental and moral maturity, they must be able to recognize the significance and scope of the interference and the waiver of the protection of legal interests. The consenting person must not be subject to any substantial defects of will (for example, as a result of deception, coercion or error). Finally, the perpetrator must subjectively act with knowledge and on the basis of the given consent.[45]

The thoroughly differentiated German criminal law thus has a number of instruments with which it can meet the requirements for the classification of the consent of the person concerned in law governing sexual offenses. The question is which of these instruments is the most suitable one. To evaluate this, it is first necessary to understand German criminal sexual law in its entirety.

GERMAN LAW GOVERNING SEXUAL OFFENSES: REFORMS, DEVELOPMENT AND CURRENT LEGAL SITUATION

As already explained, German law governing sexual offenses has been controversially discussed and reformed, especially in recent years. However, the criminalization of assaultive[46] sexual behavior is by no means new; rather, today's law governing sexual offenses is based on a long history of development and reform. This normative genesis has always reflected changes in social values, sexuality[47] and images of women: The idea that women, like men, are allowed to initiate and reject sexual contacts in a self-determined manner is much younger than law governing sexual offenses as such and only emerged in the 20th century.[48] In order to be able to formulate a comprehensive critique of the current legal situation of sexual offenses law, it is necessary to look at the development of the norms and reforms with their underlying role and sexual images (I.), whereupon the current legal situation can be explained (II.) and its dogmatic and social problems identified (III.).

From Sexuality Owned by Man to Free Sexual Self-Determination

The *Constitutio Carolina Criminalis* of 1532 is considered the first German criminal code.[49] The norms of this Code were considered "God-given" or "natural." This also applied to law governing sexual offenses. Due to religious influences, sexuality as such was only recognized within a heterosexual marriage. A woman's sexuality always belonged to a man—her father or her husband.[50] The term "sexual honor" also comes from this period, describing the requirements for female impeccability.[51] Immaculateness at this point does not mean virginity, but extramarital unspoiledness.[52] These religious ideas of purity are also perceptible in the criminalization of homosexuality[53] or adultery.[54] The suppression of female sexuality is particularly evident in the offense of "fornication" (*Notzucht*), according to which only those who take the feminine honor (ergo sexual honor) of married women, widows or virgins by force or threat are punished.[55]

In the Penal Code from 1870 to 1953, one can further see these basic attitudes in sexual offenses. The division of the sexual offenses is titled as "crimes against morality."[56] According to § 175 (fornication), anyone who coerces a "female person" into acquiescence by force or by threat of present danger to life or limb is punishable. The extramarital coitus is also punished according to § 176 StGB, even if the female person (*Frau*) is put into an unconscious state for this purpose.[57]

These general attitudes remain intact even in the reform processes of the 1950s. This can be seen in the explanatory memorandum to the government's draft of a penal code, in which it is stated that it is an "indisputable realization" that "the purity and health of sexual life is an extraordinarily important prerequisite for the existence of the nation and the preservation of the natural order of life."[58] In the judgment of the Federal Constitutional Court on the prohibition of male homosexuality, it is stated that this prohibition does not violate the principle of equality, because the "biological difference of the sexes so differently characterizes the circumstances. [. . .] These differences of the sexual life make themselves felt possibly even more strongly with same-sex than with heterosexual relations, since the organism of the woman, which is designed for motherhood, shows the way to act in a figurative social sense in a womanly-maternal way, even if she is biologically not a mother, while a corresponding compensation is missing with the man. Thus, the lesbian woman succeeds more easily in maintaining sexual abstinence, while the homosexual man tends to fall prey to an unrestrained sexual desire."[59]

In this decision, persons perceived as masculine are described as fundamentally instinct-driven beings who cannot control themselves, to such an extent that criminal limits must be set. Furthermore, women are not attributed their own sex drive. The Federal Constitutional Court only sees such a drive in combination with a male partner.

In the 1960s, some offenses were abolished (adultery, homosexuality among adults, fornication with animals, procuring extramarital coitus), but the offense of extramarital sexual intercourse and the moral attitudes associated with it remained.[60] An important step towards a modern law governing sexual offenses was the 4th Penal Reform Act of 23.11.1973, the section of sexual offenses was renamed to offenses against sexual self-determination. Thus, from that time on, sexual self-determination is the underlying legal interest of all offenses in the 13th section.[61] In addition to sexual self-determination, other protected interests such as physical integrity or freedom, both freedom of movement and freedom of choice, are of course also regularly restricted. Sexual self-determination is only emphasized here because (as an offshoot of the right of personality) it includes the other violations as well as others and also includes sexual autonomy, which is significantly impaired by imposed sexual behavior.[62]

Terms such as "fornication" and "lewd acts" were replaced by neutral terms such as "sexual acts." "Fornication" was replaced by the term "rape." The restriction of the crime victims to "blameless girls" in § 182 StGB was abolished. The injustice of procuration (*Kuppelei*) was also rethought, towards preventing the exploitation of prostitutes.[63] Despite all these reforms, certain traditional imprints remained unreflected; the coercive context remained a prerequisite for the offense of rape, even though it was no longer titled "fornication." Men were also still not included in the group of victims of this offense. Thus, a differentiated understanding of sexual self-determination still did not exist.[64] It was not until 1997, with the 33rd Penal Reform Act, that men were included in the circle of victims of § 177 StGB.[65] In the years that followed, there were minor changes and reforms, primarily for the protection of children and adolescents or the pornography offenses.[66] The next (and to date last) major reform of law governing sexual offenses came in 2016 with the 50th Penal Reform Act ("Improving the Protection of Sexual Self-Determination").[67]

Current Legal Situation and the Latest Major Reform

This major reform of law governing sexual offenses was partly prompted by the events of New Year's Eve 2015. During the night of December 31, 2015, to January 1, 2016, there was an increase in sexual assaults throughout Germany, especially in Cologne. Six hundred sixty-one women reported sexual crimes after the night, 28 of the reports involved attempted or completed rape.[68] After this event, there was an outcry among the population, and special attention was paid to the laws on sexual self-determination and their inadequacies.[69] There was great pressure for reform.[70]

Sexual offenses are regulated in the 13th division of the Criminal Code, namely in §§ 174–1841 StGB. §§ 174–176e of the StGB criminalize the sexual abuse of wards, victims in other power dynamics, and children. The central norm of German law governing sexual offenses is § 177 StGB, which covers sexual assault, sexual coercion, and rape. This is followed by § 178 StGB, which supplements the basic offense of § 177 StGB with a qualification of success (at least recklessly causing the death of the victim). In the course of the reform, the offenses of sexual harassment (§ 184i StGB) and group offenses (§ 184j StGB) were introduced. § 177 StGB arguably underwent the most fundamental alteration. The essentially still contained, traditionalist understanding of rape as forcibly overcoming physical resistance to enable sexual intercourse[71] was replaced: While § 177 para 1 StGB in its old version required the use of force or threat with which the perpetrator tolerated or performed sexual acts on the victim, this context of coercion is no longer necessary since the reform. According to the current version of § 177 para 1 StGB, the performance[72] of a sexual act on another person against their recognizable will is sufficient for criminal liability. The previously required coercive context has thus been replaced by the so-called "no-means-no" rule,[73] which requires the overcoming of an explicit refusal.[74]

The coercion of the victim by threat of a serious evil is equated to that in § 177 para 2 No. 5 StGB. Likewise, the commission of the offense by taking advantage of various conditions or situations of the victim that are considered worthy of protection has been included in § 177 para 2 Nos. 1–4 StGB, and thus the regulatory content of § 179 StGB (which has been repealed) has essentially been integrated into § 177 StGB.[75] The acts under § 177 para 1 and 2 StGB are punishable by imprisonment of six months to five years and are thus "only" classified as misdemeanors. Threats of present danger to life or limb and the use of force, on the other hand, are now punishable by a term of imprisonment of at least one year in § 177 V StGB; they are thus classified as crimes. It was only with this reform that the protected right of *sexual self-determination* was redefined as a free decision about the place, time, form and partner of a sexual encounter.[76]

The norm of § 177 StGB is now divided into eight paragraphs:

Table 4.2. Section 177: Sexual Assault; Sexual Coercion; Rape

(1) Whoever, against a person's discernible will, performs sexual acts on that person or has that person perform sexual acts on them, or causes that person to perform or acquiesce to sexual acts being performed on or by a third person incurs a penalty of imprisonment for a term of between six months and five years.

(2) Whoever performs sexual acts on another person or has that person perform sexual acts, or causes that person to perform or acquiesce to sexual acts being performed on or by a third person incurs the same penalty if

1. the offender exploits the fact that the person is not able to form or express a contrary will,

(continued)

Table 4.2. (*continued*)

2. the offender exploits the fact that the person is significantly impaired in respect of the ability to form or express a will due to said person's physical or mental condition, unless the offender has obtained the consent of that person,
3. the offender exploits an element of surprise,
4. the offender exploits a situation in which the victim is threatened with serious harm in case of offering resistance or
5. the offender has coerced the person to perform or acquiesce to the sexual acts by threatening serious harm.

(3) The attempt is punishable.

(4) The penalty is imprisonment for a term of at least one year if the inability to form or express a will is due to the victim's illness or disability.

(5) The penalty is imprisonment for a term of at least one year if the offender

1. uses force against the victim,
2. threatens the victim with a present danger to life or limb or
3. exploits a situation in which the victim is unprotected and at the mercy of the offender's influence.

(6) In especially serious cases, the penalty is imprisonment for a term of at least two years. An especially serious case typically occurs where

1. the offender has sexual intercourse with the victim or has the victim have sexual intercourse or commits such similar sexual acts on the victim or has the victim commit them on them which are particularly degrading for the victim, especially if they involve penetration of the body (rape), or
2. the offense is committed jointly by more than one person.

(7) The penalty is imprisonment for a term of at least three years if the offender

1. carries a weapon or other dangerous implement,
2. otherwise carries an instrument or other means for the purpose of preventing or overcoming the resistance of another person by force or threat of force or
3. places the victim at risk of serious damage to health.

(8) The penalty is imprisonment for a term of at least five years if

1. the offender uses a weapon or other dangerous implement during the commission of the offence or
2. the offender
   a) seriously physically abuses the victim during the offense or
   b) by committing the offense places the victim in danger of death.

In less serious cases under subsections (1) and (2), the penalty is imprisonment for a term of between three months and three years, in less serious cases under subsections (4) and (5) imprisonment for a term of between six months and 10 years, and in less serious cases under subsections (7) and (8) imprisonment for a term of between one year and 10 years.

Source: Table 4.2 was provided by the Authors. The data from the translated version of this section can be found here <https://www.gesetze-im-internet.de/englisch_stgb/> accessed March 11, 2023).

In addition to the provisions of subsection 1, particular attention should also be paid to those of § 177 para 2 no 2 StGB. By implementing an "only-yes-means-yes" solution, this norm contains a provision according to which sexual contact with the persons designated therein is punishable if the perpetrator has not assured themselves of the consent of this person, i.e., the sexual partners involved must have consented in advance to each individual sexual act—including any that occurs within the same sexual contact.[77] The solution implemented there protects the sexual self-determination rights of people who are capable of forming or expressing a natural will but are significantly limited in this ability due to their physical or mental condition.[78] The legislative justification for § 177 para 2 no 2 StGB and the consensus solution implemented therein is particularly interesting in light of the issues examined in this chapter. It states that the increased need for protection of the protected group of persons makes a "yes-means-yes" solution necessary; however, the sexual acting out by the protected persons is respected if this corresponds to their natural will. Thus, the norm takes into account the importance of the personality right, because whoever assures themselves of the person's consent to the sexual act does not make themselves liable to prosecution.[79] The natural will can be declared verbally or conclusively, but must be unambiguous from an objective point of view; ambivalent declarations are not sufficient.[80] The perpetrator is also liable to prosecution if the protected person subsequently states that they performed the sexual act voluntarily, but the defendant did not ascertain this in advance—the waiver of prior consent entails "the abstract risk that the protected person's sexual self-determination will be violated."[81] German criminal law on sexual offenses thus already knows a consensual solution, which to date, however, has only been implemented for the particularly protected group of persons under § 177 para 2 no 2 StGB.

Doctrinal Problems

Moving away from a required coercive context and introducing a "no-means-no" solution as the basis for the rest of the law governing sexual offenses was already a significant step towards better protection of sexual self-determination. When the law was enacted, however, not only were the considerations of the expert commission on reforming law governing sexual offenses disregarded, but the federal government's draft was also ignored.[82] Instead, a hastily drafted bill from the Bundestag's legal committee was drafted and enacted. The current law governing sexual offenses still has both dogmatic and fundamental societal problems.

Due to the aforementioned rapid adoption of the 50th Penal Reform Act, the current law governing sexual offenses contains many dogmatic problems.[83] In § 177 StGB, the distinction of subsections 1 and 2 is partly confusing. According to these, the expression of refusal is a sufficient, but not a necessary condition for criminal liability under § 177 StGB. The legislator recognizes that in some cases, rejection cannot be communicated or communication would be unreasonable. The distinction is partly not plausible.[84] According to para 1 of § 177 StGB, the opposing will must also be "recognizable." This means, from the perspective of an objective third party, that the express or implied refusal has been declared by the person concerned. Is the declaration necessary? Or can the opposing will also be recognizable if the concerned person has no communication behavior? [85]

For § 177 StGB, intent (regardless of the degree) is required. However, the evidence as to whether the perpetrator actually recognized the opposing intent is often a problem. However, this was already a problem before the draft bill, and would also pose one in the case of a different regulation or possible criminal liability for negligence. Another difficulty is the distinction between the absolute inability to form or express the will (e.g., due to unconsciousness) pursuant to § 177 para 2 no 1 StGB and No. 2, where the perpetrator must be certain of express consent if the person concerned is significantly limited in forming or expressing their will due to their condition.[86] Within No. 2, it is also not clear what the use of force means, as it is not present and not defined in the basic offense.[87] The definition of mental condition is equally uncertain. [88]

The term "sexually determined act" from § 184i StGB (sexual harassment) is also subject to criticism, as it is determined by the sexual motivation of the perpetrator and thus opens up many gray areas.[89] Due to the required physical touch, any verbal[90] sexual harassment falls outside the scope of punishability.[91] These and other problems show that the legal situation leads to many uncertainties and gaps in punishability. By the time active rejection can be communicated, the assault oftentimes has already occurred. Thus, the current legal situation must resolve such cases via "surprise attacks."[92] Also, the demarcation of the ability to form or express the will exists mainly because the rejection is assumed. The many special rules, definitions and discussions, such as the punishability of violating intimate parts of body by taking photographs or other images (§ 184k StGB), sexual harassment (§ 184i StGB), offenses committed out of groups (§ 184j StGB), etc. are all necessary because a gap has been identified in the protection of sexual self-determination that cannot be closed by an underlying "no-means-no" solution.

Ultimately, the comparison with other legal rights shows that the "no-means-no" solution underlying German law governing sexual offenses de lege lata is foreign matter in the national dogmatics of consent even in civil law: e.g., the right to property in § 903 para 1 of the German Civil Code (BGB) as a right to dispose of a certain object and to exclude unauthorized persons gives the owner positive freedom of decision as to whom to give, transfer or lend property to or to whom not to grant corresponding rights of use.[93] The victim of a theft is not subject to 'self-protection obligations'; the theft remains punishable, regardless of whether the door is locked or unlocked.[94] Whoever takes away another's property, i.e., breaks another's custody, without the consent of the entitled person, commits theft. If the perpetrator breaks open a door or uses force in the process, the wrong is only intensified.[95] Thus, the non-consent solution is overall not dogmatically convincing.

Societal Problems

The aforementioned dogmatical problems are still based on the same understanding of sexuality that can be observed in previous laws up to the Constitutio Criminalis Carolina. This can be seen in criminal offenses such as exhibitionism (§ 183 StGB), which to this day can only be committed by men.[96] The Bundestag justifies this with the fact that exhibitionistic acts by women "can hardly ever have the negative effects emanating from exhibitionistic acts by a man."[97] This is also reflected in the "no-means-no" solution: according to this rule, the refusal must be "recognizably" expressed by gestures or verbally and is thus based on the responsibility of the person concerned.[98] An opposing will must be clearly discernible to an objective third party.[99] One problem with this is that this rule does not respect a mutual, reciprocal, responsible action in a joint act. The responsibility lies with the "passive" part to communicate a possible refusal.

In no other area of criminal law must a negative boundary be drawn as clearly as in law governing sexual offenses. In all other areas of society, fundamental boundaries are perfectly clear. They are shaped by (partly unwritten, i.e., not articled) generally accepted rules of conduct and social values, which are reflected in the law, at least in the case of other legally protected rights: A person does not have to forbid others to take their possessions. The owner of a property does not have to explicitly express their will that the property may not be entered,[100] the blackmailed person does not have to emphasize several times that they do not want to be blackmailed.[101] Only in law governing sexual offenses do these limits not exist because of the underlying stereotypes. There is an image of femininely perceived persons who arbitrarily and insanely make their decisions and therefore have to make their unwillingness explicitly clear, but who also "feign" unwillingness in order to appear more attractive, there is the myth of the "masochistic woman."[102] Opposed to this is the aggressively advancing man who is infantile and insane at the mercy of his drives and therefore needs direct, active boundaries from his environment in order to be able to behave appropriately.[103] Neither of these images does justice to self-determined and freely acting persons.[104] A consensual sexual contact rather consists of two (or more) active partners who are sure or must be sure of each other's consent. §§ 174ff StGB do not take this into account *de lege lata*:

the norms imply that the absence of a "no" is equivalent to a "yes."[105] This conceals not only a large gray area between the two contrary statements, but also the different fundamental meanings about sexual contact that these two limits give. The need to refuse unwanted sexual contact assumes an aggressive part and a passive part, the passive part is responsible for showing and communicating its boundaries, for at least explicitly resisting the actions of the active part. This also ignores the fact that the boundary transgression has often already happened by the time it needs to be formulated and defended. The protection according to mutual consensus, on the other hand, assumes that two freely deciding people face each other on equal footing with equal interest in sexual acts, without hierarchy or boundary transgressions.

THE IMPLEMENTATION OF "YES-MEANS-YES" IN GERMAN CRIMINAL LAW

Based on such a picture, the implementation of a consensus solution could also solve dogmatic problems of German law governing sexual offenses and achieve improved protection of sexual self-determination.

Introduction: The Concept of "Yes-Means-Yes" in International and National (Criminal) Law

A look at the requirements of international legal sources[106] for German law governing sexual offenses shows that these necessitate the implementation of the consensus solution: Art. 3 and 8 of the European Convention on Human Rights (ECHR) and Art. 36 of the IC are particularly relevant. According to the case law of the European Court of Human Rights (ECtHR), the former obligates the contracting states to ensure effective prosecution of sexual offenses.[107] In this regard, the positive obligations of the member states under Art. 3 and 8 ECHR are to be understood in accordance with current standards and trends, and "*any non-consensual sexual act*, including in the absence of physical resistance by the victim" must be penalized and effectively prosecuted.[108] These guidelines of the ECHR jurisprudence were incorporated in the Istanbul Convention.[109] Art 36 para 1 IC obliges the criminalization of non-consensual penetration of the body of another person (Art 36 para 1 lit a IC) as well as other non-consensual sexually determined acts with another person (Art 36 para 1 lit b IC). Art 36 para 2 IC provides that consent must be given *voluntarily as a result of the person's free will*; this will is "assessed in the context of the relevant surrounding circumstances." In the opinion of the expert panel GREVIO, the current provision of § 177 StGB does not fully comply with these requirements. The wording of the norm does not allow for prosecution if the victim does not consent to the sexual act but remains passive (i.e., does not express a contrary will). This means that criminal proceedings focus on the victim's actions rather than those of the accused, which creates the risk of reviving gender stereotypes and rape myths.[110] GREVIO therefore appeals to the German legislator to monitor and evaluate the implementation of the new Sexual Offenses Act, and in particular § 177 StGB, so that the definition of consent is further aligned with that in Art 36 para 2 IC.[111] Even from the perspective critical of the consensus model, it is partly conceded that Art 36 para 2 IC calls for such a "yes-means-yes" solution.[112]

The basic idea of the "yes-means-yes" solution is that of a consensus-based law governing sexual offenses. A consensual solution is not unknown to German criminal law, but rather underlies the dogmatics of legal interests protected by criminal law. As already explained, the consent of the injured person is recognized as a factor for criminal liability. It must first be clarified how exactly this factor can be located in law governing sexual offenses and how the consensual solution can be structured. Following the wording of Art. 36 para 1 lit. a, b IC ("non-consensual"), the model of assent excluding the elements of the offense (*tatbestandsausschließendes Einverständnis*) is convincing.[113] According to this, sexual contact without the consent of the other person(s) would be punishable—in a comprehensive implementation of this principle, this would apply regardless of the existence of a limitation of the capacity to form or express will. Insofar as all persons involved in the sexual contact agree, there is no punishable sexual act, but rather a consensual sexual contact between consenting, free, autonomous persons.[114]

According to the principles of natural, free will, there is also no consensual sexual contact if the contact is simply tolerated because resistance at the time seems futile or even dangerous, because then the decision is neither wanted nor free.[115] According to the dogmatics of consent in German criminal law and case law, consent is also neither generally given for all future scenarios, nor is it irrevocable.[116] These constellations are relevant to criminal sexual law: Consent to sexual contact must be given anew each time and be present over the entire period of contact. Sexual contact does not necessarily mean physical touching, as required by § 184i StGB. Even non-physical sexual harassment can principally constitute sexual contact, as in the case of certain image recordings (so-called "upskirting"/"downblousing") or verbal sexual harassment. According to the current regulations of law governing sexual offenses, criminal liability is limited to intentional commission. It remains to be clarified whether this can remain within the concept of a "yes-means-yes" solution or if it would virtually require the introduction of criminal liability for negligence.[117] A comparison with other offenses, such as bodily injury, shows that the introduction of a negligence penalty is conceivable. In the sexual context, the violation of sexual self-determination occurs even if the perpetrator does not intend it—precisely according to the dogmatics of the consensual solution, it is the responsibility of the sexual partners to be sure of their respective consent.[118]

Criticism of "Yes-Means-Yes" from the National Legal System's Perspective

While the non-consent solution ("no-means-no") has already been criticized for its considerable dogmatic shortcomings as a result of the "hasty" reform,[119] the proposal to introduce a "yes-means-yes" solution is also facing criticism on various levels. On the one hand, there are weighty legal policy objections to the implementation of the "yes-means-yes" solution: it is criticized to be based on the "antiquated idea" that sexual contact is fundamentally undesirable or worthy of disapproval; sexual contact loses the stigma of being punishable only through consent.[120] According to this opinion, sex, unlike the taking of an object, is rarely undesirable and these approaches would equate sex with the crimes of bodily harm or theft.[121] In addition, the consensus model is said to be based on an image of active and passive partner, thus also reproducing heteronormative role models.[122]

Furthermore, the closure of every loophole by criminalizing all human behavior is not regarded as a primary goal of criminal law, but rather the recording of punishable injustice.[123] According to this, the "no-means-no" provision would already be too broad, since sexual self-determination as a legal right was not sufficiently separated from other encroachments on freedom of action or personal freedom.[124] An intrusion of sexual self-determination could rarely reach the quality that distinguishes punishable from merely unpleasant behavior.[125] Particularly in law governing sexual offenses, the change in society's view of "victim status" would also be partly responsible for the desire for harsher punishments. While victimization used to be associated with stigma, today the "victim status" is claimed to be associated with empathy and recognition.[126]

With regard to a phrasing based on Art 36 para 1 IC, it is also assumed that this could result in an indeterminate expansion of the offense definition to the accused's detriment: it would no longer be recognizable to the accused when a sexual act crosses the line to criminal liability if its criminal liability were made dependent solely on the consent of the victim.[127] Furthermore, at the procedural level, there are fears of either evidentiary difficulties, a constitutionally inacceptable facilitation of reasoning, or even false charges. This was already feared about the introduction of the "no-means-no" solution;[128] regarding the consensus model, these concerns are even more present.[129] In legal practice, attrition can be observed, which in the area of sexual offenses can be attributed to an intensified prosecutorial selection process due to evidence problems, among other things.[130]

In addition to dogmatic, legal policy and practical objections, the question of the suitability and necessity of criminal law as a regulatory system in the field of sexuality can ultimately be raised. Under aspects of critique of the state and punishment itself, the evaluation of punitiveness must also be attentive to problems of the state and the punishment system.[131] Racist, sexist, and queerphobic prejudice and discrimination are so entrenched in society that they are also contained within the patriarchal power structures of the state apparatus.[132] Taking intersectionality into account, it must be considered whether introducing new criminal offenses grants law enforcement institutions more power to exercise punishment against marginalized population groups within these discriminatory structures.[133] It should be noted that patriarchal structures instill certain patterns of (sexual) behavior in the first place. The role of the aggressive man who sexualizes women and abuses them against their will for his own gratification is instilled or at least encouraged by society, education, and sexist structures. In the case of a reform of law governing sexual offenses—no matter what kind of behavior—it must be asked whether (solely) criminal law is the right place for the re-education of entire generations.[134]

Reasons to Implement "Yes-Means-Yes" into German Criminal Law

To the latter objection, it must be conceded that there may be reasons to use a sanctioning mechanism other than criminal law even if a violation of rights has occurred in the victim. It is also true that effective prevention of sexual offenses can only succeed if the penal norms are supported by other measures. However, it is clear that while non-criminal legal instruments (such as the Protection Against Violence Act, the Equal Treatment Act and law of delict) and social regulatory mechanisms are important for protecting sexual self-determination at other levels, effective and comprehensive protection of this legal right cannot succeed without criminal law.[135] It should also be kept in mind that legislation in the area of law governing sexual offenses in particular has often been the result of charged social debates. Like hardly any other area of (criminal) law, law governing sexual offenses is the subject of controversial and often occasion-related public debate. Insofar, a social and political symbolic effect must be granted to (sexual) criminal law that should not be underestimated, a signal of a change in social values.[136] Criminal law must therefore be part of a comprehensive and integral approach to sex education and the further development of society's understanding of consent, but it is ultimately an important instrument for holding sex offenders responsible and establishing accountability.

Evaluative Analysis of the Critical Views on "Yes-Means-Yes"

The other objections can also be refuted. The aforementioned view that sexual contacts would be "stigmatized as punishable" by implementing a consensus solution and equated with bodily injury offenses or theft,[137] cannot be agreed with. Adducing this comparison is not a matter of substantively equating the elements of crime or the legal interests, but rather a matter of comparing the dogmatic discussion of the protected interests. Furthermore, it is not a *consensual* sexual contact[138] that is equated with bodily injury or theft, but rather a *non-consensual sexual* contact—just as a consensual sexual contact and a consensual bodily injury (e.g., a life-saving surgical measure) or consensual sexual contact and the consensual taking of another's property (e.g., in the form of a gift) can be compared. It is not consensual sexual acts as such that have a "stigma of being punishable," but intrusions into sexual self-determination. A sexual act that takes place with the consent of the person concerned is no more punishable or stigmatized than a consensual medical procedure or boxing match would be even according to the "yes-means-yes" solution. Similarly, the consensus solution does not assume "active" and "passive" parts; rather, it is based on the idea of two (or more) equal, responsible, consenting participants in a sexual act.

Likewise, the argument relating to difficulties in providing evidence is not convincing. Especially in the case of sexual offenses, the presentation of evidence is difficult anyway—usually, there are no uninvolved witnesses, and there are opposing statements.[139] However, this difficulty is not peculiar to law governing sexual offenses,[140] but "exists wherever the facts of a crime depend on the will of the injured person and the act occurs between only two persons."[141] Even the implementation of the consensus solution, however, would change little in this regard: The question to be answered in the court's establishment of the case's facts would no longer be whether the victim did not say "no," but whether they verbally or conclusively consented to the performance of the sexual act.[142] Also, a fundamental distinction must be made between substantive criminal law and procedural evidentiary difficulties: "It is not the task of criminal law to minimize evidentiary problems, but to protect legal positions."[143]

The argument that the accused would no longer be able to recognize the limit of punishability if it were based on consent is only convincing if the legal figure of assent (*tatbestandsausschließendes Einverständnis*) as a whole were to be declared unsuitable. In other constellations, the recognizability of social or penal limits for the perpetrator is not questioned. In contrast to justifying consent, the requirements for an effective assent are less strict; only the natural will capacity of the assenting person is necessary.[144] It should also be considered that the constellation in which a sexual offense is committed out of actual (physical, financial or other) necessity is rather rare in contrast to other offenses (e.g., theft, bodily harm or similar, where situations of self-defense, necessity as justification or defense or social implications are conceivable). Apart from constellations of coercive necessity (*Nötigungsnotstand*), the commission of sexual offenses does not tend to occur against the background of legally or socially comprehensible personal situations of the perpetrator, but rather regularly out of selfish drive satisfaction.

Lastly, the legislative justification for the consensus solution implemented in § 177 para 2 no 2 StGB should be particularly considered. According to this, the acting out of sexuality by the protected persons is respected by the norm. The group of persons mentioned there can be expected to express their consent to sexual acts verbally or conclusively despite their considerable limitations in forming or expressing their will, taking appropriate account of the significance of the right of personality.[145] From this it can be derived as an argumentum a fortiori that in situations of sexual contact between persons who are *not* (significantly) limited in their ability to form or express their will, both the obtaining of consent and the (verbal or implied) expression of unambiguous consent to the sexual acts is all the more expectable without disproportionately impeding consensual sexuality.

An Interdisciplinary and Intersectional Perspective

Sexualities,[146] gender and sexual identity, and the free (non-)expression of sexuality are core areas of human life. The WHO defines sexuality as a "central aspect of being human throughout life" that encompasses "sex, gender identities and roles, sexual orientation, eroticism, pleasure, intimacy and reproduction" and is influenced by "the interaction of biological, psychological, social, economic, political, ethical, legal, religious and spiritual factors."[147] Unlike (purely) social-legal constructs such as property and ownership, the legal right to sexual self-determination is based on scientifically researched and verifiable physical and psychological processes inherent to being human. Like the right to physical integrity, sexual self-determination is inseparably linked to physical and mental human sensations. It is the task of law governing sexual offenses to take these processes and feelings into account. In doing so, especially the right to (sexual) self-determination must always be seen in the context of a patriarchal society. Particularly in the context of the gender dimension, a balance must be found between protection and paternalism.[148]

It should also be kept in mind that non-consensual sexual contact regularly affects more than just the protected right of sexual self-determination. The fact that the use of force or an infection with sexually transmitted diseases also affects the physical integrity of the victim is probably largely undisputed. However, potential pregnancy must also be taken into consideration. Legal interests of the victim affected in such cases go well beyond that of sexual self-determination. § 218a StGB articles exception provisions in regard to the general punishability of an abortion. In § 218a para 3 StGB, the so-called criminological indication refers to §§ 176–178 StGB. Due to this connection, in regard to the risk of an (unwanted) pregnancy resulting from a non-consensual sexual act, the specific configuration of sexual offenses is relevant beyond the norm complex itself. Consequently, criminalizing sexual offenses on the basis of the consensus solution does affect rights to abortion.

From an interdisciplinary perspective and in comparison to § 177 para 2 no 1 StGB, it becomes clear that the consensus model is better suited to protect sexual self-determination. With this provision, the legislator recognizes that exploiting a (temporary) incapacity to form or express an opposing will is worthy of punishment. In this context, the victim must be absolutely incapable of forming or expressing any will.[149] This is the case for persons who are in a state of profound disturbance of consciousness (e.g., fainting, sleep, anesthesia, severe intoxication), as well as for persons for whom communication is generally no longer possible.[150] Mere restrictions on the ability to form or express a will (e.g., due to intimidation) are not sufficient.[151] However, the incapacity or restriction in the ability to express the will may precisely result from the situation of unwanted sexual contact.[152] Whether the phenomena of *freezing* or so-called *tonic immobility* are covered by § 177 para 2 no 1 StGB has not been conclusively clarified. However, a comparison with § 177 para 1 StGB, which requires the victim, who is generally capable of forming and expressing their will, to clearly express an opposing will, only allows the conclusion that taking advantage of such a shock paralysis[153] is not punishable *de lege lata.*[154]

With regard to the requirement of active (internal) consent before intruding into the legal rights of another person, it should ultimately be noted that this is a functional, socially and legally recognized and lived concept. The fundamental unconditionality[155] of the recognition of subjective legal rights of others and the requirement of active consent as legitimization of an intervention are understood as basic prerequisites for a self-determined approach to subjective legal rights. From a social perspective, too, the area of sexuality is one of the few areas in which mature legal subjects are not (yet) expected to assume full responsibility for their behavior and, *vice versa*, in which those affected are not (yet) granted full autonomy.

CONCLUSION: ONLY YES IS YES—NEED FOR REFORM

The criticism of a consensus solution does not withstand thorough scrutiny. The examined international legal sources call for the improvement of the protection of sexual self-determination. From this dogmatic as well as from an interdisciplinary perspective, only the implementation of the consensus model meets the requirements of a functional sexual criminal law oriented by the standards of self-determined sexuality and effectively protecting sexual autonomy. Criminal law must not over-regulate where there is no violation of legal rights at all or hinder the free, consensual expression of sexuality in an educated society. In order to be able to guarantee free sexuality for *all* legal subjects, however, the behavioral boundaries of the ones must be drawn where the legal interests of others are reached. (Only) the other can consent to the crossing of their boundary, and only then will sexuality be truly free and self-determined. We need the decisive step towards protecting sexual self-determination: the reform of sexual offenses by "only yes-means-yes."

NOTES

1. The authors would like to sincerely thank *Prof. Dr. Liane Wörner, LL.M. (UW-Madison)* for enabling and supporting the writing of this chapter, as well as *mag. iur. Belgin Aktas* and *stud. iur. Isabel Wörner* for their helpful remarks.

2. E.g., the "Cologne New Year's Eve 2015", see text to n 67ff below.

3. E.g., the #MeToo debate or the petition "Ban #upskirting in Germany!" initiated by Hanna Seidel and Ida-Marie Sassenberg <https://www.change.org/p/verbietet-upskirting-in-deutschland> accessed March 10, 2023.

4. The so-called Istanbul Convention (hereinafter cited as: "IC") entered into force in Germany on 01.02.2018, cf Ministry of Justice, *Federal Law Gazette* (17.07.2017), BGBl. 2017 II, 1026–1027; Ministry of Justice, *Federal Law Gazette* (05.04.2018), BGBl. 2018 II, 142.

5. Sections of the German Criminal Code (Strafgesetzbuch, StGB) will be cited as §§.

6. See BKA, 'PCS 2021—Tables, Cases—Basic Table—2021', key 100000 ("offenses against sexual self-determination in total") <https://www.bka.de/EN/CurrentInformation/Statistics/PoliceCrimeStatistics/2021/pcs2021_node.html> accessed March 13, 2023.

7. This was effected by the 50th Act to Amend the Criminal Code—improving the Protection of Sexual Self-Determination of 04.11.2016, cf Ministry of Justice, *Federal Law Gazette* (09.11.2016) BGBl 2016, 2460; for more details, see text to n 67ff below.

8. As is the assumption of the expert panel "GREVIO", cf GREVIO, 'Baseline Evaluation Report Germany' (published 07.10.2022) 71, assessment no 251

<https://rm.coe.int/report-on-germany-for-publication/1680a86937> accessed March 13, 2023.

9. ibid. This should not be misunderstood as a positive assessment of the rising number of cases of crimes against sexual self-determination. Rather, it is encouraging to see an apparent increase in the willingness to report crimes.

10. Cf Lena Stadler, Steffen Bieneck and Christian Pfeiffer, 'Repräsentativbefragung Sexueller Missbrauch 2011' (KFN-Forschungsberichte Nr. 118, 2011), 42, Tab 24 <https://kfn.de/wp-content/uploads/Forschungsberichte/FB_118.pdf> accessed March 13, 2023. In 2005, a reporting rate of only 11% in cases of sexual violence was found, see Ursula Müller and Monika Schröttle, 'Lebenssituation, Sicherheit und Gesundheit von Frauen in Deutschland' (conducted on behalf of the Federal Ministry for Family Affairs, Senior Citizens, Women and Youth 2005) 208–209 <https://www.bmfsfj.de/bmfsfj/studie-lebenssituation-sicherheit-und-gesundheit-von-frauen-in-deutschland-80694> accessed March 13, 2023; see also Jo Lovett and Liz Kelly, 'Different systems, similar outcomes? Tracking attrition in reported rape cases across Europe' (2009) 20 <https://www.researchgate.net/publication/228847968_Different_systems_similar_outcomes_Tracking_attrition_in_reported_rape_cases_in_eleven_countries> accessed March 13, 2023.

11. Statistisches Bundesamt Destatis, Rechtspflege; Strafverfolgung 2019 (Fachserie 10, Reihe 3, 29.10.2020) 24 <https://www.destatis.de/DE/Themen/Staat/Justiz-Rechtspflege/Publikationen/Downloads-Strafverfolgung-Strafvollzug/strafverfolgung-2100300197004.html> accessed March 10, 2023.See also in detail Lovett and Kelly (n 9) 20ff, 57–58; Brigitte Sick and Joachim Renzikowski, 'Lücken beim Schutz der sexuellen Selbstbestimmung aus menschenrechtlicher Sicht' in Britta Bannenberg and others (eds), Über allem: Menschlichkeit. *Festschrift für Dieter Rössner* (Nomos 2015) 928, 930.

12. As already the claim with the abortion solution.

13. The scope of this chapter is limited to sexual contacts between adults. Constellations in which a minor is involved are not covered.

14. In this respect, this chapter only covers persons who are generally unrestrictedly capable of forming and expressing a natural will. Persons who are protected by § 177 para 2 no 2 StGB due to a mental or physical restriction of their ability to form or express a will are not covered by the scope of this work.

15. Elisa Hoven and Andrew Dyer, '„Only Yes means Yes"? Aktuelle Entwicklungen im australischen Sexualstrafrecht und Folgerungen für die deutsche Diskussion' (2020) 132 (1) ZStW 250, 251; Tatjana Hörnle, 'Warum § 177 Abs. 1 StGB durch einen neuen Tatbestand ergänzt werden sollte' (2015) 4 ZIS 206, 213.

16. Tatjana Hörnle, 'Sexuelle Selbstbestimmung: Bedeutung, Voraussetzungen und kriminalpolitische Forderungen' (2015) 127 (4) ZStW 851, 868; Tatjana Hörnle, 'Das Gesetz zur Verbesserung des Schutzes sexueller Selbstbestimmung' (2017) NStZ 13, 14; Joachim Renzikowski, 'Nein! – Das neue Sexualstrafrecht' (2016) NJW 3553, 3555; Thomas Fischer, *Strafgesetzbuch mit Nebengesetzen* (Beck'sche Kurz-Kommentare, 69th edn, C.H. Beck 2022) § 177 margin number 9.

17. See below text to n 24ff.

18. Volker Haas, '§ 13 StGB' in Holger Matt and Joachim Renzikowski (eds), *StGB; Strafgesetzbuch Kommentar* (2nd edn, Vahlen 2020) margin numbers 1, 33; Jörg Eisele, '§ 13 StGB' in Albin Eser (ed), *Schönke/Schröder Strafgesetzbuch; Kommentar* (30th edn, C.H. Beck 2019), margin numbers 15ff with further references; Claus Roxin and Luís Greco, *Strafrecht Allgemeiner Teil*, vol 1: *Grundlagen. Der Aufbau der Verbrechenslehre* (5th edn, C.H. Beck 2020) para 10 margin numbers 19ff.

19. See § 15 StGB. Negligent acts are only punishable if the law explicitly punishes negligent behavior, e.g., § 222 StGB (negligent homicide).

20. See §§ 32, 34 StGB. Regarding the differentiation between justification and excuse see Albin Eser, 'Justification and Excuse' (1976) 24 (4) The American Journal of Comparative Law 621.

21. See § 19 StGB.

22. See §§ 20, 21 StGB.

23. If this awareness is lacking, cf § 17 StGB.

24. Such as §§ 33, 35 StGB.

25. Whether this distinction is necessary at all is disputed; cf e.g., Horst Schlehofer, 'Vor §§ 32ff StGB' in Volker Erb and Jürgen Schäfer (eds), *Münchener Kommentar zum Strafgesetzbuch*, vol 1 (4th edn, C.H. Beck München 2021) margin numbers 144–145 and 146ff with further references.

26. E.g., §§ 218, 248b StGB.

27. Cf e.g., Roland Schmitz, '§ 242 StGB' in Volker Erb and Jürgen Schäfer (eds), *Münchener Kommentar zum Strafgesetzbuch*, vol 4 (4th edn, C.H. Beck München 2021), margin number 49 with further references.

28. Cf e.g., Urs Kindhäuser, '§ 242 StGB' in Urs Kindhäuser, Ulfrid Neumann and Hans-Ullrich Paeffgen, *Strafgesetzbuch* (Nomos Baden-Baden 2017) vol 3, margin number 41 with further references.

29. Cf e.g., ibid 43 with further references; BGH 26.6.2008 – 3 StR 182/08, published in NStZ 2008, 624, 625 with further references.

30. Detlev Sternberg-Lieben, 'Vorbemerkungen zu den §§ 32 ff.' in Albin Eser (ed), *Schönke/Schröder Strafgesetzbuch; Kommentar* (30th edn. Beck München 2019), margin number 31.

31. ibid 32a.

32. BayOLG 10.10.1978 – 3 St 230/78 published in NJW 1979, 729 with further references; OLG Düsseldorf 7.9.1987 – 5 Ss 276/87 - 221/87 I, published in NJW 1988, 83; Schlehofer (n 24), 177.

33. Sternberg-Lieben (n 29), 31–33.

34. Rudolf Rengier, *Strafrecht Allgemeiner Teil* (14th edn, C.H. Beck München 2022), para 23 margin number 24; Johannes Wessels, Werner Beulke and Helmut Satzger, *Strafrecht Allgemeiner Teil* (52nd edn, C.F. Müller Karlsruhe 2022) margin number 573.

35. Sternberg-Lieben (n 29), 31; Volker Erb, '§ 32 StGB' in Volker Erb and Jürgen Schäfer (eds), *Münchener Kommentar zum Strafgesetzbuch*, vol 1 (4th edn, C.H. Beck 2020), margin number 52.

36. Wessels, Beulke and Satzger (n 33), margin number 565.

37. ibid 580.

38. Detlev Sternberg-Lieben (n 29), 33.

39. ibid 36.

40. A common legal interest is e.g., the safety of road traffic, see ibid; Schlehofer (n 24), 155.

41. E.g., § 228 StGB: The consent of the injured person to the infliction of bodily harm only has a justifying effect if the act does not offend common decency.

42. Rengier (n 33), para 23 margin number 13.

43. Wessels, Beulke and Satzger (n 33), para 11 margin number 575.

44. ibid 554.

45. Erb (n 34), 52.

46. Due to differing moral concepts, sexuality as such was also criminalized for a long time. E.g., § 175 StGB (old version) can be considered, which criminalized homosexual acts and was repealed in 1994 with the 29th Penal Law Amendment Act, cf Ministry of Justice, *Federal Law Gazette* (10.06.1994), BGBl. I 1994, 1168.

47. See also Lara Herning and Johannah Illgner, '"Ja heißt ja"—Konsensorientierter Ansatz im deutschen Sexualstrafrecht' (2016) ZRP 77, 78.

48. Hörnle (2017), NStZ (n. 15) 13, 14.

49. Brigitte Sick, *Sexuelles Selbstbestimmungsrecht und Vergewaltigungsbegriff: ein Beitrag zur gegenwärtigen Diskussion einer Neufassung des § 177 StGB unter Berücksichtigung der Strafbarkeit de lege lata und empirischer Gesichtspunkte* (Duncker & Humblot 1993), 38.

50. ibid 60; Erol Rudolf Pohlreich, *"Ehrenmorde" im Wandel des Strafrechts* (Duncker & Humblot 2009), 58.

51. RG 2.6.1893—966/93, published in RGSt 24, 201, 202; RG 3.10.1895—2926/95, published in RGSt 27, 366, 368; Sick (n 48), 60.

52. Sick (n 48), 60.

53. The Scrupulous Court Rules of Charles V of Prussia (Carolina), p. 78.

54. ibid 80.

55. Sick (n 48), 38.

56. ibid 57; Thomas Vormbaum and Jürgen Welp (eds), *Das Strafgesetzbuch; Sammlung der Änderungsgesetze und Neubekanntmachungen,* vol 1: 1870–1953 (BWV 2004) Section: Verbrechen wider die Sittlichkeit.

57. Vormbaum and Welp (n 55), § 176 para 1 no 2; Sick (n 48), 53.

58. Draft bill 1962, Bundestagsdrucksache (Parliament Papers of the German Bundestag) of 4 October 1962 -IV/650, 359.

59. BVerfG 10.5.1975 – 1 BvR 550/52, para 152.

60. Sick (n 48), 64, 67.

61. Martin Heger, *Lackner/Kühl/Heger Strafgesetzbuch; Kommentar* (30th edn, C.H. Beck 2023), Vorbemerkung 13. Abschnitt margin number 1; Dana-Sophia Valentiner, *Das Grundrecht auf sexuelle Selbstbestimmung* (Nomos Baden-Baden 2021), 74.

62. Valentiner (n 60), 74.

63. Sick (n 48), 79.

64. ibid 82.

65. Heger (n 60), 9; Valentiner (n 60), 75.

66. Jörg Eisele, 'Vorbemerkungen zu den §§ 174 ff' in Albin Eser (ed), *Schönke/ Schröder Strafgesetzbuch; Kommentar* (30th edn, C.H. Beck 2019), margin number 8; Heger (n 60), Vorbemerkung 13. Abschnitt margin number 11ff.

67. Eisele (n 65), 13; Joachim Renzikowski, 'Vorbemerkung zu § 174' in Erb V and Schäfer J (eds), *Münchener Kommentar zum Strafgesetzbuch*, vol 4 (4th edn, C.H. Beck 2021), margin number 105.

68. E.g., Bosen, 'Fünf Jahre danach: Lehren aus der Kölner Silvesternacht', (Dec. 31, 2020) DW, <https://p.dw.com/p/3mt0b> accessed March 13, 2023. Information on the number of cases varies greatly depending on the source. On the instrumentalization of the event and further information see Behrendes, Die Kölner Silvesternacht 2015/2016 und ihre Folgen: Wahrnehmungsperspektiven, Erkenntnisse und Instrumentalisierungen' (2016) NK 322–343.

69. Elisa Hoven, 'Reform des Sexualstrafrechts—Ad-hoc-Gesetzgebung und Diskursstrategien' (2018) NK 392, 397.

70. Hoven (n 68), 396.

71. Hörnle, 'Das Gesetz zur Verbesserung des Schutzes sexueller Selbstbestimmung' (n 15), 13.

72. The perpetrator is considered to have performed a sexual act on the victim if they have the victim perform the act or order the victim to perform or tolerate the sexual act on or by a third person.

73. Hörnle, 'Das Gesetz zur Verbesserung des Schutzes sexueller Selbstbestimmung' (n 15), 14

74. Joachim Renzikowski, '§ 177 StGB' in Erb V and Schäfer J (eds), *Münchener Kommentar zum Strafgesetzbuch*, vol 4 (4th edn, C.H. Beck 2021), margin number 48; Ralf Eschelbach, '§ 177 StGB' in Holger Matt and Joachim Renzikowski (eds), *StGB; Strafgesetzbuch Kommentar* (2nd edn, Vahlen 2020), margin number 27.

75. Eschelbach (n 73), § 177 margin number 2.

76. Fischer (n 15), Vor § 174 margin number 5; Renzikowski (n 66), Vor § 174 margin number 7; Elisa Hoven and Thomas Weigend, '"Nein heißt nein"—und viele Fragen offen. Zur Neugestaltung der Strafbarkeit sexueller Übergriffe' (2017) JZ 182, 183; Boris Burghardt, Anja Schmidt and Leonie Steinl, 'Der strafrechtliche Schutz der sexuellen Selbstbestimmung vor nicht-körperlichen Beeinträchtigungen' (2022) JZ 502, 503.

77. Thus expressly Bundestagsdrucksache (Parliament Papers of the German Bundestag) of 6 July 2016 – 18/9097, 25.

78. ibid 24.

79. ibid 24–25.

80. ibid 24.

81. ibid 25.

82. Hoven (n 68), 395; Hörnle, 'Das Gesetz zur Verbesserung des Schutzes sexueller Selbstbestimmung' (n 15), 14.

83. E.g., Hörnle, 'Das Gesetz zur Verbesserung des Schutzes sexueller Selbstbestimmung' (n 15), 14; Eschelbach (n 73), § 177 margin number 7.

84. Renzikowski (n 73), § 177 margin number 4; Heger (n 60) § 177 margin number 2; Hörnle, 'Das Gesetz zur Verbesserung des Schutzes sexueller Selbstbestimmung' (n 15), 15.

85. Hörnle, 'Das Gesetz zur Verbesserung des Schutzes sexueller Selbstbestimmung' (n 15), 15; Jörg Eisele, '§ 177 StGB' in Albin Eser (ed), *Schönke/Schröder Strafgesetzbuch; Kommentar* (30th edn, C.H. Beck 2019), margin number 20.

86. Eschelbach (n 73), § 177 margin number 40; Hörnle, 'Das Gesetz zur Verbesserung des Schutzes sexueller Selbstbestimmung' (n 15), 17.

87. Hörnle, 'Das Gesetz zur Verbesserung des Schutzes sexueller Selbstbestimmung' (n 15), 16.

88. ibid 17.

89. ibid 20.

90. This includes not only literal statements, but also sexual gestures, sounds and other sexually connoted behavior.

91. Martin Heger, '§ 184i StGB' *Lackner/Kühl/Heger Strafgesetzbuch; Kommentar* (30th edn, C.H. Beck 2023), margin number 2; Joachim Renzikowski, '§ 184i StGB' in Erb V and Schäfer J (eds), *Münchener Kommentar zum Strafgesetzbuch*, vol 4 (4th edn, C.H. Beck 2021), margin number 10.

92. Tatjana Hörnle, 'Wie § 177 ergänzt werden sollte' (2015) GA 313, 323.

93. Renzikowski (n 66), Vor § 174, margin number 7; Jonas Brückner, '§ 903 BGB' in Franz Jürgen Säcker and others (eds), *Münchener Kommentar zum Bürgerlichen Gesetzbuch*, vol 8 (9th edn, C.H. Beck 2023), margin number 1; Christian Berger, '§ 903 BGB' in Rolf Stürner (ed), *Jauernig Bürgerliches Gesetzbuch* (18th edn, C.H. Beck 2021), margin number 3; Hans Schulte-Nölke, '§ 903 BGB' in Reiner Schulze (ed), *Bürgerliches Gesetzbuch; Handkommentar* (11th edn, Nomos 2021), margin number 1.

94. As Hoven and Weigend (n 75), 185, who recognize this despite a critical perspective on the non-consensus as well as the consensus solution.

95. Which can be seen in the legal system of §§ 242, 243 StGB; Roland Schmitz, '§ 243 StGB' in Volker Erb and Jürgen Schäfer (eds), *Münchener Kommentar zum Strafgesetzbuch*, vol 4 (4th edn, C.H. Beck München 2021), margin number 92; Heger (n 60), § 243 margin number 24; Nikolaus Bosch, '§ 243 StGB' in Eser A (ed), *Schönke/Schröder Strafgesetzbuch; Kommentar* (30th edn, Beck München 2019), margin number 4; Jens Schmidt, '§ 243 StGB' in Holger Matt and Joachim Renzikowski (eds), *StGB; Strafgesetzbuch Kommentar* (2nd edn, Vahlen 2020), margin number 23.

96. Ralf Eschelbach, '§ 183 StGB' in Holger Matt and Joachim Renzikowski (eds), *StGB; Strafgesetzbuch Kommentar* (2nd edn, Vahlen 2020), margin number 4; Jörg Eisele, '§ 183 StGB' in Albin Eser (ed), *Schönke/Schröder Strafgesetzbuch; Kommentar* (30th edn, C.H. Beck 2019), margin number 2.

97. Bundestagsdrucksache (Parliament Papers of the German Bundestag) VI/3521, 53; BVerfG 22.5.1999 – 2 BvR 398/99, in which the Federal Constitutional Court refers to its above-mentioned (n 58) decision on male homosexuality with regard to role models.

98. Hörnle, 'Sexuelle Selbstbestimmung: Bedeutungen, Voraussetzungen und kriminalpolitische Forderungen' (n 15), 868; Hörnle, 'Das Gesetz zur Verbesserung des Schutzes sexueller Selbstbestimmung' (n 15), 14; Fischer (n 15), § 177 margin number 6; Wolfgang Mitsch, 'Die erkennbare Willensbarriere gem. § 177 Abs. 1 StGB' (2018) KriPoZ 334, 335.

99. Hörnle, 'Das Gesetz zur Verbesserung des Schutzes sexueller Selbstbestimmung' (n 47), 15; Joachim Renzikowski, 'Nein! - Das neue Sexualstrafrecht' (2016) NJW 3553, 3553; Fischer (n 15), § 177 margin number 10; Mitsch (n 98), 335.

100. Heribert Ostendorf, '§ 123 StGB' in Urs Kindhäuser, Ulfrid Neumann and Hans-Ullrich Paeffgen, *Strafgesetzbuch* (Nomos 2017) vol 2, margin number 32; Burkhard Feilcke, '§ 123 StGB in Volker Erb and Jürgen Schäfer (eds), *Münchener Kommentar zum Strafgesetzbuch*, vol 4 (4th edn, C.H. Beck München 2021), margin number 27.

101. Thomas Maier, '§ 253 StGB' in Holger Matt and Joachim Renzikowski (eds), *StGB; Strafgesetzbuch Kommentar* (2nd edn, Vahlen 2020), margin number 7.

102. Sick (n 48), 178, 180.

103. ibid 179, 187.

104. ibid 179.

105. Cf Herning and Illgner (n 46), 78.

106. For more details see Sick and Renzikowski (n 10), 935ff.

107. First MC v Bulgaria App no 39272/98 (ECtHR, 4 December 2003) para 153. This has been confirmed several times, e.g., by IG v Moldova App no 53519/07 (ECtHR, 15 May 2012 para 45; DJ v Croatia App no 42418/10 (ECtHR, 24 July 2012) para 86; NA v Moldova App no 13424/06 (ECtHR, 24 September 2013) para 71; Osman Isfen, 'Zur gesetzlichen Normierung des entgegenstehenden Willens bei Sexualdelikten' (2015) ZIS 217, 220–221.

108. MC v Bulgaria App no 39272/08 (ECtHR, 4 December 2003) para 166. On the significance of the standards established by the ECtHR for German legal practice, see Isfen (n 106), 221 with further references.

109. Isfen (n 107), 221.

110. GREVIO (n 7), assessment no. 252.

111. ibid 253.

112. E.g., Hoven (n 68), 394–395.

113. For a detailed discussion see Kempe, Lückenhaftigkeit und Reform des deutschen Sexualstrafrechts vor dem Hintergrund der Istanbul-Konvention (Duncker & Humblot 2018), 230ff; Herning and Illgner (n 46), 80 suggest "without consent" as the wording.

114. Sick (n 48), 166.

115. ibid.

116. ibid, 169.

117. In this regard see Rita Vavra, *Die Strafbarkeit nicht-einvernehmlicher sexueller Handlungen zwischen erwachsenen Personen*, (Sexualität in Recht und Gesellschaft vol 2, Nomos Baden-Baden 2020), 253ff.

118. Regarding the design as consent excluding the offense, the error about the consent would lead to a mistake of fact according to § 16 StGB, cf ibid 254. Thus, questions of mistake would also be easier to clarify.

119. See text to n 82ff above as well as e.g., Hoven (n 68), 397 ff; Hoven and Weigend JZ (n 75), 186.

120. Hoven (n 68), 395; Hoven and Weigend (n 75), 186. Similarly Birgit Cirullies, 'Stellungnahme zu dem Antrag [. . .] BT-Drucksache 18/1969' (statement of 26 January 2015 on Bundestagsdrucksache (Parliament Papers of the German Bundestag) of 2 July 2014 – 18/1969), 2.

121. Cirullies (n 120), 2; Hoven (n 68), 395; Hoven and Weigend (n 75), 185.

122. Hoven (n 68), 395.

123. Thomas Fischer, 'Anhörung zu dem Antrag [. . .] BT-Drs. 18/1969' (statement of 14 January 2015 on Bundestagsdrucksache (Parliament Papers of the German Bundestag) of 2 July 2014 – 18/1969), 9 ff; Fischer (n 15), § 177 marginal number 4ff.

124. Thomas Fischer, 'Noch einmal: § 177 StGB und die Istanbul-Konvention' (2015) ZIS 312, 315.

125. ibid 316.

126. Hoven (n 68), 396.

127. Fischer (n 123), 9ff; Cirullies (n 120), 2.

128. Cf e.g., Fischer (n 123), 12ff; Hoven and Weigend (n 75), 185.

129. Hoven and Weigend (n 75): 'practically unsolvable difficulties of evidence' (p. 186) or, with regard to the (now implemented) "yes-means-yes" draft on § 177 para 2 no 2 StGB: 'unacceptably shifting the burden of proof' (p. 188, fn. 56).

130. In detail Vavra (n 117), 37ff.

131. Anna Terwiel, 'What is Carceral Feminism?' (2020) 48 (4), Political Theory 421, 422; Boris Burghardt and Leonie Steinl, 'Sexual Violence and Criminal Justice in the 21st Century' (2021) 22, German Law Journal 691, 697.

132. Terwiel (n 131), 422; Amia Srinivasan *The Right to Sex; Feminism in the Twenty-First Century* (Picador 2022), 4.

133. Terwiel (n 131), 426; Srinivasan, (n 132), 17; Bianca Fileborn and F Vera-Gray, 'I want to be able to walk the street without fear: Transforming Justice for Street Harassment' (2017) 25 Feminist Legal Studies 203, 207.

134. Srinivasan (n 132), 29.

135. Cf Vavra (n 117), 208ff.

136. As also Monika Frommel, '§ 177 StGB' in Urs Kindhäuser, Ulfrid Neumann and Hans-Ullrich Paeffgen, *Strafgesetzbuch* (Nomos Baden-Baden 2017) vol 2, margin number 14; Herning and Illgner (n 46) 80.

137. See text to n 122 above; esp Hoven and Weigend (n 75), 185.

138. Hoven and Weigend (n 75), 185, too, presuppose the consensuality of a sexual contact for it to not be perceived as unwanted or as an unwelcome assault (like the taking away of an object).

139. Frommel (n 136), 1; Herning and Illgner (n 46), 80; Isfen (2015) ZIS (n 107) 217, 232. Franziska Drohsel, 'Das Sexualstrafrecht—aktueller Novellierungsbedarf'

(2018) NJOZ 1521, e.g., cites this circumstance as a reason why many victims shy away from legal proceedings.

140. Differing opinion: Isfen (n 107), 232, which nevertheless 'cannot be regarded as an obstacle to a sensible extension of protection'.

141. Thomas Fischer, 'Ja, Nein, Vielleicht' (2022) JJZG 63, 64.

142. Similarly Fischer (2022) JJZG (n 141) 63, 64.

143. Joachim Renzikowski, 'Lücken beim Schutz der sexuellen Selbstbestimmung aus menschenrechtlicher Sicht' (statement of 26 February 2015 on Bundestagsdrucksache (Parliament Papers of the German Bundestag) of 2 July 2014—18/1969), 2; similarly Sick and Renzikowski, (n 106), 930.

144. See text to n 24ff above.

145. German Parliament, Official Record (BT-Drs.) 18/9097, 24–25. For more detail see text to n 77ff above.

146. On the concept of sexualities (pl.) see e.g., Valentiner (n 60), 31–32 with further references.

147. WHO (2006) 'Defining sexual health; Report of a technical consultation on sexual health' (Sexual health document series, Geneva 28–31 January 2002), 5 <https://www.cesas.lu/perch/resources/whodefiningsexualhealth.pdf> accessed March 13, 2023.The WHO's working definition of sexuality can also be found here: <https://www.who.int/teams/sexual-and-reproductive-health-and-research/key-areas-of-work/sexual-health/defining-sexual-health> accessed March 10, 2023.

148. For an analysis of "autonomy as a feminist concept" and "self-determination between enabling and paternalism," see Dana-Sophia Valentiner, 'Geschlecht und Recht' (2022) JuS 1094, 1097ff.

149. Eisele (n 85), § 177 margin number 26; Renzikowski (n 73), § 177 margin number 68.

150. Eschelbach (n 73), § 177 margin number 36; Renzikowski (n 73), § 177 margin number 69 with further references.

151. Renzikowski (n 73), § 177 margin number 68.

152. See GREVIO (n 7), assessment no. 252.

153. Which is not to be confused with an element of surprise, as the exploitation of that is covered in § 177 para 2 no 3 StGB.

154. This is also the conclusion of the GREVIO report (n 7), assessment no. 252; similarly Eschelbach (n 73), § 177 margin number 37.

155. In the sense of independence from an active claim or assertion, let alone an active defense against encroachments on the respective legal asset.

BIBLIOGRAPHY

Behrendes U, 'Die Kölner Silvesternacht 2015/2016 und ihre Folgen: Wahrnehmungsperspektiven, Erkenntnisse und Instrumentalisierungen' (2016) NK 28, 322–343.

Berger C, '§ 903 BGB' in Stürner R (ed), *Jauernig Bürgerliches Gesetzbuch* (18th edn, C.H. Beck 2021).

Bosch N, '§ 243 StGB' in Eser A (ed), *Schönke/Schröder Strafgesetzbuch; Kommentar* (30th edn, Beck München 2019).

Bosen R, 'Fünf Jahre danach: Lehren aus der Kölner Silvesternacht' (31.12.2020) DW <https://p.dw.com/p/3mt0b >accessed March 13, 2023.

Brückner J, '§ 903 BGB' in Säcker F J and others (eds), *Münchener Kommentar zum Bürgerlichen Gesetzbuch*, vol 8 (9th edn, C.H. Beck 2023).

Bundeskriminalamt (BKA), Police Crime Statistics, *Cases—Basic Tables* (2013–21) <https://www.bka.de/EN/CurrentInformation/Statistics/PoliceCrimeStatistics/policecrimestatistics_node.htmll> accessed March 13, 2023.

Burghardt B and Steinl L, 'Sexual Violence and Criminal Justice in the 21st Century' (2021) 22, German Law Journal 22, 691–702.

Burghardt B, Schmidt A and Steinl L, 'Der strafrechtliche Schutz der sexuellen Selbstbestimmung vor nicht-körperlichen Beeinträchtigungen' (2022) JZ 10, 502–511.

Cirullies B, statement of 26 January 2015 on Bundestagsdrucksache (Parliament Papers of the German Bundestag) of 2 July 2014 – 18/1969.

Drohsel F, 'Das Sexualstrafrecht – aktueller Novellierungsbedarf' (2018) NJOZ 1521–1525.

Eisele J, '§ 13 StGB' in Eser A (ed), *Schönke/Schröder Strafgesetzbuch; Kommentar* (30th edn, C.H. Beck 2019).

Eisele J, 'Vorbemerkungen zu den §§ 174 ff.' in Eser A (ed), *Schönke/Schröder Strafgesetzbuch; Kommentar* (30th edn, C.H. Beck 2019).

Eisele J, '§ 177 StGB' in Eser A (ed), *Schönke/Schröder Strafgesetzbuch; Kommentar* (30th edn, C.H. Beck 2019).

Eisele J, '§ 183 StGB' in Eser A (ed), *Schönke/Schröder Strafgesetzbuch; Kommentar* (30th edn, C.H. Beck 2019).

Erb V and Schäfer J (eds), *Münchener Kommentar zum Strafgesetzbuch*, vol 1 (4th edn, C.H. Beck 2020).

Erb V and Schäfer J (eds), *Münchener Kommentar zum Strafgesetzbuch*, vol 3 (4th edn, C.H. Beck 2021).

Erb V and Schäfer J (eds), *Münchener Kommentar zum Strafgesetzbuch*, vol 4 (4th edn, C.H. Beck 2021).

Erb V, '§ 32 StGB' in Erb V and Schäfer J (eds), *Münchener Kommentar zum Strafgesetzbuch*, vol 1 (4th edn, C.H. Beck 2020).

Eschelbach R, '§ 177 StGB' in Matt H and Renzikowski J (eds), *StGB; Strafgesetzbuch Kommentar* (2nd edn, Vahlen 2020).

Eschelbach R, '§ 183 StGB' in Matt H and Renzikowski J (eds), *StGB; Strafgesetzbuch Kommentar* (2nd edn, Vahlen 2020).

Eser A, 'Justification and Excuse' (1976) 24 (4) The American journal of comparative law, 621–637.

Feilcke B, '§ 123 StGB' in Erb V and Schäfer J (eds), *Münchener Kommentar zum Strafgesetzbuch*, vol 3 (4th edn, C.H. Beck 2021).

Fileborn B and Vera-Gray F, 'I want to be able to walk the street without fear: Transforming Justice for Street Harassment' (2017) 25 Feminist Legal Studies 203–227.

Fischer T, Statement of 14 January 2015 on Bundestagsdrucksache (Parliament Papers of the German Bundestag) of 2 July 2014 – 18/1969.

Fischer T, 'Noch einmal: § 177 StGB und die Istanbul-Konvention' (2015) ZIS 6, 312–319.

Fischer T, *Strafgesetzbuch mit Nebengesetzen* (Beck'sche Kurz-Kommentare, 69th edn, C.H. Beck 2022).

Fischer T, 'Ja, Nein, Vielleicht' (2022) 2 JJZG 63–65.

Frommel M, '§ 177 StGB' in Kindhäuser U, Neumann U and Paeffgen H (eds), *Strafgesetzbuch* (Nomos 2017) vol 2.

GREVIO, 'Baseline Evaluation Report Germany'(published 07.10.2022) <https://rm.coe.int/report-on-germany-for-publication/1680a86937> accessed March 13, 2023.

Haas V, '§ 13 StGB' in Holger Matt and Joachim Renzikowski (eds), *StGB; Strafgesetzbuch Kommentar* (2nd edn, Vahlen 2020).

Heger M, *Lackner/Kühl/Heger Strafgesetzbuch; Kommentar* (30th edn, C.H: Beck 2023).

Herning L and Illgner J, '„Ja heißt Ja"—Konsensorientierter Ansatz im deutschen Sexualstrafrecht' (2016) 3, 77–80.

Hörnle T, 'Sexuelle Selbstbestimmung: Bedeutung, Voraussetzungen und kriminalpolitische Forderungen' (2015) ZStW 127, 851–887.

Hörnle T, 'Wie § 177 StGB ergänzt werden sollte' (2015) GA 313–328.

Hörnle T, 'Warum § 177 Abs. 1 StGB durch einen neuen Tatbestand ergänzt werden sollte' (2016) ZIS 206–215.

Hörnle T, 'Das Gesetz zur Verbesserung des Schutzes sexueller Selbstbestimmung' (2017) NStZ 1, 13–21.

Hoven E and Dyer A, '„Only Yes means Yes"? Aktuelle Entwicklungen im australischen Sexualstrafrecht und Folgerungen für die deutsche Diskussion' (2020) ZStW 132, 250–263.

Hoven E and Weigend T, '„Nein heißt Nein" – und viele Fragen offen' (2017) JZ 4, 182–191.

Hoven E, 'Reform des Sexualstrafrechts – Ad-hoc-Gesetzgebung und Diskursstrategien' (2018) NK 4, 392–409.

Isfen O, 'Zur gesetzlichen Normierung des entgegenstehenden Willens bei Sexualdelikten' (2015) ZIS 217–233.

Kempe A, *Lückenhaftigkeit und Reform des deutschen Sexualstrafrechts vor dem Hintergrund der Istanbul-Konvention* (Duncker & Humblot 2018).

Kindhäuser U, '§ 242 StGB' in Kindhäuser U, Neumann U and Paeffgen H (eds), *Strafgesetzbuch* (Nomos 2017) vol 3.

Kindhäuser U, Neumann U and Paeffgen H (eds), *Strafgesetzbuch* (Nomos 2017) vol 2.

Kindhäuser U, Neumann U and Paeffgen H (eds), *Strafgesetzbuch* (Nomos 2017) vol 3.

Lovett J and Kelly L, 'Different systems, similar outcomes? Tracking attrition in reported rape cases across Europe' (2009) <https://www.researchgate.net/publica

tion/228847968_Different_systems_similar_outcomes_Tracking_attrition_in_reported_rape_cases_in_eleven_countries> accessed March 13, 2023.

Maier T, '§ 253 StGB' in Matt H and Renzikowski J (eds), *StGB; Strafgesetzbuch Kommentar* (2nd edn, Vahlen 2020).

Matt H and Renzikowski J (eds), *StGB; Strafgesetzbuch Kommentar* (2nd edn, Vahlen 2020).

Mitsch W, 'Die erkennbare Willensbarriere gem. § 177 Abs. 1 StGB' (2018) KriPoZ 334–338.

Müller U and Schröttle M, 'Lebenssituation, Sicherheit und Gesundheit von Frauen in Deutschland' (conducted on behalf of the Federal Ministry for Family Affairs, Senior Citizens, Women and Youth 2005) <https://www.bmfsfj.de/bmfsfj/studie-lebenssituation-sicherheit-und-gesundheit-von-frauen-in-deutschland-80694> accessed March 13, 2023

Ostendorf H, '§ 123 StGB' in Kindhäuser U, Neumann U and Paeffgen H (eds), *Strafgesetzbuch* (Nomos 2017) vol 2.

Pohlreich ER, *"Ehrenmorde" im Wandel des Strafrechts* (Duncker & Humblot 2009).

Rengier R, *Strafrecht Allgemeiner Teil* (14th edn, C.H. Beck, 2022).

Renzikowski J, statement of 26 February 2015 on Bundestagsdrucksache (Parliament Papers of the German Bundestag) of 2 July 2014 – 18/1969.

Renzikowski J, 'Nein!—Das neue Sexualstrafrecht' (2016) NJW 49, 3553–3558.

Renzikowski J, 'Vorbemerkung zu § 174' in Erb V and Schäfer J (eds), *Münchener Kommentar zum Strafgesetzbuch*, vol 4 (4th edn, C.H. Beck 2021).

Renzikowski J, '§ 177 StGB' in Erb V and Schäfer J (eds), *Münchener Kommentar zum Strafgesetzbuch*, vol 4 (4th edn, C.H. Beck 2021).

Renzikowski J, '§ 184i StGB' in Erb V and Schäfer J (eds), *Münchener Kommentar zum Strafgesetzbuch*, vol 4 (4th edn, C.H. Beck 2021).

Roxin C and Greco L, *Strafrecht Allgemeiner Teil*, vol 1: *Grundlagen. Der Aufbau der Verbrechenslehre* (C.H. Beck 2020).

Säcker F and others (eds), *Münchener Kommentar zum Bürgerlichen Gesetzbuch*, vol 8 (C.H. Beck 2023).

Schlehofer H, 'Vorbemerkung zu § 32' in Erb V and Schäfer J (eds), *Münchener Kommentar zum Strafgesetzbuch*, vol 1 (4th edn, C.H. Beck 2022).

Schmidt J, '§ 243 StGB' in Matt H and Renzikowski J (eds), *StGB; Strafgesetzbuch Kommentar* (2nd edn, Vahlen 2020).

Schmitz R, '§ 242 StGB' in Erb V and Schäfer J (eds), *Münchener Kommentar zum Strafgesetzbuch*, vol 4 (4th edn, C.H. Beck 2021).

Schmitz R, '§ 243 StGB' in Erb V and Schäfer J (eds), *Münchener Kommentar zum Strafgesetzbuch*, vol 4 (4th edn, C.H. Beck 2021).

Schönke A and Schröder H, Strafgesetzbuch. Kommentar (C.H. Beck 2019).

Schulte-Nölke H, '§ 903 BGB' in Schulze R (ed), *Bürgerliches Gesetzbuch; Handkommentar* (11th edn, Nomos 2021).

Sick B, *Sexuelles Selbstbestimmungsrecht und Vergewaltigungsbegriff: ein Beitrag zur gegenwärtigen Diskussion einer Neufassung des § 177 StGB unter Berücksichtigung der Strafbarkeit de lege lata und empirischer Gesichtspunkte* (Duncker & Humblot 1993).

Sick B and Renzikowski J, 'Lücken beim Schutz der sexuellen Selbstbestimmung aus menschenrechtlicher Sicht' in Bannenberg B and others (eds), Über allem: Menschlichkeit; Festschrift für Dieter Rössner (Nomos 2015), 928–942.

Srinivasan A, *The Right to Sex; Feminism in the Twenty-First Century* (Picador 2022).

Stadler L, Bieneck S and Pfeiffer C, 'Repräsentativbefragung Sexueller Missbrauch' (kfn-Forschungsberichte No. 118, 2011) <https://kfn.de/wp-content/uploads/Forschungsberichte/FB_118.pdf> accessed March 13, 2023.

Statistisches Bundesamt Destatis, Rechtspflege; Strafverfolgung 2019 (Fachserie 10, Reihe 3, 29.10.2020) <https://www.destatis.de/DE/Themen/Staat/Justiz-Rechtspflege/Publikationen/Downloads-Strafverfolgung-Strafvollzug/strafverfolgung-2100300197004.html> accessed March 10, 2023.

Sternberg-Lieben D, 'Vorbemerkungen zu den §§ 32 ff.' in Eser A (ed), *Schönke/Schröder Strafgesetzbuch; Kommentar* (30th edn, Beck München 2019).

Terwiel A, 'What is Carceral Feminism?' (2020) 48 (4) Political Theory 421–442.

Valentiner D-S, *Das Grundrecht auf sexuelle Selbstbestimmung. Zugleich eine gewährleistungsdogmatische Rekonstruktion des Rechts auf die freie Entfaltung der Persönlichkeit* (Nomos 2021).

Valentiner D-S, 'Geschlecht und Recht' (2022) 12 JuS 1094–1098.

Vavra R, *Die Strafbarkeit nicht-einvernehmlicher sexueller Handlungen* (Sexualität in Recht und Gesellschaft vol 2, Nomos 2020).

Vormbaum T and Welp J (eds), *Das Strafgesetzbuch; Sammlung der Änderungsgesetze und Neubekanntmachungen*, vol 1: 1870–1953 (BWV 2004).

Wessels J, Beulke W and Satzger H, *Strafrecht Allgemeiner Teil* (52nd edn, C.F. Müller 2022).

5

The Legal Framework as a Way of Correcting Attrition in Sexual Offenses

Lessons Learned from Sweden?

Dennis Martinsson

This chapter[1] focuses on the Swedish regulation on rape, with emphasis on a statutory law reform in 2018 that introduced involuntariness as the essential part of the *actus reus* element of rape, and also the new offence of negligent rape. To analyze the current Swedish legal framework on rape, a contextual understanding of the socio-political setting is necessary. The chapter therefore begins by portraying these features. There follows an overview of the *actus reus* elements of rape, including a brief historical and political background of the 2018 reform, and also an overview of the *mens rea* element of intentional rape and negligent rape. Following this, the chapter highlights and discusses the areas of attrition present in the current Swedish provisions on rape.

CONTEXTUAL BACKGROUND

Sweden, like the other Nordic countries, often ranks well internationally in regard to gender equality.[2] One possible explanation is that Sweden is considered a social democratic version of a welfare state,[3] characterised by policies concerning the individual's private realm and where both "soft" and "hard" legal instruments are commonly used as means of implementing social norms. This is evident in matters concerning gender equality.[4] Welfare state policies affect how work and family commitments are combined; thereby also affecting gender equality.[5] Hence, to improve and to promote gender equality, Sweden has adopted policies in various areas, including criminal law. Consequently, legal reforms have been adopted within a political context where gender equality has, inter alia, resulted in addressing violence against women as a matter of criminal justice.[6] This gradual development has accelerated since the 1970s. It is against this backdrop that the current Swedish provision on rape needs to be understood.[7]

The provision was reformed in 2018, right in the middle of the #MeToo movement, and marked an important shift, introducing involuntariness (instead of coercion or force) as the essential *actus reus* element of rape,[8] and also the offence of negligent rape.

To grasp the Swedish provision on rape, one always needs to view Swedish criminal law through a Nordic lens. Generally, the welfare states in the Nordic region have had great bearing on legal thinking in the Nordic countries, in which a Scandinavian legal tradition of realism, pragmatism and practical considerations in legal reasoning is preferred to theoretical thinking.[9] Further, the legislative procedure is similar and, seen internationally, unique. The procedure is rather slow and complex process, and includes the government's appointment of a commission of inquiry responsible for creating a legislative proposal. The procedure includes mandatory consultations with external parties, such as government agencies and universities.[10] The result of the legislative procedure is the *travaux préparatoires*; a set of documents providing the judicial and political reasoning behind a piece of legislation and its provisions. Although *travaux préparatoires* are not a binding legal source, the courts often refer to them since they often provide support for legal argumentation.[11] Further, statutory law is emphasized and the courts generally have a limited role in the judicial system—at least if viewed from a common law perspective.[12] Given these common features, legal comparisons are often made among the Nordic countries, and the closeness of the Danish, Swedish and Norwegian languages particularly promotes intra-Nordic comparisons. Consequently, a legal reform in one Nordic country (in any legal area) is commonly inspired or influenced by the regulation in another.[13] This is particularly true for criminal law and policy.[14]

In a criminal law and policy context the Nordic welfare state model, with its emphasis on socioeconomic reforms aiming to balance out the consequences of inequality, on social policy and on alternatives to imprisonment, has contributed to the concept of "Scandinavian/Nordic exceptionalism," i.e., low prison rates, low sentencing regimes and humane prison conditions.[15] However, this has been criticised:[16] welfare state policies can also be used to legitimize a far-reaching degree of incarceration.[17] The concept of Scandinavian/Nordic Exceptionalism has, particularly during the last decade, been criticised also for other reasons.[18] This is perhaps not the accurate forum to discuss whether the concept actually exist or even existed in the first place. Nevertheless, one should note that the Nordic countries have introduced comparatively harsh sentencing regimes for sexual offences.[19] For instance, as recently as 1 August 2022, a stricter Swedish sentencing regime was introduced in relation to (intentional) rape.[20]

When focusing on the Swedish statutory rape law, one notes that in the Nordic welfare state, gender equality and criminal law policy have been intertwined and given a prominent role.[21] This has been evident in recent years where the Nordic countries have witnessed a shift in the regulation of rape: from coercion and/or force as prerequisites for criminal responsibility towards a regulation based on involuntariness or consent. Iceland adopted consent-based legislation in 2018,[22] Denmark amended its rape law in 2021[23] and Finland amended, inter alia, the provision on rape in 2022, which entered into force 1 January 2023.[24] Norway has not yet reformed its regulation on rape, but a statutory reform has been launched there.[25] These reforms are part of an international development where several jurisdictions seem to be moving towards a regulation based on consent or involuntariness in relation to sexual offences.[26] The Danish, Finnish and Swedish provisions on rape presuppose a lack of voluntariness—not a lack of consent—as the essential requirement for the *actus reus* element. Since this chapter focuses on the Swedish provision and for consistency, "involuntariness" not "consent" will be used when reviewing the provision.[27]

The double purpose of the present chapter is to review the current provision on rape in Swedish criminal law and to identify challenges with the provision, particularly in relation to attrition. Attrition in the Nordic region is often analyzed in terms of a need for legislative revision.[28] Since the Swedish statutory rape law was recently revised, the present text—in line with a Nordic tradition—focuses on the legal framework. Some challenges are identified when reviewing the statutory law (and its implications) in relation to the policy background of the current provisions. The review identifies two areas of attrition: (1) the construction of the statutory law, (2) the discrepancy between the statutory law, its policy background and application of the provisions in the case law. Consequently, due to the existing ambiguity, one might question whether Swedish criminal law, in fact, offers effective legal protection for potential victims of rape.

THE *ACTUS REUS* ELEMENT: THE WIDE DEFINITION OF WHAT SEXUAL ACTS CONSTITUTES RAPE

Before turning to the 2018 reform and the introduction of "involuntariness" as an *actus reus* element, one should briefly mention what sexual acts constitute rape according to Swedish criminal law. In 2022 the statutory law was amended and the provision on rape (Swedish Criminal Code, ch 6 s 1) now states that the following sexual acts are a part of the *actus reus* element: "*vaginal*, *anal* or *oral intercourse*, or some *other sexual act* that in view of the seriousness of the violation is comparable to sexual intercourse . . ."[29] Notably, the 2022 amendment resulted in the inclusion in the statutory law of anal and oral intercourse. Prior to the amendment, "intercourse" was defined as (heterosexual) vaginal intercourse. However, anal and oral sex were previously included in the phrasing "other sexual act" and were thereby a part of the *actus reus* element of rape. Thus, the 2022 amendment marked a shift: from defining "intercourse" as exclusively heteronormative to an inclusive, gender-neutral, legal definition of the notion of "intercourse."

The statutory law is wide in its definition of what sexual acts constitute rape. The scope of "intercourse" is even wider since, regarding vaginal and anal intercourse, penetration is not required. Vaginal or anal intercourse occurs already when the perpetrator's and the victim's genitals touch, and oral intercourse occurs when, for instance, the perpetrator's tongue touches the victim's genitals.[30]

As already mentioned, "other sexual acts" are included in the *actus reus* element of rape. Prior to the 2022 amendment, the courts should assess whether the relevant sexual act—in the view of the seriousness of the violation—was comparable to (heterosexual) vaginal intercourse. Today, the relevant comparison is the widened meaning of intercourse, which includes anal and oral intercourse. Consequently, the 2022 amendment has probably narrowed the meaning of "other sexual act" in the provision. However, the government has stated that the scope of "other sexual act" needs be clarified in the case law and that prior statements in the case law and the *travaux préparatoires* are still of relevance.[31] From Supreme Court precedents it follows, for instance, that touching a woman's genitals (without penetration) is considered an "other sexual act," but not masturbating another man's penis.[32]

Further, a sexual act that constitutes the *actus reus* element of rape does not require that the perpetrator and the victim are physically present at the same place when the offence is committed. Hence, no bodily contact between the perpetrator and the victim is needed and a sexual act can, for instance, be committed online by the victim performing or conducting a sexual act on her- or himself.[33]

In conclusion, when reviewing what sexual acts establish the *actus reus* element of rape in Sweden, the rape provision is rather extensive. From an international perspective the Swedish provision includes sexual acts that are perhaps not considered as rape or perhaps not even considered as another sexual offence in other jurisdictions.[34] In this regard, the Swedish provision offers a far-reaching legal protection for sexual autonomy and sexual integrity. Hence, an extensive definition of what sexual acts constitute the *actus reus* element of rape is one way of correcting attrition in sexual offences.

THE *ACTUS REUS* ELEMENT AND THE 2018 REFORM: THE INTRODUCTION OF INVOLUNTARINESS

From the Outside Looking In: A Swedish Version of Affirmative Consent

The question of constructing involuntariness or consent as the essential *actus reus* element of rape is a normative one.[35] However, the challenge is to define what involuntariness/consent actually *is*—or ought to be.[36] The literature on involuntariness or consent as an *actus reus* element in relation to sexual offences is vast and the literature is sometimes very detailed when analyzing different models of involuntariness or consent. It includes rather refined definitions of models and hypothetical situations that are seemingly similar. However, this is not perhaps the right forum for a review of the vigorous international philosophical and legal discussion on involuntariness and consent.[37] But to categorize the Swedish provision on rape in relation to the international scholarly discussion of models of involuntariness or consent, the most accurate description is that this provision represents a version of affirmative consent.[38] A regulation on rape based on affirmative consent is often described as "(only) yes means yes," meaning that a lack of explicit consent is the decisive element for criminal liability.[39] The Swedish provision can be categorized as a version of affirmative consent because the statutory law does not state that criminal liability for rape presupposes that the victim did not say yes. Hence, criminal liability can be awarded in a situation where there is an absence of an explicit expression of involuntariness from the victim.[40]

The Historical and Political Context of the 2018 Reform

As mentioned, the current Swedish provision on rape needs to be understood in relation to a gradual, historical development regarding sexual offences and in a political context where gender equality has been a priority. Using the three theories of rape described by Burgess-Jackson, it is clear that the Swedish provision has shifted from a "conservative theory" (where rape is considered a property offence) to a "liberal theory" (where rape is considered an unwanted infringement of the victim's integrity as an individual person and where autonomy is central for the ability to consent).[41] Yet developments in the 1900s and early 2000s illustrate that the "liberal" construction of the rape provision has continuously progressed, highlighted by the introduction of involuntariness as the crucial *actus reus* element in 2018.

Historically, the shift from a "conservative" to a "liberal" theory of rape occurred in Sweden in 1864, with a provision aimed at protecting the victim's individual freedom.[42] Rape was previously considered a property offence, aimed at harming the victim's family honour.[43] However, it was not until 1965—when the modernized Swedish Criminal Code entered into force—that rape was considered a sexual offence. The *travaux préparatoires* explicitly mark this move, defining the protected legal interest (*Rechtsgut*) as individual integrity in a sexual context.[44] Another landmark in 1965 was that marital rape was criminalized.[45] Note that the 1965 provision was exclusively heteronormative, since the statutory law explicitly stated that only a man could rape a woman. A reform in 1984 made the provision on rape gender-neutral.[46] These examples illustrate that a consecutive development has occurred in Sweden regarding rape (and other sexual offences), and the development since the 1970s is clear: amendments to the statutory law have explicitly been made to enhance the protection of sexual autonomy and sexual integrity.[47] This development has, at least partly, been influenced by cases receiving media attention and which, in turn, have generated a public debate on the provision on rape and other sexual offences.[48]

Turning to developments closer to the present-day Swedish provision on rape, at least ten *travaux préparatoires* have been published since 1995, each aiming, to some extent, at amending the statutory law.[49] Not all resulted in an amendment; the question of whether involuntariness or consent should be introduced as an *actus reus* element has been discussed previously in the *travaux préparatoires*.[50] So why was involuntariness introduced as an *actus reus* element of rape in 2018 and not earlier?

There are mainly three explanations. First, the previous *travaux préparatoires* concluded that there was—from a legal point of view—no need for involuntariness or consent as an *actus reus* element and for some time there was no political demand for introducing involuntariness or consent.[51] Second, the #MeToo movement during the autumn of 2017 created strong public demand for political action to improve gender equality in Sweden. There were petitions to introduce involuntariness or consent as an *actus reus* element in the Swedish provision on rape and to introduce negligent rape as an offence in Swedish criminal law. Third, the demands raised by the #MeToo movement offered a great political opportunity for the Swedish government at the time—which was made up of two parties: the Social Democrats and the Green Party. The government coalition was formed after the 2014 general election and claimed to be a "feminist government."[52] Consequently, the demands springing from #MeToo in the autumn of 2017 converged with the political ambition of the Swedish government at the time. In March 2018 the government hastily published a government bill proposing e.g., "involuntariness" as an *actus reus* element of rape, which was submitted to the Swedish Parliament. At the vote in May 2018, all political parties unanimously adopted the proposed government bill. Hence, when introducing "involuntariness" as the essential part of the provision on rape, the Swedish government skilfully used political momentum, combining #MeToo with the ambition of being a feminist government.

The Construction of Involuntariness as an *Actus Reus* Element

Three Situations That Are Always Involuntary

The 2018 reform resulted in a statutory amendment, and the provision on rape (Swedish Criminal Code, ch 6 s 1) now specifies three situations where participation is always deemed involuntary:

1. [if] their participation is a result of assault, other violence or a threat of a criminal act, a threat to bring a prosecution against or report another person for an offence, or a threat to give detrimental information about another person;
2. the perpetrator improperly exploits the fact that the person is in a particularly vulnerable situation due to unconsciousness, sleep, grave fear, the influence of alcohol or drugs, illness, bodily injury, mental disturbance or otherwise in view of the circumstances; or
3. the perpetrator induces the person to participate by seriously abusing the person's position of dependence on the perpetrator.[53]

However, the three situations in the statutory law stipulating when participation is always involuntary, were not new.[54] In fact, prior to the 2018 reform, these three situations were *already* criminalized. Situation (1) was specified in the prior provision on rape (where coercion or force was an essential part of the *actus reus* element of rape) and so was situation (2). Situation (3) was previously a separate sexual offence. Consequently, the three situations in the statutory law now explicitly stating when participation always is involuntary, did not—except from portraying them within the umbrella concept of "involuntariness"—change the scope of the provision on rape. Hence, prior Supreme Court precedents and statements in the *travaux préparatoires* are still valid.[55]

Involuntariness in Other Situations

The legal significance of the 2018 reform was an amendment of the statutory law regarding situations which do not qualify for any of the three above-mentioned situations where participation is always involuntary. For situations outside these three situations, the provision on rape stipulates that the *actus reus* element can still be fulfilled under certain circumstances.[56] In that case, the provision states the following:

> Whether participation is voluntary or not, particular consideration is given to whether voluntariness was expressed by word or deed or in some other way.[57]

This quotation explicitly marks the normative shift that the government sought to achieve, both in the statutory law and in the Swedish society.[58]

Although the quotation sends a clear normative shift, its scope is unclear.[59] The government stated, for instance, that it is neither possible nor appropriate to clarify the (legal) meaning of "involuntariness" in the statutory law. Instead, the government left to the development in the case law to clarify the meaning.[60] However, the government made some statements in the *travaux préparatoires* regarding the interpretation of the above-mentioned quotation.

When assessing whether participation is involuntary, the point of departure is the actual participation, not a person's inner will.[61] Therefore, according to the government, voluntary participation in intercourse or a sexual act can be either active or passive. Although passive participation is often a sign of involuntariness, this is not always the case. If someone does not express his or her participation by word or deed, the assessment should focus on whether the participation was expressed in "some other way," i.e., facial expression or body language.[62] Consequently, the government admitted that it is generally not possible to distinguish a case of involuntary passive participation from a case of voluntary passive participation.[63] Relating to the question of passive participation, silent consent could negate involuntariness.[64]

Note that, since actual participation is of great importance when assessing whether participation is involuntary, participation resulting from persuasion or pressure is not considered involuntary. As long as a person was able to readily decide whether to participate and he or she did so after persuasion, participation is not considered involuntary.[65]

Also discussed in the *travaux préparatoires* was sexual deceptions,[66] also known as "fraud in the factum" and "fraud in the inducement."[67] The discussion was rather detailed, distinguishing between situations which are involuntary and those which are not. Without going into detail, it seems to matter what someone was deceived about.[68] Somewhat simplified, if a person is deceived about the sexual act as such or if the perpetrator is pretending to be the victim's partner, the participation is deemed involuntary. However, if someone is deceived regarding e.g. the use of contraception[69] or sexually transmitted diseases or pretending to be a celebrity, this does not negate involuntariness and is therefore lawful.

Lastly, not all situations where participation is always involuntary are considered unlawful. As mentioned above, a situation where the perpetrator exploits a victim who is asleep, is a case of involuntariness. However, there are exceptions. The government has, for instance, stressed that it is not uncommon in a relationship that one person awakens his or her partner by performing sexual advances. In that case, criminal liability should not be awarded.[70]

In conclusion, when reviewing involuntariness in the Swedish provision on rape, the 2018 reform of the statutory law sends a normative message: sex should be voluntary. Although the statutory law stipulates three situations which are always involuntary, it lacks clarity in relation to cases that fall outside these three situations. Consequently, the umbrella concept of involuntariness is partly ambiguous. Therefore, one could argue that the concept of involuntariness in the Swedish provision on rape is—at first glance—a way of correcting attrition in sexual offences. However, the ambiguity leads to uncertainties regarding the scope of the protection of sexual autonomy and sexual integrity. This is discussed further in the last section of this chapter.

The *Mens Rea* Element in Relation to Rape

The Mens Rea Element of Intentional Rape

When one look into the *mens rea* element of rape, the standard *mens rea* requirements are applied. Since the 2018 reform introduced the offence of negligent rape, one should therefore note that two types of *mens rea* generally exist in Swedish criminal law: intent and negligence. Intent is the standard *mens rea* requirement while negligence can only be applied if a certain provision explicitly states that this form of *mens rea* suffices to establish criminal liability.[71] Although Sweden is a civil law jurisdiction emphasizing statutory law, no provision in Swedish criminal law defines intent. Instead, the different forms of intent have been developed by the Supreme Court and in the literature, and the development has focused on the lowest form of intent (as how to distinguish intent from negligence). Today, Sweden recognizes three forms of intent: direct intent, indirect intent and reckless intent.[72] Unless otherwise stated, reckless intent is sufficient to prove that the defendant acted with intent.[73]

Since direct intent is only relevant in relation to *actus reus* elements which express a particular result or effect, it cannot be applied in relation to rape. However, indirect intent can be applied, meaning that the defendant is practically aware that an effect will occur or that a condition exists.[74] In relation to rape and involuntariness, indirect intent is when the defendant was certain that the victim's participation was involuntary, for example by being aware of the specific circumstances that made participation involuntary, such as intoxication, unconsciousness or use of violence.

Further, the lowest form of intent—reckless intent—is applicable in relation to rape. Reckless intent was formally established in a Supreme Court precedent pronounced in 2004. Two condictions must be met.[75] First, the defendant must be indifferent to the existence of a certain effect, result or circumstance, which is another way of stating that the defendant must be aware or have knowledge of the risks relating to the deed he or she performed. Second, the defendant must be indifferent to the realization of the effect, result or circumstance in the sense that he or she accepts the effect, result or circumstance that occurs—or might occur—because of his or her conduct.[76] Regarding rape and involuntariness, reckless intent is when the defendant is aware of a risk that participation is involuntary, but is indifferent to whether this insight is true or not and therefore initiates or continues to perform a sexual act with someone whose participation might be involuntary.

The Introduction of Negligent Rape

Partly inspired by Norway,[77] the 2018 reform introduced into Swedish criminal law a new offence: negligent rape. The Swedish provision on negligent rape (Swedish Criminal Code ch 6 s 1A) stipulates the following:

> A person who commits an act referred to in Section 1 and is grossly negligent regarding the circumstance that the other person is not participating voluntarily is guilty of negligent rape . . . [78]

The construction of negligent rape deserves further explanation. First, the *actus reus* element is the same as for intentional rape. Second, negligent rape is only applicable (as a *mens rea* element) in relation to involuntariness, not in relation to the sexual component (intercourse or other sexual act). Third, the statutory law states that only "gross negligence" can establish criminal liability. Generally, "gross negligence" is equivalent to "conscious" negligence, meaning that the defendant is aware or has knowledge of the risks relating to the deed performed (i.e., the first, but not the second, requirement of reckless intent is fulfilled). Hence, negligent rape is where the defendant was aware of the risk that participation was involuntary, but nevertheless performed intercourse or a sexual act.[79] However, the *travaux préparatoires* to the 2018 reform stress that "gross negligence" also includes "unconscious" negligence, meaning that the defendant is unaware or lacks knowledge of the risks relating to the deed performed, but should have been aware of these risks.[80] Consequently, this signals that everyone has a duty to investigate whether someone is participating voluntarily or not, and often it is sufficient to simply ask the other person if he or she agrees for the sexual act to be performed. Further, the more clear signs of involuntariness there are, the heavier the duty to investigate.[81]

Although the introduction of negligent rape was a significant part of the 2018 reform and only "clearly reprehensible" cases of unconscious negligence are covered by the provision, the government provided no guidelines for the courts on how to assess the *mens rea* element of negligence. Instead, it left to the case law to further develop whether a case of negligent rape can result in criminal liability.[82]

Since the 2018 reform, the Supreme Court has adjudicated three cases, of which two are relevant in this context.[83] These cases illustrate a clear uncertainty regarding when criminal liability should be awarded for intentional rape, or negligent rape or should lead to an acquittal (of rape, not necessarily other sexual offences). Therefore, the Supreme Court precedents, arguably, reflect the ambiguity present in the statutory law regarding intentional and negligent rape. In its first precedent, the Court repeated the statements in the *travaux préparatoires* and did not clarify the *mens rea* element.[84] The Court only concluded that the defendant fulfilled the first, but not the second, requirement of reckless intent; hence, the defendant was guilty of negligent rape. In the second precedent concerning negligence as the *mens rea* element, the ambiguity is clearly visible in the reasoning.[85] On the one hand, the Court concluded that there were clear signs (the victim being passive and the defendant being rough) indicating that the defendant should have been aware that it was a case of involuntariness. On the other hand, the Court stated that on this particular occasion, it could not be required that the defendant was aware of this. Yet the Court stated that in any case the negligence was not "remarkably reprehensible." Therefore, the defendant was acquitted.

Since the Supreme Court precedents reflect the ambiguity present in the statutory law, one might question whether this ambiguity is also present in the case law. A 2020 report by the Swedish National Council for Crime Prevention analyzed the case law from Sweden's 48 district courts and six courts of appeal concerning intentional and negligent rape adjudicated in 2019, where the victim was a woman.[86] Reviewing the development in the case law, the Council noted some tendencies. Here it is relevant to focus on the *mens rea* element. Based on the judgments scrutinized in the review, the Council concluded that there clearly exists an ambiguity in the case law about the application of reckless intent and negligence. The Council stressed that the application of reckless intent is particularly ambiguous since application of both the first and the second requirement of reckless intent is far from clear. Similarly, although only 12 cases of negligent rape were adjudicated in 2019, the Council concluded that the application of negligent rape was unclear.[87] Consequently, there is an apparent need to clarify the *mens rea* element in this context.

SOME CHALLENGES IN RELATION TO ATTRITION WITH THE CURRENT SWEDISH PROVISIONS ON RAPE

From the review above, it follows that the 2018 reform at first glance gives the impression that the protected legal interest (*Rechtsgut*) in the statutory law is designed in a particular way. However, regarding several essential legal requirements in the statutory law, no guidelines are available in the *travaux préparatoires* and the case law is ambiguous. Hence, the review suggested that two areas of attrition can particularly be identified in relation to the Swedish provisions on rape: (1) in the construction of the statutory law, (2) in the discrepancy between the statutory law and its policy background and the application of the provisions in the case law. It is therefore relevant to discuss why these forms of attrition are present in relation to the Swedish provisions on rape.

When identifying attrition in this context, one starting point is that the protected legal interest has successively been transformed. Seemingly, the protected legal interest regarding rape has shifted: from covering a concrete, physical harm relating to the victim's body to an abstract understanding of sexual integrity where emphasis is on "violation" in a wider sense. Hence, the protected legal interest is also transformed in relation to the victim, since emphasis is on the abstract: the victim *qua* individual is not as important; rather, the victim is viewed as representing a collective (of potential victims): the victim *qua* a member of society is put at the centre.[88] Alternatively, one might argue that the protected legal interest of sexual autonomy and sexual integrity has been emphasized since 1965, but the concept of sexual integrity has changed. If this is so, it would offer an explanation as to why the statutory law and the case law have widened the comprehension of when a violation of sexual integrity has occurred.[89]

Regardless, there seems to be agreement that the protected legal interest has shifted to a more abstract idea of sexual integrity and under what circumstances it is violated. As a result of a more abstract protected legal interest, specific issues are not pronounced adequately in the *travaux préparatoires*, and this in turn creates a risk of a legal vacuum when courts adjudicate rape cases. Several aspects regarding the current Swedish provision on rape illustrate this, particularly the design of involuntariness and the *mens rea* element of negligence, where the government left to the courts to clarify the scope and the meaning of the central parts of the 2018 reform. Considering the emphasis on the statutory law and that Swedish courts generally have a limited role in the judicial system, there is a risk that not much development in the case law will occur. One can thus discern a discrepancy: on the one hand, the government did not clarify the 2018 reform enough to achieve legal certainty; on the other, Swedish courts lack a mandate to create law-making through case law—the mandate is basically confined to applying the statutory law in individual cases. Drawing on these reflections, one might criticize the Swedish government for investing political capital to introduce the 2018 reform without providing guidelines and without assuring that the reform would result in designing the statutory law to harmonize better with legal certainty.

However, the discrepancy outlined here might be of a different kind. Some argue that it is a misconception to assume that the concept of sexual autonomy could be reformed on the basis of prior statutory law, bearing with it a tradition from previous legislation. Since the concept of autonomy was formerly not as pronounced as today (prior statutory law was not designed to protect sexual autonomy) it might lead to clashes within the legal system: the old roots of the statutory law and its application correspond poorly with modern, normative concepts of sexual autonomy and sexual integrity. Consequently, the statutory law needs not to be reformed but redesigned from scratch.[90] One could argue that the conflict between the "old roots" and the current statutory law on rape is present in Swedish criminal law. The continuum of development of the rape provision bears its tradition into new legislative reforms, and this is particularly true for the 2018 reform. As mentioned, some changes in the statutory law were not new. Rather than redesigning the provision on rape from scratch and outlining the statutory law based on present-day conceptions of sexual autonomy and sexual integrity, the Swedish government reformed the statutory law without clarifying core concepts. Hence, the 2018 reform did not fully incorporate the concept of sexual autonomy and sexual integrity. This is one explanation of the attrition present in the Swedish rape provision.

The idea that the statutory law, to fully incorporate the concept of sexual autonomy and sexual integrity, should be redesigned from scratch resembles feminist criticism of the concept of consent (and *mutas mutandis*, involuntariness). Though the Swedish government at the time of the 2018 reform claimed to be a feminist one and that the reform was motivated by improving gender equality, the reform is not necessarily accepted by feminist theorists as a feminist one. According to some scholars, the concept of consent is flawed since it presupposes two equal partners and since there exists a sexual hierarchy—which is a part of a patriarchal society—the legal concept of consent in a context of sexual offences cannot adjust the societal inequality between the sexes.[91] Therefore, these scholars suggest that a new framework on sexual offences needs to be created, which centres around inequality and how to adjust it. From this perspective, the Swedish government has not transformed the current Swedish provision from a "liberal theory" of rape to a "radical theory" of rape framing the offence within a theory and practice of recognizing it as part of structural inequality. Hence, the policy background of the Swedish provision on rape does not correspond with feminist legal theory in this regard.

Additionally, the current Swedish framework on rape does, arguably, not correspond with feminist legal theory on the distinction between the victim's inner and external actions. When assessing whether it was a case of involuntariness, the point of departure for Swedish courts is the actual participation, not a person's inner will. According to some feminist scholars, inner will is connected with emotions and is a cognitive state. If the assessment of involuntariness is based (purely) on the external participation and external signs whether it was a case of involuntariness, the assessment thereby ignores if—in fact—the victim participated by an inner will to do so. Hence, the assessment presupposes that an external participation automatically equals to a person's inner will to participate voluntarily. Consequently, focusing (purely) on the external participation could risk that the assessment concentrates on whether the defendant interpreted external signs from the victim as voluntary participation and not whether the victim actually—from an emotional point of view—willingly wanted to participate.[92]

Lastly, the areas of attrition identified in the review shows that it exists a lack of legal certainty, particularly concerning foreseeability. As demonstrated above, one cannot foresee when a deed should be considered a case of intentional rape, or negligent rape or a lawful act. Evidently, this is deeply problematic for the defendant who might have difficulties in the preparation of his or her defence. However, the lack of forseeability might also directly affect the (potential) victim negatively. Since the statutory law and the case law are unclear regarding the 2018 reform, from a victim's perspective it might be difficult to be recognized as a victim thereby losing the potential rights of a victim. Consequently, the existing attrition might lead to a wider discrepancy between the (potential) victim's expectations (who through the 2018 reform might assume that the legal protection is wider than it seems to be) and the legal assessment in the individual case.

CONCLUSIONS

In Sweden, the welfare state and gender equality have fused, as illustrated by e.g., prioritizing gender equality in several policy areas, which to a high extent include criminal law and policy. Hence, since the 1970s reforms concerning sexual offences have been supported by gender-equality arguments. The 2018 reform that introduced involuntariness as the essential *actus reus* element and the new offence of negligent rape symbolize this exceptionally well, particularly since the reform was introduced by a government who at the time defined itself as "feminist."

In line with Nordic tradition, the present review focuses on attrition in the legal framework. The review shows that two areas of attrition are present in regard to the Swedish provisions on rape: (1) the construction of the statutory law, (2) the gap between the statutory law, its policy background and the case law. Consequently, there are disconnects between, on one hand, the construction of the statutory law and its application, and on the other the political ambition of the 2018 reform. This, in turn, results in ambiguity in the application of the rape provisions, suggesting a lack of legal certainty and foreseeability. Evidently, although the 2018 reform politically marked an important normative shift, several legal issues were left unsolved. Until adjusted, the attrition identified in the review, will remain.

NOTES

1. The author would like to thank Marie Kagrell and Annika Suominen for reading and commenting on a previous version of the present text. Since the present text is the result of research involving personal data relating to criminal offences, court cases in criminal law matters, sentencing and administrative deprivation of liberty, and was conducted in Sweden, an application for ethical review was submitted to the Swedish Ethical Review Authority. On 14 February 2023, the application was approved, see the Swedish Ethical Review Authority, reference number 2022-07186-01.

2. See e.g., Global Gender Gap Report 2022, where Iceland, Finland, Norway and Sweden rank top 5 in the world regarding gender equality.

3. See e.g., Gøsta Esping-Andersen, *The Three worlds of Welfare Capitalism* (Polity 1990), 27–28; Andreas Bergh, 'The Universal Welfare State: Theory and the Case of Sweden' (2004) 54 Political Studies 745; Emanuel Ferragina and Martin Seeleib-Kaiser, 'Welfare regime debate: past, present, futures?' (2011) 39 Policy & Politics 583.

4. See generally Helga Hernes, *Welfare state and woman power* (Norwegian University Press 1987), who links the Nordic welfare state with feminism. See also e.g., Annette Borchorst and Birte Siim, 'Woman-friendly policies and state feminism: Theorizing Scandinavian gender equality' (2008) 9 Feminist Theory 207.

5. See generally Christina Bergqvist, 'The Welfare State and Gender Equality' in Jon Pierre (ed) *The Oxford Handbook of Swedish Politics* (OUP 2016).

6. See e.g., Monica Burman, 'The Ability of Criminal Law to Produce Gender Equality: Judicial Discourses in the Swedish Criminal Legal System' (2010) 16 Violence Against Women 173, 175. Additionally, note that the EU has recognized rape as part of gender-based violence, see Directive 2012/29/EU, recital 17.

7. See e.g., Madeleine Leijonhufvud, *Svensk sexualbrottslag. En framåtsyftande tillbakablick* (Norstedts 2015).

8. However, some argue that although involuntariness was not a part of the statutory law on rape, consent was relevant prior to the 2018 reform, for instance in the form of a consent defence by the defendant and as a hypothesis of consent applied by the courts, see Ulrika Andersson, 'The Unbounded Body of the Law of Rape: The Intrusive Criterion of Non-Consent' in Kevät Nousiainen et al (eds) *Responsible Selves: Women in the Nordic legal culture* (Aldershot 2001) 337–345.

9. See e.g., Pia Letto-Vanamo and Ditlev Tamm, 'Nordic Legal Mind' in Pia Letto-Vanamo and Ditlev Tamm (eds) *Nordic Law in European Context* (Springer 2019); Jaakko Husa, Kimmo Nuotio and Heikki Pihlajamäki, 'Nordic Law—Between Tradition and Dynamism' in Jaakko Husa, Kimmo Nuotio and Heikki Pihlajamäki (eds) *Nordic Law—Between Tradition and Dynamism* (Intersentia 2007).

10. See generally Olof Petersson, 'Rational Politics: Commissions of Inquiry and the Referral System in Sweden' in Jon Pierre (ed) *The Oxford Handbook of Swedish Politics* (OUP 2016) 650–662; Mauro Zamboni, 'Methods of Ex-Ante Evaluation in Legislation: The Swedish Model' in Kim Kye-Hong (ed) *Goals and Methods of Ex-Ante Evaluation of Legislation* (KLRI 2019) 3–31.

11. See e.g., Mauro Zamboni, '(Absence of) Omnibus Legislation in Sweden: When Legislative Drafting Affects the Political Discourse' in Ittai Bar-Siman-Tov (ed) *Comparative Multidisciplinary Perspectives on Omnibus Legislation* (Springer 2021) 321–324.

12. The two Supreme Courts in Sweden are, for instance, viewed as a part of the public administration rather than as independent actors, see generally Mauro Zamboni, 'The Positioning of the Supreme Courts in Sweden—A Democratic Oddity?' (2019) 15 European Constitutional Law Review 668.

13. An intra-Nordic comparison is commonly made in the legislative procedure of each jurisdiction. For examples of intra-Nordic comparisons regarding reforms concerning rape and other sexual offences, see e.g., the Finnish *travaux préparatoires* RP 13/2022 rd, 77–84; the Swedish *travaux préparatoires* SOU 2016:60, 142–154; the Icelandic *travaux préparatoires* Þingskjal 552–419. mál, 146. löggjafarþing 2016–2017, 7–9; the Norwegian *travaux préparatoires* NOU 2022:21, 85–107.

14. On Nordic cooperation in criminal law matters, see generally e.g., Tapio Lappi-Seppälä and Kimmo Nuotio, 'Crime and Punishment' in Pia Letto-Vanamo and Ditlev Tamm (eds) *Nordic Law in European Context* (Springer 2019); Sakari Melander, 'Nordic Criminal Justice Policy—Single Path or Separate Ways?' in Jaakko Husa, Kimmo Nuotio and Heikki Pihlajamäki (eds) *Nordic Law—Between Tradition and Dynamism* (Intersentia 2007).

15. See e.g., John Pratt, 'Scandinavian Exceptionalism in an Era of Penal Excess. Part I: The Nature and Roots of Scandinavian Exceptionalism' (2008) 48 British Journal of Criminology 119; John Pratt, 'Scandinavian Exceptionalism in an Era of Penal Excess: Part II: Does Scandinavian Exceptionalism have a Future?' (2008) 48 British Journal of Criminology 275.

16. See e.g., Vanessa Barker, 'Nordic Exceptionalism revisited: Explaining the paradox of a Janus-faced penal regime' (2013) 17 Theoretical Criminology 5; Thomas Uglevik, 'Seeing like a welfare state: Immigration control, statecraft, and a prison with double vision' in Katja Aaas Franko and Mary Bosworth (eds) *The borders of punishment: Migration, citizenship and social exclusion* (OUP 2013); Robert Andersson, 'A culture of intervention—Vagrancy and drug treatment in Sweden from the late 19th century until today' in Peter Smith Scharff and Thomas Uglevik (eds) *Scandinavian Penal History, Culture and Prison Practice: Embraced by the Welfare State?* (Palgrave 2017).

17. See e.g., Peter Smith Scharff and Thomas Uglevik, 'Punishment and Welfare in Scandinavia' in Peter Smith Scharff and Thomas Uglevik (eds) *Scandinavian Penal History, Culture and Prison Practice: Embraced by the Welfare State?* (Palgrave 2017) 513.

18. For an overview regarding the critique of the concept that has developed during the last decade, see e.g., Mikkel Jarle Christensen, Kjersti Lohne & Magnus Hörnqvist, 'Introduction: Nordic criminal justice in a global context' in Mikkel Jarle Christensen, Kjersti Lohne & Magnus Hörnqvist (eds) *Nordic criminal justice in a global context. Practices and promotion of exceptionalism* (Routledge 2022) 4–5.

19. See e.g., Tapio Lappi-Seppälä, 'Nordic Sentencing' (2016) 45 Crime and Justice 17, 25–31.

20. The sentencing regime for rape (of the standard degree) was changed in the statutory law and the minimum penalty increased from imprisonment for two years to three years, while the penalty for rape that is "less gross" changed from custodial sentence to imprisonment for six months. The political reason for introducing the new sentencing regime was purely to increase the level of punishment and not—for instance—by arguing that there was a need for reforming the sentencing regime based on a too restrictive application of the sentencing regime in the case law. See the *travaux préparatoires* prop. 2021/22:231, 48–51, 84.

21. See e.g., Johanna Niemi, 'Promoting Gender Equality' in Pia Letto-Vanamo and Ditlev Tamm (eds) *Nordic Law in European Context* (Springer 2019); May-Len Skilbrei, Kari Stefansen and Bruvik Heinskou, 'A Nordic research agenda on rape and sexual violence' in May-Len Skilbrei, Kari Stefansen and Bruvik Heinskou (eds) *Rape in the Nordic countries. Community and change* (Routledge 2019), 3–6. Several Swedish scholars have analyzed criminal law matters concerning sexual offences and sexual violence from a feminist perspective, see e.g., Ulrika Andersson, *Hans (ord) eller hennes? En könsteoretisk analys av straffrättsligt skydd mot sexuella övergrepp* (Bokbox 2004); Monica Burman, *Straffrätt och mäns våld mot kvinnor. Om straffrättens förmåga att producera jämställdhet* (Iustus 2007); Kerstin Berglund, *Straffrätt och kön* (Iustus 2007); Linnea Wegerstad, *Skyddsvärda intressen och straffvärda kränkningar. Om sexualbrotten i det straffrättsliga systemet med utgångspunkt i brottet ofredande* (Lunds universitet 2015).

22. The Icelandic Penal Code, s 194. See further Ragnheiður Bragadóttir, 'Legislation on the offence of rape in Icelandic criminal law' (2020) 8 Bergen Journal of Criminal Law & Criminal Justice 54, 70–77.

23. See the Danish Penal Code, s 216. See further Jørn Vestergaard, 'The rape law revision in Denmark: Consent or voluntariness as the key criterion?' (2020) 8 Bergen Journal of Criminal Law & Criminal Justice 5.

24. Criminal Code of Finland, ch 20 s 1. The provision was amended through Act 316/1994 on Amendment to the Criminal Code of Finland ch 20. See also the Finnish *travaux préparatoires* RP 13/2022 rd, 52–54, 71–72, 93–102, 144. See further Daniela Alaattinoğlu, Heini Kainulainen and Johanna Niemi, 'Rape in Finnish criminal law and process—A discussion on, and beyond, consent' (2020) 8 Bergen Journal of Criminal Law & Criminal Justice 33. Note that the Finnish 2023 reform also resulted in amendments in regard to other sexual offences.

25. See the Norwegian *travaux préparatoires* NOU 2022:21, 145–213, presenting the proposals by commission of inquiry. A government bill is yet to be presented. For an overview of the discussion in Norway to reform the provision on rape, see e.g., Jørn Jacobsen and May-Len Skilbrei, 'Reforming the Rape Offence in Norwegian criminal Law' (2020) 8 Bergen Journal of Criminal Law & Criminal Justice 78, 87–92.

26. See e.g., Vanessa Munro and Clare McGlynn (eds) *Rethinking Rape Law: International and Comparative Perspectives* (Routledge 2010); Eithne Dowds, 'Towards a Contextual Definition of Rape: Consent, Coercion and Constructive Force' (2020) 83 Modern Law Review 35; Janet Halley, 'Currents: Feminist Key Concepts and Controversies: The Move to Affirmative Consent' (2016) 42 Signs: Journal of Women in Culture and Society 257. Regarding the development in the EU, see e.g., Carlotta Rigotti, 'A long way to end rape in the European Union: Assessing the commission's proposal to harmonize rape law, through a feminist lens' (2022) 13 New Journal of European Criminal Law 153.

27. Note that the statutory law states the *actus reus* element, in this regard, as a "person who is not participating voluntarily" (Swedish Criminal Code, ch 6 s 1). To formulate this more efficiently, the phrase "involuntariness" is used throughout the present chapter. One could of course also use "lack of voluntariness" as an alternative phrasing. Apart from the fact that "involuntariness" does not necessarily have the same meaning as "consent," consent as a justification is regulated in the statutory law (Swedish Criminal Code, ch 24 s 7). However, the scope of the provision on consent as a justification is extremely narrow and is not—and has never been—applicable in relation to sexual offences. Note that some claim that the concept of consent was relevant prior to the 2018 reform, see Ulrika Andersson, 'The Unbounded Body of the Law of Rape: The Intrusive Criterion of Non-Consent' in Kevät Nousiainen et al (eds) *Responsible Selves: Women in the Nordic legal culture* (Aldershot 2001) 337–345.

28. May-Len Skilbrei, Kari Stefansen and Bruvik Heinskou, 'A Nordic research agenda on rape and sexual violence' in May-Len Skilbrei, Kari Stefansen and Bruvik Heinskou (eds) *Rape in the Nordic countries. Community and change* (Routledge 2019) 5.

29. [Emphasis added.] English translation offered by the Swedish government <https://www.government.se/4a4563/contentassets/7a2dcae0787e465e9a2431554b5eab03/the-swedish-criminal-code.pdf> accessed March 14, 2023.

30. See e.g., the *travaux préparatoires* prop. 2021/22:231, 84.

31. The *travaux préparatoires* prop. 2021/22:231, 84.

32. Supreme Court cases NJA 2008 s. 482 I and II.

33. See Supreme Court case NJA 2015 s. 501 and the *travaux préparatoires* prop. 2017/18:177, 43–45, 79.

34. International comparisons regarding e.g. official statistics are almost impossible, since different jurisdictions vary significantly in their definition of what sexual acts can establish the *actus reus* element of rape. It is sometimes—wrongfully—claimed that Sweden is the "rape capital of the world": however, many factors affect the number of reported cases of (alleged) rape, amongst them the construction of the *actus reus* elements, the willingness to report sexual offences, various methods of

reporting statistics, the level of denunciation from rape myths, the level of gender equality, etc. See generally Stina Holmberg, 'Det sexuella våldet i ett jämförande perspektiv' in Amir Rostami and Jerzy Sarnecki (eds) *Det svenska tillståndet* (Studentlitteratur 2022).

35. The Swedish government argued that the introduction of involuntariness sent a clear normative message: "sex must be voluntary," see the *travaux préparatoires* prop. 2017/18:177, 22–23. See also Donald Dripps, 'For a Negative Normative Model of Consent, with a Comment on Preference-Scepticism' (1996) 2 Legal Theory 113, 116, suggesting that "consent"—just as normative concepts like "equality"—is rather elusive.

36. See e.g., Deborah Tuerkheimer, 'Rape On and Off Campus' (2015) 65 Emory Law Journal 1, 3: "Indeed, it is virtually axiomatic that nonconsensual sex is rape; the challenge outstanding is to define consent." See however Alan Wertheimer, *Consent to sexual relations* (CUP 2003) 119, suggesting that the relevant question is not what consent is, but "the condition under which consent is *morally transformative* in the relevant way." [Emphasis in original.]

37. For an analysis of voluntariness or consent as an *actus reus* element of rape and other sexual offences, see e.g., Keith Burgess-Jackson, *Rape—A Philosophical Investigation* (Aldershot 1996); Alan Wertheimer, *Consent to sexual relations* (CUP 2003); Kimberly Kessler Ferzan, 'Consent, culpability and the law of rape' (2016) 13 Ohio State Journal of Criminal Law 397. For a review of the consent literature, see e.g. Melanie A. Beres 'Spontaneous sexual consent: an analysis of sexual consent literature' (2007) 17 Feminism & Psychology 93. For an analysis in relation to Swedish criminal law, see Petter Asp, *Sex och samtycke* (Iustus 2010).

38. See also Linnea Wegerstad, 'Sex must be voluntary: sexual communication and the new definition of rape in Sweden' (2021) 22 German Law Journal 734, 741.

39. See generally e.g., Deborah Tuerkheimer, 'Affirmative Consent' (2016) 13 Ohio State Journal of Criminal Law 441.

40. See the *travaux préparatoires* prop. 2017/18:177, 80. The Swedish government explicitly opposed a construction built on a model of 'pure' affirmative consent, see the *travaux préparatoires* prop. 2017/18:177, 31–33. For a related Supreme Court precedent, see case NJA 2019 s. 668.

41. Keith Burgess-Jackson, *Rape—A Philosophical Investigation* (Aldershot 1996) 43–64. The "radical theory" is the third theory, where rape is considered a systemic crime which reinforces sexual hierarchy and where the crime is aimed at women (not a woman). Those advocating a "radical theory" argue that "consent" should be replaced with another prerequisite or, at least, should be defined to exclude consent which has been coerced or manipulated. From a "radical" theorist point of view, the concept of consent presupposes two equal partners and since there exists a sexual hierarchy (which is a part of a patriarchal society), that presumption is an illusion, see e.g., Catharine A MacKinnon, *Toward a Feminist Theory of the State* (HUP 1989) 174–175; Susan Brownmiller, *Against Our Will* (Penguin 1976), 383–387. Cf. Michelle Madden Dempsey and Jonathan Herring, 'Why Sexual Penetration Requires Justification' (2007) 27 Oxford Journal of Legal Studies 467, 468–471, who

distinguish between "the orthodox view" and "the alternative view" when discussing whether sexual penetration requires justification.

42. The 1864 rape provision was placed in a chapter named "On crimes against the freedom of another," thereby clearly signalling a shift. See the *travaux préparatoires* Förslag till Allmänn Criminallag. Andra upplagan med de förändringar, hwilka Lag-Committeen wid slutlig granskning af förslaget infört, Motiver, 1839, 63. This shift occurred gradually during the seventeenth and eighteenth centuries, where rape shifted from being considered a property offence toward being viewed both as an offence of violence and a public order offence, see e.g., Karin Hassan Jansson, *Kvinnofrid. Synen på våldtäkt och konstruktionen av kön i Sverige 1600–1800* (Acta Universitatis Upsaliensis 2002).

43. See e.g., Åsa Bergenheim, *Brottet, offret och förövaren. Vetenskapens och det svenska rättsväsendets syn på sexuella övergrepp mot kvinnor och barn 1850–2000* (Carlssons 2005) 26–40.

44. See the *travaux préparatoires* SOU 1953:14, 228.

45. In Nordic comparison, marital rape was, for instance, criminalized in Norway in the case law in 1974, where the Norwegian Supreme Court Rt 1974 s. 1121 stated that "rape cannot be excluded (from criminal liability) on the grounds that the defendant and the victim are married and are living together" and in Finland in 1994 (Act 316/1994 on Amending the Finnish Criminal Code Chapter 20). In Denmark, the statutory law made it possible in 1930 to punish marital rape—however, the statutory law made some exemptions from marital rape that were partially removed. Thus, in 1967 it was no longer possible to lower the sentence for marital rape, and it was not until 2013 that the last exemptions were removed in the statutory law. In other jurisdictions, marital rape was criminalized in Canada in 1983 (Bill C-127, s 246.8, now regulated in the Canadian Criminal Code 1985, s 278). In the UK, marital rape was deemed criminal in the case law in 1991 (*R v R* [1991] 3 WLR 767) but it was not until 2003 that the UK statutory law (Criminal Justice and Public Order Act 1994, s 142) explicitly stated that marital rape is a crime.

46. See the *travaux préparatoires* prop. 1983/84:105, 16–18, 51. The 1984 reform must be seen in the light of the progress of the lgbtq-movement in the 1960s, 1970s and 1980s, both internationally and in Sweden, with strong demands for equal rights, see e.g., the *travaux préparatoires* SOU 1982:61: "To differ between homosexual and heterosexual deeds could not be more foreign in contemporary society."

47. For a thorough analysis, see Linnea Wegerstad, *Skyddsvärda intressen och straffvärda kränkningar. Om sexualbrotten i det straffrättsliga systemet med utgångspunkt i brottet ofredande* (Lunds universitet 2015) 141–210.

48. See e.g., Gabriella Nilsson, 'Towards involuntariness in Swedish rape law: Hyper-medialised group rape cases and the shift in the legal discourse' in May-Len Skilbrei, Kari Stefansen and Bruvik Heinskou (eds) *Rape in the Nordic countries. Community and change* (Routledge 2019).

49. See the following *travaux préparatoires*: SOU 1995:15; SOU 1995:60; SOU 2001:14; SOU 2010:71; SOU 2011:75; Ds 2015:49; SOU 2016:42; SOU 2016:60; SOU 2016:70; SOU 2021:43.

50. See the following *travaux préparatoires*: SOU 2001:14, 123–138; 2010:71, 123–160, 197–257. For a description of the process resulting in the 2018 reform, see Moa Bladini and Wanna Svedberg Andersson, 'Swedish rape legislation from use of force to voluntariness—critical reflections from an everyday life perspective' (2020) 8 Bergen Journal of Criminal Law & Criminal Justice 95, 98–109; Monica Burman, 'Rethinking rape law in Sweden. Coercion, consent or non-voluntariness?' in Vanessa Munro and Clare McGlynn (eds) *Rethinking Rape Law: International and Comparative Perspectives* (Routledge 2010).

51. This was the position of the Swedish government in 2013, see the *travaux préparatoires* prop. 2012/13:111, 18–23. The position was motivated by, inter alia, the difficulty in defining "involuntariness" or "consent" which would result in difficulties regarding foreseeability and could therefore also lead to problems during the pre-trial investigation. For some time only one political party, the Green Party, in the Swedish Parliament demanded a regulation based on involuntariness or consent. The Greens ordered their own report on the question of introducing a model based on involuntariness or consent, written by Professor Madeleine Leijonhufvud. She suggested a model based on involuntariness, see further Madeleine Leijonhufvud, *Samtyckesutredningen* (Thomson 2008).

52. See the Prime Minister's key note speech on 3 October 2014, where (former) Prime Minister Stefan Löfven first expressed this officially.

53. English translation offered by the Swedish government <https://www.government.se/4a4563/contentassets/7a2dcae0787e465e9a2431554b5eab03/the-swedish-criminal-code.pdf> accessed March 14, 2023.

54. For a more thorough overview of these situations, see Linnea Wegerstad, 'Sweden' in Elsa Hoven and Thomas Weigend (eds) *Consent and Sexual Offenses—Comparative Perspectives* (Nomos 2022), 259–266.

55. See the *travaux préparatoires* prop. 2017/18:177, 80–83.

56. This was clearly the government's position, see the *travaux préparatoires* prop. 2017/18:117, 37–38.

57. English translation offered by the Swedish government <https://www.government.se/4a4563/contentassets/7a2dcae0787e465e9a2431554b5eab03/the-swedish-criminal-code.pdf> accessed March 14, 2023.

58. The *travaux préparatoires* prop. 2017/18:177, 22–23.

59. The statutory law was formulated in this way after receiving criticism. During the legislative procedure the proposed amendment was criticized by the Council on Legislation, according to which the boundary between an unlawful act (involuntariness) and a lawful act (voluntariness) was blurred. Hence, the Council stressed that the proposal lacked foreseeability—arguing that the assessment of whether participation was involuntary was to be determined by the normative conception of the individual judge regarding what kind of participation in sexual acts should and should not be viewed as involuntary. Although the government partly accepted the Council's criticism, one could argue that the final amendment of the statutory law still lack precision, as the Council had argued during the legislative procedure.

60. The *travaux préparatoires* prop. 2017/18:177, 33.

61. The *travaux préparatoires* prop. 2017/18:177, 78–79. This suggests that the government views involuntariness as a performative act. Since silent consent can negate involuntariness, viewing involuntariness as a performative act is contradictory.

62. The *travaux préparatoires* prop. 2017/18:177, 80.

63. The *travaux préparatoires* prop. 2017/18:177, 34.

64. The *travaux préparatoires* prop. 2017/18:177, 34, 80.

65. The *travaux préparatoires* prop. 2017/18:177, 78.

66. The *travaux préparatoires* prop. 2017/18:177, 30–31, 42–43, 79.

67. See e.g., Alan Wertheimer, *Consent to sexual relations* (CUP 2003) 195–196; David Archard, *Sexual Consent* (Routledge 1998) 56; Patricia J Falk, 'Rape by Fraud and Rape by Coercion' (1998) 64 Brooklyn Law Review 39, 157–172.

68. For an analysis of sexual deceptions in relation to the 2018 reform, see Marie Kagrell, 'Sexuella vilseledanden' in Andreas Anderberg, Dennis Martinsson and Erik Svensson (eds) *Teori och politik—straffrätt i omvandling* (Iustus 2022). For a discussion prior to the 2018 reform, see Petter Asp, *Sex och samtycke* (Iustus 2010) 147–155.

69. On the matter of stealthing (non-consensual condom removal) in Swedish criminal law, see Linnea Wegerstad, 'Är det straffbart att ta av kondomen utan samtycke? Rättsläget efter den svenska våldtäktsreformen 2018' (2021) Tidskrift utgiven av Juridiska föreningen i Finland 353.

70. The *travaux préparatoires* prop. 2017/18:177, 40.

71. Swedish Criminal Code, ch 1 s 2, para 1.

72. For a fairly recent overview in English of intent in Swedish criminal law, see Ebba Lekvall and Dennis Martinsson, 'The *Mens Rea* Element of Intent in the Context of International Criminal Trials in Sweden' (2020) 66 Scandinavian Studies in Law 99, 104–108.

73. See e.g., Ivar Strahl, *Allmän straffrätt i vad angår brotten* (Norstedt 1976) 110, stating that the lowest form of intent is sufficient to prove that the defendant acted with intent. See also Petter Asp, Magnus Ulväng and Nils Jareborg, *Kriminalrättens grunder*, 2nd edn (Iustus 2013) 287.

74. See e.g., Supreme Court cases NJA 2004 s. 176, 194–195; NJA 1977 s. 630, 638.

75. See Supreme Court case NJA 2004 s. 176. Note that the Court prior to the 2004 precedent, has reasoned in terms of reckless intent, see e.g. NJA 1975 s. 594; NJA 1985 s. 757; NJA 1990 s 210; NJA 1996 s. 509.

76. From a common law perspective, reckless intent might seem rather peculiar, since its meaning—at least partly—resembles how recklessness as a *mens rea* element is perceived in some common law jurisdictions, see e.g., Jeremy Horder, *Ashworth's Principles of Criminal Law*, 10 edn (OUP 2022) 217–224; Andrew P Simester and Warren J Brookbanks, *Principles of Criminal Law*, 5th edn (Thomson Reuters 2019) 141–154.

77. See the Norwegian *travaux préparatoires* Ot.prp. Nr. 28 (1999–2000), 30–38, 157, 175. The Norwegian provision on negligent rape entered into force on 1 August 2000.

78. English translation offered by the Swedish government <https://www.government.se/4a4563/contentassets/7a2dcae0787e465e9a2431554b5eab03/the-swedish-criminal-code.pdf> accessed March 14, 2023.

79. The *travaux préparatoires* prop. 2017/18:177, 85.

80. The *travaux préparatoires* prop. 2017/18:177, 85.

81. The *travaux préparatoires* prop. 2017/18:177, 85.

82. The *travaux préparatoires* prop. 2017/18:177, 85.

83. Supreme Court cases NJA 2019 668; NJA 2021 s. 536 and NJA 2022 s. 237. Note that the 2021 precedent only concerned the sentencing.

84. Supreme Court case NJA 2019 s. 668, particularly at paras 24–28.

85. Supreme Court case NJA 2022 s. 237, particularly at paras 17–21.

86. Brå, Rapport 2020:6: Den nya samtyckeslagen i praktiken. En uppföljning av 2018 års förändringar av lagreglerna rörande våldtäkt. An English summary of the report is available at <https://bra.se/download/18.7d27ebd916ea64de53065cff/1614334312744/2020_6_The_new_consent_law_in_practice.pdf> accessed March 14, 2023.

87. See also Lisa Wallin, Sara Uhnoo, Åsa Wettergren and Moa Bladini, 'Capricious credibility—legal assessments of voluntariness in Swedish negligent rape judgements' (2021) 22 Nordic Journal of Criminology 3, 10–13, agreeing with the Council's conclusion.

88. Claes Lernestedt, 'Sexualitet är i betraktarens öga? Tendenser i svensk sexualstraffrätt, sedda bl.a. genom ett rättsfall och debatten kring det' (2004) Tidskrift utgiven av Juridiska föreningen i Finland 398, 402. Cf. Ulrika Andersson and Linnea Wegerstad, 'Det kriminaliserade området för sexuellt ofredande—kroppslig och abstrakt integritet' (2018) Juridisk Tidskrift 652, 661.

89. Marie Kagrell, 'Sexuella vilseledanden' in Andreas Anderberg, Dennis Martinsson and Erik Svensson (eds) *Teori och politik—straffrätt i omvandling* (Iustus 2022) 185.

90. Tatjana Hörnle, '#MeToo—Implications for Criminal Law?' (2018) 6 Bergen Journal of Criminal Law & Criminal Justice 115, 126–127.

91. See e.g., Catharine A MacKinnon, *Toward a Feminist Theory of the State* (HUP 1989) 174–175; Catherine A MacKinnon, *Women's Lives, Men's Laws* (HUP 2005) 240–248; Susan Brownmiller, *Against Our Will* (Penguin 1976), 383–387. See also Nicola Lacey, *Unspeakable subjects: feminist essays in legal and social theory* (Hart 1998) 117–124.

92. See e.g., Catharine A MacKinnon, 'Rape Redefined' (2016) 10 Harvard Law & Policy Review 431, 452. For a discussion on the exercise of will as a subjective mental state in this regard, see e.g., Heidi M Hurd, 'The moral magic of consent' (1996) 2 Legal Theory 121; Larry Alexander, 'The moral magic of consent (II)' (1996) 2 Legal Theory 165.

BIBLIOGRAPHY

Alaattinoğlu D, Kainulainen H and Niemi J, 'Rape in Finnish criminal law and process—A discussion on, and beyond, consent' (2020) 8 Bergen Journal of Criminal Law & Criminal Justice 33.

Alexander L, 'The moral magic of consent (II)' (1996) 2 Legal Theory 165.

Andersson R, 'A culture of intervention—Vagrancy and drug treatment in Sweden from the late 19th century until today' in Smith Scharff P and Uglevik T (eds) *Scandinavian Penal History, Culture and Prison Practice: Embraced by the Welfare State?* (Palgrave 2017).

Andersson U, 'The Unbounded Body of the Law of Rape: The Intrusive Criterion of Non-Consent' in Nousiainen K et al (eds) *Responsible Selves: Women in the Nordic legal culture* (Aldershot 2001).

Andersson U, *Hans (ord) eller hennes? En könsteoretisk analys av straffrättsligt skydd mot sexuella övergrepp* (Bokbox 2004).

Andersson U and Wegerstad L, 'Det kriminaliserade området för sexuellt ofredande—kroppslig och abstrakt integritet' (2018) Juridisk Tidskrift 652.

Archard D, *Sexual Consent* (Routledge 1998).

Asp P, *Sex och samtycke* (Iustus 2010).

Asp, P, Ulväng M and Jareborg N, *Kriminalrättens grunder*, 2nd edn (Iustus 2013).

Barker V, 'Nordic Exceptionalism revisited: Explaining the paradox of a Janus-faced penal regime' (2013) 17 Theoretical Criminology 5.

Beres M A, 'Spontaneous sexual consent: an analysis of sexual consent literature' (2007) 17 Feminism & Psychology 93.

Bergenheim Å, *Brottet, offret och förövaren. Vetenskapens och det svenska rättsväsendets syn på sexuella övergrepp mot kvinnor och barn 1850–2000* (Carlssons 2005).

Bergh A, 'The Universal Welfare State: Theory and the Case of Sweden' (2004) 54 Political Studies 745.

Berglund K, *Straffrätt och kön* (Iustus 2007).

Bergqvist C, 'The Welfare State and Gender Equality' in Pierre J (ed) *The Oxford Handbook of Swedish Politics* (OUP 2016).

Bladini M and Svedberg Andersson W, 'Swedish rape legislation from use of force to voluntariness—critical reflections from an everyday life perspective' (2020) 8 Bergen Journal of Criminal Law & Criminal Justice 95.

Borchorst A and Siim B, 'Woman-friendly policies and state feminism: Theorizing Scandinavian gender equality' (2008) 9 Feminist Theory 207.

Bragadóttir R, 'Legislation on the offence of rape in Icelandic criminal law' (2020) 8 Bergen Journal of Criminal Law & Criminal Justice 54.

Brownmiller S, *Against Our Will* (Penguin 1976).

Burgess-Jackson K, *Rape—A Philosophical Investigation* (Aldershot 1996).

Burman M, *Straffrätt och mäns våld mot kvinnor. Om straffrättens förmåga att producera jämställdhet* (Iustus 2007).

Burman M, 'Rethinking rape law in Sweden. Coercion, consent or non-voluntariness?' in Munro V and McGlynn C (eds) *Rethinking Rape Law: International and Comparative Perspectives* (Routledge 2010).

Burman M, 'The Ability of Criminal Law to Produce Gender Equality: Judicial Discourses in the Swedish Criminal Legal System' (2010) 16 Violence Against Women 173.

Christensen M J, Lohne K and Hörnqvist M, 'Introduction: Nordic criminal justice in a global context' in Christensen, M J, Lohne K and Hörnqvist M (eds) *Nordic criminal justice in a global context. Practices and promotion of exceptionalism* (Routledge 2022).

Dempsey, M M and Herring J, 'Why Sexual Penetration Requires Justification' (2007) 27 Oxford Journal of Legal Studies 467.

Dowds E, 'Towards a Contextual Definition of Rape: Consent, Coercion and Constructive Force' (2020) 83 Modern Law Review 35.

Dripps D, 'For a Negative Normative Model of Consent, with a Comment on Preference-Scepticism' (1996) 2 Legal Theory 113.

Esping-Andersen, G, *The Three worlds of Welfare Capitalism* (Polity 1990).

Falk P J, 'Rape by Fraud and Rape by Coercion' (1998) 64 Brooklyn Law Review 39.

Ferragina E and Seeleib-Kaiser M, 'Welfare regime debate: past, present, futures?' (2011) 39 Policy & Politics 583.

Ferzan K K, 'Consent, culpability and the law of rape', (2016) 13 Ohio State Journal of Criminal Law 397.

Halley J, 'Currents: Feminist Key Concepts and Controversies: The Move to Affirmative Consent' (2016) 42 Signs: Journal of Women in Culture and Society 257.

Hernes H, *Welfare state and woman power* (Norwegian University Press 1987).

Holmberg S, 'Det sexuella våldet i ett jämförande perspektiv' in Rostami A and Sarnecki J (eds) *Det svenska tillståndet* (Studentlitteratur 2022).

Horder J, *Ashworth's Principles of Criminal Law*, 10 edn (OUP 2022).

Hurd H M, 'The moral magic of consent' (1996) 2 Legal Theory 121.

Husa J, Nuotio K and Pihlajamäki H, 'Nordic Law—Between Tradition and Dynamism' in Husa J, Nuotio K and Pihlajamäki H (eds) *Nordic Law—Between Tradition and Dynamism* (Intersentia 2007).

Hörnle T, '#MeToo—Implications for Criminal Law?' (2018) 6 Bergen Journal of Criminal Law & Criminal Justice 115.

Jacobsen J and Skilbrei M-L, 'Reforming the Rape Offence in Norwegian criminal law' (2020) 8 Bergen Journal of Criminal Law & Criminal Justice 78.

Jansson K H, *Kvinnofrid. Synen på våldtäkt och konstruktionen av kön i Sverige 1600–1800* (Acta Universitatis Upsaliensis 2002).

Kagrell M, 'Sexuella vilseledanden' in Anderberg A, Martinsson D and Svensson E (eds) *Teori och politik—straffrätt i omvandling* (Iustus 2022).

Lacey N, *Unspeakable subjects: feminist essays in legal and social theory* (Hart 1998).

Lappi-Seppälä T, 'Nordic Sentencing' (2016) 45 Crime and Justice 17.

Lappi-Seppälä T and Nuotio K, 'Crime and Punishment' in Letto-Vanamo P and Tamm D (eds) *Nordic Law in European Context* (Springer 2019).

Leijonhufvud M, *Samtyckesutredningen* (Thomson 2008).

Leijonhufvud M, *Svensk sexualbrottslag. En framåtsyftande tillbakablick* (Norstedts 2015).

Lekvall E and Martinsson D, 'The *Mens Rea* Element of Intent in the Context of International Criminal Trials in Sweden' (2020) 66 Scandinavian Studies in Law 99.

Lernestedt C, 'Sexualitet är i betraktarens öga? Tendenser i svensk sexualstraffrätt, sedda bl.a. genom ett rättsfall och debatten kring det' (2004) Tidskrift utgiven av Juridiska föreningen i Finland 398.

Letto-Vanamo P and Tamm D, 'Nordic Legal Mind' in Letto-Vanamo P and Tamm D (eds) *Nordic Law in European Context* (Springer 2019).

MacKinnon C A, *Toward a Feminist Theory of the State* (HUP 1989).

MacKinnon C A, *Women's Lives, Men's Laws* (HUP 2005).

MacKinnon C A, 'Rape Redefined' (2016) 10 Harvard Law & Policy Review 431.

Melander S, 'Nordic Criminal Justice Policy—Single Path or Separate Ways?' in Husa J, Nuotio K and Pihlajamäki H (eds) *Nordic Law—Between Tradition and Dynamism* (Intersentia 2007).

Niemi J, 'Promoting Gender Equality' in Letto-Vanamo P and Tamm D (eds) *Nordic Law in European Context* (Springer 2019).

Nilsson G, 'Towards involuntariness in Swedish rape law: Hyper-medialised group rape cases and the shift in the legal discourse' in Skilbrei M-L, Stefansen K and Bruvik Heinskou M (eds) *Rape in the Nordic countries. Community and change* (Routledge 2019).

Petersson O, 'Rational Politics: Commissions of Inquiry and the Referral System in Sweden' in Pierre J (ed) *The Oxford Handbook of Swedish Politics* (OUP 2016).

Pratt J, 'Scandinavian Exceptionalism in an Era of Penal Excess. Part I: The Nature and Roots of Scandinavian Exceptionalism' (2008) 48 British Journal of Criminology 119.

Pratt J, 'Scandinavian Exceptionalism in an Era of Penal Excess: Part II: Does Scandinavian Exceptionalism have a Future?' (2008) 48 British Journal of Criminology 275.

Rigotti C, 'A long way to end rape in the European Union: Assessing the commission's proposal to harmonize rape law, through a feminist lens' (2022) 13 New Journal of European Criminal Law 153.

Skilbrei M-L, Stefansen K and Bruvik Heinskou M, 'A Nordic research agenda on rape and sexual violence' in Skilbrei M-L, Stefansen K and Bruvik Heinskou M (eds) *Rape in the Nordic countries. Community and change* (Routledge 2019).

Simester A P and Brookbanks W J, *Principles of Criminal Law*, 5th edn (Thomson Reuters 2019).

Smith Scharff P and Uglevik T, 'Punishment and Welfare in Scandinavia' in Smith Scharff P and Uglevik T (eds) *Scandinavian Penal History, Culture and Prison Practice: Embraced by the Welfare State?* (Palgrave 2017).

Strahl I, *Allmän straffrätt i vad angår brotten* (Norstedt 1976).

Tuerkheimer D, 'Rape On and Off Campus' (2015) 65 Emory Law Journal 1.

Tuerkheimer D, 'Affirmative Consent' (2016) 13 Ohio State Journal of Criminal Law 441.

Uglevik T, 'Seeing like a welfare state: Immigration control, statecraft, and a prison with double vision' in Aaas Franko K and Bosworth M (eds) *The borders of punishment: Migration, citizenship and social exclusion* (OUP 2013).

Vestergaard J, 'The rape law revision in Denmark: Consent or voluntariness as the key criterion?' (2020) 8 Bergen Journal of Criminal Law & Criminal Justice 5.

Wallin L, Uhnoo S, Wettergren Å and Bladini M, 'Capricious credibility—legal assessments of voluntariness in Swedish negligent rape judgements' (2021) 22 Nordic Journal of Criminology 3.

Wegerstad L, *Skyddsvärda intressen och straffvärda kränkningar. Om sexualbrotten i det straffrättsliga systemet med utgångspunkt i brottet ofredande* (Lunds universitet 2015).

Wegerstad L, 'Är det straffbart att ta av kondomen utan samtycke? Rättsläget efter den svenska våldtäktsreformen 2018' (2021) Tidskrift utgiven av Juridiska föreningen i Finland 353.

Wegerstad L, 'Sex must be voluntary: sexual communication and the new definition of rape in Sweden' (2021) 22 German Law Journal 734.

Wegerstad L, 'Sweden' in Hoven E and Weigend T (eds) *Consent and Sexual Offenses—Comparative Perspectives* (Nomos 2022).

Wertheimer A, *Consent to sexual relations* (CUP 2003).

Zamboni M, 'Methods of Ex-Ante Evaluation in Legislation: The Swedish Model' in Kye-Hong K (ed) *Goals and Methods of Ex-Ante Evaluation of Legislation* (KLRI 2019).

Zamboni M, 'The Positioning of the Supreme Courts in Sweden—A Democratic Oddity?' (2019) 15 European Constitutional Law Review 668.

Zamboni M, '(Absence of) Omnibus Legislation in Sweden: When Legislative Drafting Affects the Political Discourse' in Bar-Siman-Tov I (ed) *Comparative Multidisciplinary Perspectives on Omnibus Legislation* (Springer 2021).

6

Italian Criminal Justice and Sexual Offenses

Lucia Parlato and Marta Palmisano[1]

> "The attack against women's rights and gender equality is often one dimension of a broader deterioration in the situation of democracy, the rule of law and fundamental rights."[2]

The phenomenon of sexual violence in Italy is widespread and deeply rooted in the social fabric and linked to socio-cultural models that have allowed the asymmetry of power between men and women to persist over time, as reflected in gender-based violence.[3] The importance of focusing on this type of offense also stems from the fact that sexual violence violates the victim's sense of personal dignity and freedom of self-determination, thus violating fundamental constitutional principles. The main objective of this paper will therefore be to examine the reasons why this type of crime significantly contributes to fuelling the so-called "dark figure of crime," due to the disparity between the number of sexual offenses actually committed and those recorded as well as between reported sexual offenses and the low rate of conviction. In particular, in Italy, the highest percentage of recorded sexual offenses is committed against women. Therefore, this chapter pays particular attention to their protection.[4] Further, the chapter illustrates how the factors that appear to hinder the "justiciability" of sexual offenses can be traced back to socio-cultural and economic reasons, which create a distorted perception of sexual crime and of the behaviour of the victim and the aggressor as well as to procedural and criminal law elements. It, therefore, focuses on the profiles of substantive and procedural criminal law, in the Italian experience, which, in the light of the legislative and case law system, may constitute a limit to the legal initiative of the victim.[5] References to practical case law can facilitate the understanding of how the legislation is applied to specific cases and the verification of the actual evolution of the Italian system.

REGULATORY CHANGES

Sexual offense is one of the areas in which the criminal justice system has evolved the most. The 1930 Rocco Code (R.D. no. 1398 of 19 October 1930) included these offenses in Title IX among the "Crimes against public morality and public decency"[6] (Articles 519–526 of the Italian Criminal Code, CC). Among other things, the Rocco Code provided a special cause for the extinction of the crime (so-called "rehabilitating marriage," Art. 544 CC), punished only the adultery of women (Art. 559 CC) and reduced the punishment in cases of honor killing of spouses, daughters or sisters (Art. 587 CC).

The offenses envisaged reflected strongly patriarchal, authoritarian and paternalistic dimensions and women were almost considered as the property of a man (father, husband, brother).[7] Therefore, sexual violence among spouses was not conceived and the protection of the individual was relegated only to cases where it involved an offense against the collective good of public morals, also excluding women from access to the criminal justice system. When the Constitution came into force, the framework of values changed, but we had to wait for Law no. 66 of 15 February 1996, "Regulations against sexual violence" for the abrogation of that patriarchal system and for the radical reform of the subject. In fact, the latter, by introducing the crimes of sexual violence (Art. 609 *bis*-609 *decies* CC), finally placed them among the crimes against the person and personal freedom, in line with a new social and cultural perception of sexual freedom and in accordance with an egalitarian and person-oriented conception of legal protection which is typical of the Italian Constitution.[8] More attention is also paid to the victims, and their actual will and psychological dimension.[9] Among others, it is worth mentioning the introduction of the offenses of "Sexual violence" under Article 609 *bis* CC[10] and "Group sexual violence" (Art. 609 *octies* CC),[11] for which a complaint, which is irrevocable, can be filed within 12 months (Art. 609 *septies* CC). Also relevant in this regard is to mention the unification of the offenses of "rape" (Art. 519 CC) and "violent libidinal acts" (Art. 521 CC), now repealed, into the offense of "sexual violence" (Art. 609 *bis* CC). In this way, the crime of sexual violence includes both rape and all other forms of libidinal behaviour as well as, in general, any form of violence perpetrated in this context. This unification was a consequence of the affirmation of "sexual violence" as a "crime against the person." Moreover, it avoided insidious medical investigations aimed at determining the modalities of the act and identifying the specific criminal offense to be applied;[12] such investigations would, in fact, have required even more suffering from the victim, further offending the honour of the victim.[13]

This reform is, therefore, an important step towards making women more inclined to denounce violence, since they are re-evaluated as legal subjects.[14]

The subsequent Law no. 154 of 5 April 2001, "Measures against violence in family relationships," focused on domestic violence and on unlawful conduct that puts at risk the physical or moral integrity of the spouse or other cohabitant. The law introduces some criminal measures (such as the "Injunction to stay away from the family home" *ex* Art. 282 *bis* of the Italian Criminal Procedure Code, CPC) and civil measures (such as Articles 342 *bis* Art. 342 *ter* of the Italian Civil Code on "Protection orders against family abuse," coordinated with Art. 736 *bis* et seq. CPC), aimed at ensuring greater safety for victims of violence[15] also in order to facilitate the surfacing of the phenomenon of sexual violence.

Further development took place through the Law no. 38 of 23 April 2009, as amended and supplemented, which introduced the offense of "Persecutory acts," known as "stalking" (Art. 612 *bis* CC), which can be prosecuted on the basis of a complaint by the victim, which can only be revoked at trial and, in some cases, is irrevocable.[16] Measures to protect the victim are also strengthened (see Art. 282 *ter* CPC "Injunction to stay away from the places attended by the victim").[17]

The subsequent Law no. 77 of 27 June 2013, implementing the so-called Istanbul Convention of 11 May 2011 (hereinafter IC),[18] recognises violence against women as a violation of human rights and a form of discrimination (Art. 3 of the Convention).[19] The provisions are supplemented by Law no. 119 of 15 October 2013 (the so-called Femicide Law) which, within the scope of gender-based violence, identifies physical, sexual, domestic, economic and psychological violence.[20] In addition, certain aggravated circumstances are introduced if the act is committed by a spouse or person linked by a relationship of affection (on this point, see also Law no. 69/2019).

Ultimately, of particular importance is Law no. 69 of 19 July 2019 (the so-called Red Code, "Codice Rosso"), "*Amendments to the Criminal Code, to the Code of Criminal Procedure and other provisions on the protection of victims of domestic and gender-based violence*," which increases the punishment for some crimes (including for the crime of "Abuse" pursuant to Art. 572 CC[21]), introduces and reshapes some aggravating circumstances, provides for new crimes[22] and extends the time limit for filing a complaint to 12 months.[23] Moreover, an amendment to Art. 165 CC provides that the granting of suspended sentences for crimes of domestic and gender-based violence is subject to participation in specific rehabilitation programmes.[24]

With reference to sexual offenses committed against minors, who are the most vulnerable, there is enhanced protection. The Code deals with them in Articles 600 *bis* - 600 *quinquies* CC and in Art. 609 *quinquies* CC "Corruption of a minor"[25]; the offense of "Sexual acts with a minor" (Art. 609 *quater* CC) is particularly important.[26] In this regard, it is worth mentioning the intervention of Law no. 238 of 23 December 2021, which, in Art. 20, makes changes to some regulations in order to more severely repress sexual abuse of minors and child pornography.[27]

Lastly, noteworthy are the so-called spy crimes, a possible indication of a criminal inclination to commit a crime of sexual violence, represented by "Assault" (Art. 581 CC), "Personal injury," also aggravated (Art. 582–583 CC),[28] by "kidnapping" (Art. 605 CC),[29] by "private violence" (Art. 610 CC),[30] by "threats" (Art. 612 CC), by "harassment" (Art. 660 CC) and by "persecution" (Art. 612 *bis* CC).[31] Lastly, the crime of "Exploitation and aiding and abetting of the prostitution of others" (Art. 3 of the Law no. 75 of 20 February 1958, so-called Law Merlin) and the "Crimes against equality" (Articles 604 *bis* and 604 *ter* CC, Sec. I *bis*, Chapter III, XI title CC), inserted by Legislative Decree no. 21 of 1 March 2018 also emerge.[32]

Finally, among the offenses that may indirectly come to light in the field of sexual violence are the following: "Acts of indecency" (Art. 527 CC), "Practices of mutilation of female genital organs" (Art. 583 *bis* CC, introduced by Law no. 7 of 1 September 2006), "Reduction or maintenance in slavery or servitude" (Art. 600 CC) with the aim of forcing sexual services, "Trafficking in human beings" (Art. 601 CC) with the aim of inducing or forcing sexual services. On this subject, see also the aggravating circumstances referred to in Art. 602 *ter* CC. The offenses of "Homicide" (Art. 575 CC) aggravated pursuant to Articles 576 and 577 CC, and the offense of "Death or injury as a consequence of another offense" (Art. 586 CC) may also be integrated.

With the goal of reforming the current system, the recent bill C. 439 on combating violence against women and DV is of particular importance. The bill, presented on 24 October 2022, was assigned to the II Commission on Justice on 10 January 2023, where the examination is still ongoing.

SUBSTANTIVE ISSUES IN CRIMINAL LAW AND PROPOSALS

From the brief summary hereinabove, it is clear that the Italian criminal justice system is, from a regulatory perspective, sufficiently comprehensive with regard to the aims of combating sexual violence; however, it is not free from certain critical points that affect women's determination to report sexual violence. In particular, the definition of the offense of "Sexual violence" in

Art. 609 *bis* CC is highlighted. To some authors, the offense is characterised by a certain vagueness of description, with a violation of the principle of legal certainty and difficulties in assessing the seriousness of the offense.[33] Further, the offending conduct is often based on the element of compulsion, through violence, threat or abuse, leaving in place the traditional "burden of resistance" of the victims, which requires them, from an objective and subjective point of view, to prove that they physically resisted, expressing also their own dissent.[34] Therefore, it would seem appropriate to amend the definition of the offense by introducing the wording "*in the absence of a valid consent of the victim*"[35] (Art. 36 IC),[36] also making the offense a crime whose punishability is determined by the Court as being the occurrence of the criminal event itself. This would also facilitate the willingness to report. In this regard, the United Nations Special Report on Violence against Women of 2021 further suggests a reform according to which the "definitions of rape should explicitly include lack of consent and place it at its centre, stipulating that rape is any act of sexual penetration of a sexual nature by whatever means committed against a person who has not given consent."[37]

Another critical profile is represented by the lack of the specific crime of sexual harassment in Italian law (Art. 40 IC). This legislative vacuum, which predominantly affects some sectors, such as in the work and family sphere, can also be a deterrent to the possibility of reporting. Such an offense, even as a possible "spy crime," would in fact make it possible to interrupt a possible "criminal course" at an early stage.

Further considerations can be made with reference to the offense of "domestic violence" pursuant to Art. 572 CC which, due to its wording, does not seem to capture the value of the phenomenon.[38] The offense, in fact, presupposes the demonstration of a habitual nature, which is not always easy to establish (also the episodic nature or the concentration of the violent behaviour over time, the brevity of the emotional relationship and/or the timeliness of the complaint sometimes lead to the exclusion of the habitual nature of the conduct). The crime also presupposes a state of submission or subjection of the woman, which is essential, according to part of the jurisprudence, for the creation of that "vexatious lifestyle" on which the commission of the offense depends[39] and which is considered necessary for the delimitation of this case as opposed to a mere "couple conflict," to which, instead, the violent behaviour reported is often referred.[40] Often, however, these facts are reduced to minor offenses (e.g., assault, personal injury, threats) or involve the application of general mitigating circumstances (in 99 percent of cases),[41] suspended sentence and the provision of alternative measures; this often leads to the application of paltry penalties, which are inadequate to the seriousness of the facts and which often constitute an additional deterrent to reporting by the victim. Moreover, the application of minor offenses is subject to a complaint by the offended person, who is usually reluctant to file a complaint against the partner, also because of the possible negative impact of it on the family and the custody of children; in addition, complaints are often withdrawn once the violence, or cohabitation, ceases. In this regard, it might be appropriate to remove the requirement of habituality from the case of "domestic violence," punishable *ex officio*. In any case, the introduction of *ex officio* prosecution could also be considered for "minor" offenses of violence when committed in the context of an emotional relationship (Art. 55 IC).

The importance of a reform of this offense is, moreover, linked to the fact that behind abuse there are often dimensions of suffering connected to situations of violence that are not only physical but also psychological and economic, capable of compromising a person's life and integrity.

Furthermore, it should be noted that the Italian legal system does not provide for the specific case of "femicide,"[42] also because of the principle of neutrality of criminal law, which is considered, by some Italian authors, a guarantee of equality before the law.[43] Nevertheless, considering the function of cultural guidance typical of criminal law, such a provision could prove useful, also with regard to the increased visibility of the protection: this could constitute an encouragement for female victims of violence to report.[44] In this regard, on the one hand, it is undoubtedly true that the provision of an *ad hoc* criminal offense for femicide would have a strong impact, including a symbolic one, in the socio-cultural and regulatory context of reference, with a very strong value in stigmatising the phenomenon. On the other hand, account must be taken of the difficulty of normative delimitation of this phenomenon without incurring violations such as that of the criminal law principle of "determinateness."

In this context, a comparison with the Spanish legal system, which, among European countries, boasts one of the most significant experiences in combating violence against women, could be particularly interesting.[45]

Another element that negatively affects the willingness to denounce is undoubtedly linked to the lack of effectiveness of the punishment for the offender, which is a circumstance that, moreover, is not compatible with the general preventive function of the penalty. As mentioned, and as the statistical data show, for example, the granting of suspended sentences appears to be frequent. In this regard, Law no. 69/2019 makes the suspension, for some sexual offenses, conditional on participation in specific rehabilitation programmes, with a view to re-education, but without clarifying the contents of such rehabilitation programmes and the subjects responsible for their elaboration.

Another issue that could hinder the justiciability of these offenses concerns the system of prosecution; the current provision of a 12-month time limit for filing a complaint could discourage a woman who may need more time to make up her mind. The filing of the complaint could, therefore, be allowed within the statute of limitations provided for the offense.[46]

In this regard, even preventive actions may turn out to be sometimes ineffective. It is worth mentioning the scarce application in civil law of the protection orders (see Articles 342 *bis* and 342 *ter* of the Italian Civil Code) which were introduced in 2001 in order to protect a woman who suffers violence from her partner, by removing the latter from the family home or prohibiting from approaching her. Moreover, the civil protection order is a resource if it is issued quickly and without hearing the offender. It is instead risky for the woman if it is issued after a long investigation. Nevertheless, Italian judges rarely apply this measure quickly and rarely give up on hearing the abuser.[47]

The need to act against discrimination is still unquestionable, possibly by providing for aggravating circumstances;[48] in fact, all forms of marginalisation, including those due to discrimination, can be the cause of physical and psychological abuse. It is, in fact, these "discriminated" people who run the greatest risk of sexual abuse, as is also shown by the statistical data, precisely because of the loneliness in which they find themselves and the difficulty of facing a trial alone. Discrimination is, therefore, an important factor in resistance to reporting.[49]

Regarding the sexual violence suffered by non-EU women, it would also be appropriate, given the data on violence against foreign women, to repeal the crime of illegal immigration, as currently provided for in Italy; the special one-year residence permit for victims of certain sexual offenses, provided for in Art. 18 *bis,* legislative decree no. 286 of 1998, in fact, appears to be an inadequate measure to deal with this phenomenon, including discouraging the willingness to report.

In the end, the collection of data for monitoring the phenomenon and ensuring the anonymity of victims could also be important; in this regard, a contribution could also be made by the provisions of the recent Law no. 53 of 5 May 2022 on "*Provisions concerning statistics on gender-based violence.*" Furthermore, some of the critical profiles addressed are also considered, in hopes of reforming the current system, in the aforementioned bill presented to the Italian Parliament on 24 October 2022.

ECHR NORMS AND POSITIVE PROCEDURAL OBLIGATIONS

It is the right moment to address the main issues related to the criminal proceedings sphere. In this context, it is significant to consider the central role played by the European Convention on Human Rights (ECHR), which provides several norms that have dual relevance in relation to sexual offense cases. The main norms in question are Articles 2, 3, 4 and 8 ECHR: it may be appropriate to bring to mind that they respectively concern the right to life, the prohibition of torture, the prohibition of slavery and forced labor, as well as the right to respect for private and family life. According to these norms—besides the self-evident "negative duty" to abstain from behaviours that violate the above-mentioned fundamental rights—the States Parties to the Convention have "positive duties," both in the substantial sphere and in the procedural one. On the substantial side, the State is bound to incriminate the conducts which offend the rights protected by ECHR norms. On the procedural side, it is mandatory for the State to ensure the actual identification and punishment of perpetrators.[50] We intend to focus on the second group of positive obligations, namely the procedural ones. As it will be clarified—briefly highlighting the ECtHR case law—this area of positive obligations includes the duties to carry out appropriate and effective investigations: hearing the victims and using scientific/technological tools if it is possible, as well as protecting and involving the victims themselves (or their relatives) during the criminal proceedings.

Positive procedural obligations deriving from the ECHR are a cornerstone for the protection of sexual offense victims. Through the activities of the judicial authorities, the State must guarantee the right of victims and their close relatives to participate in criminal proceedings, to be heard and to introduce evidence. At the same time, victims need to be protected from "secondary victimization," which could result from the participation of the accused person in the trial or from the actual proceedings dynamics.[51]

A relevant case law of the European Court of Human Rights (hereinafter ECtHR) has been developing towards this direction. This trend stresses the necessity of protecting the victim not only "through" the justice system, but also "from" it. Violations related to procedural duties were found by the Court in several cases of sexual offense. Many judgments are noteworthy in this regard. In one case, for instance, proceedings were not brought against the perpetrator because, according to domestic law, the victim (a minor) had to make the complaint herself.[52] In this case, the violation was originated from a law gap, but in a broad range of cases it was purely resulting from procedural failures.

A specific lack of effective investigations concerned a rape case, due to the failure of the States' authorities to properly pursue an obvious line of inquiry resulting from DNA evidence.[53]

The Court repeatedly recognised violations of the ECHR in its "procedural limb," mainly related to Art. 3, because the States' authorities failed to carry out effective,[54] full and comprehensive investigations.[55] It is not enough that a national criminal norm is provided and that it incriminates the relevant conducts: it is also required that the national judicial bodies effectively engage in preventing and punishing violations. In some judgments, the ECtHR pointed out long delays in criminal proceedings, in breach of the State's duty to promptly prosecute criminal conducts.[56] In one case related to repeated sexual assaults by a family friend against a minor, the judicial proceedings unreasonably lasted seven years and resulted in severe damages to the young victim's personal integrity, producing a violation of both Articles 3 and 8 ECHR.[57] We should emphasize that the European Court acknowledged violations of the prohibition of torture and the right to respect for private and family life. The ECtHR also recognised a violation of Art. 13 ECHR, in connection to Art. 3 ECHR, in so far as criminal law and civil remedies were not made available to the victim.[58] As it is well-known, the infringed Article concerns the right to an effectively and suitable domestic remedy to challenge the alleged violation of ECHR.

SOME PROCEDURAL POINTS

Sexual offense raises several procedural issues. In this frame, it is possible to single out four problematic topics: complaint, evidence, legal aid, and language used in the trial.

A) In the light of Art. 44, para 3, of the Istanbul Convention (hereinafter IC), proceedings related to sexual offenses shall not be subordinated to the victim's complaint or its withdrawal. This rule aims to protect victims from intimidation, conditioning or brainwashing on the part of the accused and their family or of the victim's social circle. However, for some sexual offenses a complaint is needed, in order to guarantee the privacy of the victim. In Italy, the complaint is often required by the law for crimes involving the intimate sphere, but it is not withdrawable (however, for some crimes, it is withdrawable only before judicial authorities).

The actual problem is that these types of crimes do not often arise. They are not easily reported, due to the feeling of shame or the desire for privacy the victim often experiences, or because they occur secretly inside homes or as part of a family or sentimental relationship. New methods to encourage reports and new places or institutions to host and support victims in extreme cases are needed.[59]

B) The issues related to possible intimidation or the feeling of shame may arise also in the context of giving evidence. Time having passed since the facts or the complaint, the victim may try to describe the facts in a different light, leaving out relevant details or minimising the cruelty of the conducts. A victim's hearing can be affected by the same problems. A delay in the victim's hearing can result in the weakening of their statement and in the loss of useful evidence. Moreover, an unclear "declarative progression," which is intermittent and discontinuous, can affect the persecution of the crime.

In this regard, the Italian Supreme Court of Cassation clarified that these inconsistent declarations cannot by themselves undermine the reliability of the victim as a witness.[60] The above mentioned Law no. 69 of 2019 (the so-called "Codice Rosso") introduced a new norm which establishes that the victim of gender and domestic offenses shall be heard within three days after the beginning of the investigation (Art. 362 para 1 *ter* CPC). If possible, they shall not be heard several times. Moreover, the hearing shall be "protected" through precaution measures (e.g., without cross examination) and limiting the trial publicity.[61] The assessment of these crimes usually focuses mainly on the victim's hearing. However, considering the weaknesses of this type of evidence, a central role is recognised to scientific proof and, in particular, to DNA analyses. The already mentioned ECtHR case-law is noteworthy in this regard, as it clearly underlines the importance of following these investigative paths.[62]

C) The third procedural issue concerns the so-called "legal aid." The latter plays a very significant role in the frame of gender and domestic violence cases. In the period immediately following violence, many victims of gender and domestic violence are forced to leave all their belongings or their jobs without prior warning. This results in victims being devoid of financial resources. Victims often need legal aid in order to successfully claim their rights, as judicial and administrative procedures can be very complex and expensive. In fact, not all offended persons are able to bear the high costs involved in the use of justice.

In the light of Art. 57 IC, in the case of gender and domestic violence, the States "shall provide for the right to legal assistance and to free legal aid for victims under the conditions provided by their national law." This norm corresponds to the guarantees established by Directive no. 2012/20/EU, (whereas no. 37, 38, 58).

In many States (including Italy) it is not mandatory for victims to have a defence lawyer, but all too often they cannot effectively exercise their rights on their own. In Italy, a specific norm provides for legal aid in favour of gen-

der and domestic violence victims,[63] irrespective of their economical situation and without any judicial assessment.

However, an Italian judge has recently challenged this norm. The alleged defect concerned the incompatibility of the law with the principle of equality and with the right of defense. The Italian Constitutional Court was called to decide on this matter[64] and clearly reaffirmed the constitutionality of this form of legal aid. The latter—according to this decision—is the result of the legislator's unquestionable choice, aimed to support particularly vulnerable victims and to encourage them to report crimes: for these reasons, legal aid has to be ensured to all victims of gender and domestic violence regardless of their financial means. There should be no need for such a clarification, which should be taken for granted.

D) To conclude, it is appropriate to consider how important language is for the satisfaction of sexual offense victims. In the light of Directive no. 29, the sexual harassment victim is a "particularly vulnerable" one (Art. 22 Directive no. 2012/29/EU, Art. 90 *quater* It. CPC): Directive no. 29 (Art. 23) requires sensitivity on the part of those who hear the victims during the trial, to avoid "secondary victimization." According to Art. 194 It. CPC "the testimony that may be useful in defining the victim's personality shall be admitted only if the criminal act must be evaluated in connection with the victim's behaviour." However, in many cases victims are asked embarrassing questions and made to disclose aspects of their private life that are irrelevant for the ascertainment of the facts. These uncomfortable questions can result in the victim reliving the experience of violence and being discredited (for instance, on the basis of their clothing and sexual orientation). Moreover, this kind of questioning is capable of hurting the victim even if a judge intervenes relieving them from answering.[65]

Offensive language is sometimes also used in judgments. In a case of gang rape, aspects of the victim's private life were mentioned by an Italian judge, who acquitted the charged persons in a second instance: the victim's sexual orientation was discussed, as well as the underwear she was wearing when she was attacked. At the time of the assault, the young victim was an art history and drama student. The judgment also specified that, among her presumed assailants, there was a man with whom she had made a short film a few months before. In this film, she played the role of a prostitute who was abused. All these details about the victim's private life were stressed and treated as evidence by the Italian judge. Due to this decision, the ECtHR recognised that the Italian authorities had failed to protect the victim's right to respect for her private life and physical integrity. In 2021, it condemned Italy for the "words" levied by the judge (the Court of Appeal of Florence) against her. The ECtHR pointed out that judges should avoid reproducing sexist stereotypes in their decisions, minimising gender violence and exposing women to secondary victimisation.

CONCLUSION

As it has emerged from the considerations set out so far, the unwillingness to report crimes, which is so widespread in Italian society, is only partly due to flaws in the substantive and procedural law. In fact, as it has been recognised by the ECtHR and the *Group of Experts on Action Against Women and Domestic Violence* (GREVIO), the Italian criminal justice system appears, from a regulatory perspective, sufficiently complete and equipped with good legislative instruments.[66]

However, it is undoubtedly true that the matter should also be addressed in relation to the socio-economic and cultural context, still anchored to "gender" prejudices and stereotypes that govern not only the Italian society but also the judicial system itself.[67] This consideration also seems to be confirmed by the ECtHR, which, in two recent decisions,[68] criticised the Italian judiciary for its lack of awareness[69] and knowledge of the phenomenon of sexual violence against women.

Many issues have been hindering the effective and broad protection of women in the area of sexual offenses. Among those, a significant one arises, namely the still wide recourse to sexist prejudices, socio-cultural stereotypes, and patriarchal patterns. In this context, the Italian judiciary system often minimises the painful dimension of violence and produces various forms of discrimination, including indirect discrimination, and secondary victimisation.[70]

In this regard, there is no doubt that trust in justice and its effectiveness are fundamental to inducing victims of violence to report crimes.[71]

Due to the centrality of the issue, the European Parliament Resolution of 16 September 2021 is of particular importance, as it contains recommendations to the Commission concerning the identification of gender-based violence as a new sphere of crime to be included among the so-called Euro-crimes, i.e. among "areas of particularly serious crime with a cross-border dimension."[72] In particular, the European Parliament stresses that gender-based violence, both online and offline, is a particularly serious crime and a widespread violation of fundamental rights and freedoms in the European Union which needs to be addressed with greater efficiency and determination on a common basis; moreover, it points out that gender-based violence is the result of societal and systemic structural gender inequalities that have a cross-border dimension; indeed, gender-based violence affects all areas of society and it is rooted in gender stereotypes, heteropatriarchal structures, power asymmetries and structural and institutional inequalities. The European Parliament, in addition, stresses that the special need to combat violence against women and girls and other forms of gender-based violence on a common basis also results from the need to establish minimum rules concerning the definition of criminal offenses and sanctions, including a common definition of gender-based violence, as well as minimum rules concerning key issues of prevention, under-reporting, victim protection, support and reparation, and the prosecution of the perpetrator. Therefore, whereas the Council of the European Union may, on the basis of developments in crime, adopt a decision identifying areas of particularly serious crime with a cross-border dimension resulting from the nature or impact of such offenses or from a special need to combat them on a common basis, the Council has adopted the decision that "Gender-based violence is hereby identified as an area of crime that meets the criteria specified in Article 83 (1) of the Treaty on the Functioning of the European Union."

Ultimately, agreeing with the conclusions of the European Parliament, the importance of ensuring effective protection against sexual and gender-based violence is highlighted as a bulwark in the area of respect for fundamental rights and, through these, for the principles of the rule of law.

NOTES

1. The present paper is the result of a shared research. Dr. Marta Palmisano wrote the following paragraphs: Introduction, Regulatory Changes, Substantive Issues in Criminal Law and Proposals, Conclusions. Prof. Lucia Parlato wrote the following paragraphs: ECHR Norms and Positive Procedural Obligations, Some Procedural Points.

2. European Parliament, *Resolution of 16 September 2021.*

3. On this subject, Claudia Pecorella, 'Violenza di genere e sistema penale' (2019) 9 Diritto penale e processo 1181.

4. See Luciana Goisis, 'La violenza sessuale: profili storici e criminologici. Una storia di "genere"' [2012] Diritto penale contemporaneo 1–28 ff.

5. In this regard, the Istanbul Convention aims to make States aware of the need to take action on several fronts to "*eradicate prejudices and customs based on the idea of women's inferiority*" and achieve the goal of gender equality.

6. This is in accordance with a publicistic vision of the legal interest protected by the law, typical of the fascist period, according to a system of "descending progression" in the placement of legal interest within the Criminal Code; See Tullio Padovani, Luigi Stortoni, *Diritto penale e fattispecie criminose* (Il Mulino 1991) 49 ff.; Alfredo Rocco, 'Relazione a S.M. il Re del Ministro Guardasigilli Rocco, per l'approvazione del testo definitivo del Codice penale' in *Lavori preparatori del codice penale e del codice di procedura penale* IV [1929] 9 f.

7. Goisis (n 3) 12.

8. On the link between sexual freedom and Art. 2 of the Constitution, see *Italian Criminal Court of Cassation* (hereinafter *Cass. Pen.*), sec. III, judgment of 28 October 2014, no. 21020; *Cass. pen.*, sec. II, judgment of 7 February 2004, no. 37395.

9. At the same time, the reform of family law was approved, which helped to recognise the social role of women and the principles of gender equality.

10. The conduct taken into consideration is sexual violence by compulsion and violence by induction; *Cass. pen.*, sec. III, judgment of 29 August 2019, no. 36636; *Cass. pen.*, sec. III, judgment of 18 September 2019, no. 38606; *Cass. pen., Un. Sec.*, judgment of 1 October 2020, no. 27326; *Cass. pen.*, sec. III, judgment of 4 March 2021, no. 19611. In legal doctrine, see Ferrando Mantovani, *Diritto penale. Parte speciale I. I delitti contro la persona* (Cedam 2014) 441 ff. The crime can also be committed via chat; *Cass. pen.*, sez. III, judgment of 8 September 2020, no. 25266. With reference to culturally oriented crimes, see *Cass. pen.*, sec. III, judgment of 2 July 2018, no. 29613. On the pardon, see *Cass. pen.*, sec. I, judgment of 7 February 2008, no. 6072. On the concept of consensus, please refer to notes nn. 27–28.

11. See *Cass. Pen.*, sec. III, judgement 18 September 2015, no. 40366; *Cass. pen.*, sec. III, judgment of 4 October 2017, no. 45589; *Cass. pen.*, sec. III, judgment of 6 December 2020, no. 19987 See *Cass. Pen.*, sec. III, judgement 18 September 2015, no. 40366; *Cass. pen.*, sec. III, judgment of 4 October 2017, no. 45589; *Cass. pen.*, sec. III, judgment of 6 December 2020, no. 19987.

12. Today, it is also irrelevant whether the end proposed by the agent is directed at satisfying his own concupiscence or has another purpose. On these topics see, among others, Goisis (n 3) 15.

13. Luigi Delpino, *Diritto Penale Parte Speciale* (14th edn, Ed. Giuridiche Simone, 2004) 580 ff.

14. With reference to the protection of minors in sexual matters see Law no. 269 of 3 August 1998, introducing Articles 600 *bis* - 600 *septies* CC, Law no. 38 of 6 February 2006, Law no. 172 of 1 October 2012, ratifying the Lanzarote Convention of 2007 and Legislative Decree no. 39 of 4 March 2014.

15. See also Art. 291, para 2 *bis* ("Application procedure" of provisional patrimonial measures) and Art. 76.4 *ter* of Presidential Decree no. 115 of 30 May 2002 on free legal aid as an exception to income limits for victims of gender violence; See *Corte Costituzionale*, judgement 11 January 2021, no. 1.

16. Among other things, the secrecy of reporting persons is guaranteed, mandatory arrest in case of flagrante delicto in crimes of family abuse and stalking is foreseen and a hotline for assistance is set up.

17. The law, among other things, focuses on domestic violence, doubles the prescription period for certain sexual offenses, extends the offense of domestic abuse to cohabitants and introduces rules on paedophilia (Art. 609 *undecies* CC).

18. Reference is also made to the Council Decision of 11 May 2017 (2017/865/EU) and the Council Decision of 11 May 2017 (2017/866/EU).

19. The Convention introduces the concepts of "gender-base" and "domestic" violence.

20. An aggravating circumstance was introduced in the case of witnessed violence (Art. 61 no. 11 *quinquies* CC). Law no. 4 of 11 January 2018 extends the provision of Art. 577 CC to the spouse, even if legally separated, to the party to the civil union or to the person bound by an affective relationship and cohabiting on a stable basis. In addition, in case of flagrante delicto for serious offenses, the "precautionary" measure of emergency removal from the family home and the prohibition to approach the places frequented by the offended person may be applied. Legislative Decree no. 212 of 15 December 2015 then introduces Art. 90 *quater* CPC defining the state of vulnerability.

21. This crime is of particular importance as it is often within the context of psychological violence that situations leading to sexual violence occur, which women often fail to report. On the offense of abuse, *Cass. pen.*, sec. III, judgment of 7 July 2008, no. 27469; *Cass. pen.*, sec. III, judgment of 4 March 2017, no. 16543; *Cass. pen.*, sec. VI, judgment of 22 July 2019, no. 32781, *Cass. pen.*, sec. III, judgment of 14 December 2020, no. 35700. The offense may also occur in the "de facto" family, *Cass. pen.*, sec. VI, judgment of 9 May 2019, no. 19922.

22. Moreover, the following crimes have been introduced: the crime of "Disfigurement as a result of permanent injuries" (Art. 583 *quinquies* CC), the crime of "Revenge porn" (Art. 612 *ter* CC), which is aggravated if committed within the framework of a relationship, even if it has ended, or with the use of computers, the crime of "Coercion or inducement to enter marriage" (Art. 558 *bis* CC) and the crime of "Breach of the injunction to stay away from the family home and of the prohibition to visit places frequented by the offended person" (Art. 387 *bis* CC). The law speeds up criminal proceedings, giving priority to sexual offenses, and accelerates the adoption of measures to protect victims; in general, it strengthens the apparatus of prevention and repression for certain crimes in this respect.

23. Law no. 69/2019 also introduces a prohibition on the prevalence of mitigating circumstances over aggravating circumstances for having committed the act to the detriment of family members or against persons with whom there is an emotional relationship and extends the scope of the aggravating circumstances of murder aggravated by personal relationships.

24. In this regard, *Cass. pen.*, sec. I, judgment of 1 March 2018, no. 9427; *Cass. pen.*, sec. V, judgment of 29 April 2020, no. 13273.

25. On the subject of sexual offenses against minors, reference is also made to the aforementioned Law no. 269/1998, Law no. 38/2006, Law no. 172/2012 and Legislative Decree no. 39/2014.

26. The legal interest protected is "*physical and psychological integrity, for the purpose of the proper development of one's sexuality*." This offense is not dependent on consent, since violence is presumed. On this subject, *Cass. pen.*, sec. III, judgment of 30 September 2014, no. 6168; *Cass. pen.*, sec. III, judgment of 14 December 2011, no. 12464; *Cass. pen.*, sez. III, ord. judgment of 22 April 2021, no. 25334.

27. Art. 20 of Law no. 238/2021 introduces amendments to bring Italian legislation into line with Directive no. 2011/92/EU. With this law, an attempt is made to bypass two infringement procedures, contested against Italy by the European Commission for not having correctly transposed Directive no. 2011/93/EU.

28. On the application of Art. 582 CC to the employer, see *Cass. pen.*, sec. IV, judgment of 8 October 2018, no. 44890.

29. Kidnapping can be absorbed into sexual violence; *Cass. pen.*, sec. III, judgment of 13 September 2019, no. 38014.

30. On private violence, see *Cass. pen.*, sec. V, judgment of 31 July 2009, no. 31758.

31. On stalking, see *Cass. pen.*, sec. V, judgment of 3 January 2018, no. 104; *Cass. pen.*, sec. I, judgment of 14 March 2018, no. 11604; *Cass. pen.*, sec. III, judgment of 21 August 2019, no. 36307; *Cass. pen.*, sec. V, judgment of 21 January 2021, no. 2496; *Cass. pen., Un. Sec.*, prel. hear., judgment of 15 July 2021. The offense can also take place through social networks and via WhatsApp; *Cass. pen.,* sec. V, judgment of 6 November 2019, no. 45141; *Cass. pen.,* sec. V, judgment of 28 January 2019 no. 3989. The complaint is irrevocable only if the threats are serious and repeated; *Cass. pen.*, judgment of 6 February 2020, no. 5092.

32. The legislative decree transposes the provisions of Law no. 654 of 13 October 1975, amended by Law no. 205 of 25 June 1993 (Mancino Law).

33. The assessment of the crime may also require humiliating investigations of the woman's body, discouraging the complaint, Alberto Cadoppi and others (eds.), *Commentario delle norme contro la violenza sessuale e della legge contro la pedofilia* (Cedam 2002) 35 f.

34. In this regard, indeed, a "presumption of consent to sexual acts" seems to exist; *Tribunal Busto Arsizio*, 26 January 2022. On the contrary, *Cass. pen.,* sec. III, judgment of 19 November 2021, no. 1559; *Cass. pen.,* sec. III, judgment of 17 December 2019, no. 12628, for which, instead, a "presumption of dissent" is considered. For instance, Austria, Montenegro, Portugal and Sweden have defined rape as a lack of consent.

35. On consent, see *Cass. pen.,* sec. III, judgment of 23 May 2013, no. 29725; *Cass. pen.,* sec. II, judgment of 16 January 2014, no. 5768; *Cass. pen.,* sec. III, judgment of 15 October 2019, no. 42118; *Cass. pen.,* sec. III, judgment of 26 March 2021, no. 11631.

36. In fact, many women do not put up any kind of resistance. Consider the cases of the so-called date rape (sexual violence between subjects linked at least by bonds of an acquaintance) in which it is more difficult to detect dissent; Maria Virgilio, 'Corpo di donna e legge penale. Ancora sulla legge sulla violenza sessuale?!' [1996] 1 Democrazia e diritto 166.

37. Andrea Niccolò Pinna, 'Violenza sessuale e ricerca del dissenso della vittima: la difficoltà dei giudici di merito a recepire gli insegnamenti della Corte di Cassazione' [8 March 2022] Sistema Penale, 5.

38. Claudia Pecorella and Patrizia Farina, 'La risposta penale alla violenza domestica: un'indagine sulla prassi del tribunale di Milano in materia di maltrattamenti contro familiari e conviventi (art. 572 c.p.)' (2018) Diritto penale contemporaneo 1–26.

39. In the current system, there would therefore be no "abuse" when the victim appears to be able, by character or culture, to react to the abuse, interrupting the relationship or resorting to denunciation; *Cass. pen.*, sec. VI, judgment of 13 November

2015, no. 5258 [2016] 8 Diritto & Giustizia 43 ff. See *Cass. pen.*, sec. VI, judgment of 13 February 2009, no. 6490.

40. On this point *Cass. pen.*, sec. VI, judgment of 20 January 2009, no. 9531; *Cass. pen.*, sec. VI, judgment of 2 July 2019, no. 6126.

41. The recognition of general mitigating circumstances is often based on an assessment of the defendant's behaviour in court, his weak points, his "cultural roots," his lack of criminal records and his good reputation.

42. Similarly, one could question the appropriateness of classifying sex crimes in an autonomous category under the heading of "offenses against sexual freedom."

43. See Fabrizio Filice, 'Diritto penale e genere' [11 September 2019] 9 Diritto penale e uomo 11 ff.; Emanuele Corn, 'Il femminicidio come reato. Spunti per un dibattito italiano alla luce della dell'esperienza cilena' [14 September 2013] Diritto penale contemporaneo 16.

44. On the issue, see Senato della Repubblica, *Commissione Parlamentare di inchiesta* (2022) <http://www.senato.it/service/PDF/PDFServer/DF/420984.pdf> accessed April 15, 2022. For a debate and a critical analysis on this topic see, among the others, Antonella Merli, 'Violenza di genere e femminicidio' (2015) 1 Diritto penale contemporaneo—Rivista trimestrale 436; Marco Venturoli, 'La protezione della vittima del reato quale autonomo scopo del diritto penale' in *Sistema penale e tutela delle vittime tra diritto e giustizia* (2015) 11; Emanuele Corn, 'Il femminicidio come fattispecie penale' [2017] in *Collana della facoltà di giurisprudenza—Università di Trento* 113 ff.; Sara Spanò, 'Il problema penale del Femminicidio. Analisi di un fenomeno' [March 2021] De Iustitia 1–30.

45. Consider, for example, the provisions of Ley Orgánica (L.O.) no. 1 of 28 December 2004 "Medidas de Protección Integral contra la Violencia de Género" which, among other things, introduce the Title II "Derechos de las mujeres víctimas de violencia de género." Also, consider the numerous aggravating circumstances that come into play when the offense is committed against a woman (see, e.g., Articles 148, 153, 171 of the Spanish Criminal Code) or the establishment of special Courts of Violence against Women. The recent L.O. no. 10 of 6 September 2022 "de garantía integral de la libertad sexual" is also a particularly important and historic law protecting women against all sexual assaults. The new law, among other things, expressly refers to sexual femicide in Art. 3. In sexual offenses, the law is also based on affirmative consent; on this topic see, among the others, Anna Mara Maugeri, 'Le 'aggravanti' nei confronti degli uomini autori di 'violenza di genere' nella disciplina spagnola: possibile strategia politico criminale o strumento di una politica della 'sicurezza' discriminatoria?' [2016] Rivista di filosofia del diritto internazionale e della politica globale <http://www.juragentium.org/forum/violenzadonne/it/maugeri.html> accessed 15 April 2022.

46. Goisis (no. 3) 19.

47. Cardinale, 'Il rapporto del GREVIO sull'applicazione in Italia della Convenzione di Istanbul: il lavoro ancora da fare' [13 May 2021] <https://www.criminaljusticenetwork.eu/it/post/il-rapporto-del-grevio-sullapplicazione-in-italia-della-convenzione-di-istanbul-il-lavoro-ancora-da-fare> accessed 15 April 2022.

48. In particular, measures to prevent violence against women who may be subject to discrimination (women with disabilities, minorities, migrants and asylum seekers, LGBT, elderly, prostitutes and drug users) could be strengthened.

49. In this regard, the draft law S. 2005 (D.d.l. Zan) against discrimination, which was rejected by the Italian Senate on 17 October 2021, was resubmitted again in Parliament on 27 April 2022; among other things, it proposes an amendment to Articles 604 *bis* CC ("Propaganda and incitement to commit crimes on grounds of racial, ethnic and religious discrimination") and 604 *ter* CC ("Aggravating circumstance"), with the aim of extending them to grounds of discrimination based on sex, gender, gender identity and sexual orientation.

50. Emanuele Nicosia, *Convenzione europea dei diritti dell'uomo e diritto penale* (Giappichelli 2006) 62 f.

51. Lucia Parlato, *Il contributo della vittima tra azione e prova* (Torri del Vento 2012) 25 f.; Parlato, 'Vulnerabilità e processo penale,' in Antonella Marandola and Giorgio Spangher (eds.), *La fragilità della persona nel processo penale* (Giappichelli 2021) 427 ff.

52. *X and Y v. the Netherlands* App no 8978/80 (ECtHR, 26 March 1985).

53. *Y v. Bulgaria* App no 41990/18 (ECtHR, 20 February 2020).

54. *Maslova and Nalbandov v. Russia* App no 839/02 (ECtHR, 24 January 2008); *I.G. v. the Republic of Moldova* App no 53519/07 (ECtHR, 15 May 2012); *M. and Others v. Italy and Bulgaria* App no 40020/03 (ECtHR, 31 July 2012); *I.P. v. the Republic of Moldova* App no 33708/12 (ECtHR, 28 April 2015).

55. *B.V. v. Belgium* App no 61030/08 (ECtHR, 2 May 2017).

56. *W.v. Slovenia* App no 24125/06 (ECtHR, 23 January 2014); *M.A. v. Slovenia and N.D. v. Slovenia* App no 16605/09 (ECtHR, 15 January 2015); *S.Z. v. Bulgaria* App no 29263/12 (ECtHR, 3 March 2015).

57. *Y v. Slovenia* App no 41107/10 (ECtHR, 28 May 2015).

58. I.P. v. the Republic of Moldova App no 33708/12 (ECtHR, 28 April 2015).

59. Matteo Antonio Sacco and others, 'The impact of the Covid-19 pandemic on domestic violence: The dark side of home isolation during quarantine' [2020] 88(2) Medico-Legal Journal 71.

60. *Cass. Pen.*, sec. III, judgment of 31 July 2020, no. 23419, <http/penaledp.it> accessed 15 April 2022.

61. Among others, Egle Pilla, 'L'incidente probatorio e l'audizione protetta' [13 January 2019] www.giustiziainsieme.it accessed 15 April 2022.

62. *Y v. Bulgaria* App no 41990/18 (ECtHR, 20 February 2020).

63. Art. 76, para 4 *ter*, "Consolidated Act on Justice Costs," D.P.R. no. 115 of 30 May 2022.

64. See *Corte Costituzionale*, judgment of 11 January 2021, no. 1.

65. Paola Emilia Cicerone, 'Violenza sessuale ai danni di due studentesse americane: il caso di Firenze' [11 March 2020] <http://dirittopenaleuomo.org> accessed 15 April 2022.

66. In this regard, the GREVIO report of 2020 expressed mostly positive evaluations towards the Italian legislation that, over time, has been expanding the regulatory

tools to prevent and combat gender-based violence. The recommendations concerning the national discipline are, therefore, rather limited.

67. Human sexual behaviour is indeed variable because it also depends on the consciousness and will of the subject, oriented by cultural, historical, social, religious and geographical parameters; "*sexual behavior is thus both instinctive and social,*" Berislav Pavisic, Davide Bertaccini, *The Other Criminal Procedures. Transitions in criminal procedural systems* I (Giappichelli 2002) 305. See also the *Convention on the Elimination of All Forms of Discrimination against Women* (1979) and the *Declaration on the Elimination of Violence against Women* (1993).

68. Reference is made to the ECtHR *Talpis against Italy* (2017) judgment, which recently condemned Italy for violating Articles 2, 3 and 14 ECHR, due to the ineffectiveness of the Italian protection system in relation to acts of intra-familiar violence. The Court also reiterated what had already been stated in the 2009 *Opuz vs Turkey* judgment, according to which the "generalised and discriminatory passivity of the police" that created "a climate favouring such violence" entailed a violation of Art. 14 of the Convention and substantial discrimination against women. Reference is also made to the *Affaire J.L. vs Italy* App no 5671/16 (ECtHR, 27 May 2021) which condemned Italy for the violation of Article 8 ECHR. On the Italian case law, see also Paola Di Nicola Travaglini, 'Trib. Roma, Sez. V, sent. 4 ottobre 2021 (dep. 23 novembre 2021), n. 11019' [11 January 2022] Sistema penale 1–15. According to the author, Italian judicial authorities do not often value the "gender motive," do not ascertain the power relations in the couple, contextualise the violent episode and distinguish between family quarrels (in a peer context) and domestic violence (in a continuous overpowering context).

69. See, for instance, *Cass. pen.*, sec. III, judgment of 24 March 2020, no. 10596, whereby the aggravating circumstance of Art. 609 *ter*, para 1, no. 2, CC does not apply if the victim of the abuse has taken alcohol and drugs spontaneously.

70. The same critical issues are highlighted by the *Committee on the Elimination of Discrimination against Women*, which, in its ruling *A.F. v. Italy* (148/2019) of 20 June 2022, held that Italian judicial authorities had violated Articles 2, 3, 5 and 15 of the *Convention on the Elimination of All Forms of Discrimination against Women (CEDAW)*. The Committee explained that the inequality faced by women resides "*also in the lack of capacity and awareness of judicial and quasi-judicial institutions to adequately address violations of women's human rights*" and that "*stereotypes and gender bias in the judicial system have far-reaching consequences for women's full enjoyment of human rights (. . .) they distort perceptions and lead to decisions based on preconceived beliefs and myths rather than relevant facts (. . .) Stereotypes also affect the credibility of women's voices, arguments and testimony as parties and witnesses.*" With specific reference to the sphere of criminal law, stereotypes make "*perpetrators not being held legally accountable for violations of women's rights, thereby upholding a culture of impunity. In all areas of law, stereotypes compromise the impartiality and integrity of the justice system.*" United Nations, CEDAW/C/82/D/148/2019, 18 July 2022, § 7.5.

Therefore, the woman who reported violence was not only left unprotected by the Italian judicial system but suffered moral and social damage precisely because of the sexist stereotypes used by the judiciary.

71. In this regard, the authorities assessed the low rate of criminal trials and convictions in Italy, which is linked to the low number of complaints, stating that it is in the courtrooms that a crucial role in combating gender-based violence and discrimination is played.

72. Noemi Maria Cardinale, 'Il Parlamento europeo chiede l'inserimento della violenza di genere tra i c.d. eurocrimini ai sensi dell'art. 83, §1, co. 2 del TFUE' [7 December 2021] Sistema Penale 1–7.

BIBLIOGRAPHY

Cadoppi A. and others (eds.), *Commentario delle norme contro la violenza sessuale e della legge contro la pedofilia* (Cedam 2002) 35 f.

Cardinale, N. M., 'Il Parlamento europeo chiede l'inserimento della violenza di genere tra i c.d. eurocrimini ai sensi dell'art. 83, §1, co. 2 del TFUE' [7 December 2021] Sistema Penale 1–7.

———, 'Il rapporto del GREVIO sull'applicazione in Italia della Convenzione di Istanbul: il lavoro ancora da fare' [13 May 2021] <https://www.criminaljusticenetwork.eu/it/post/il-rapporto-del-grevio-sullapplicazione-in-italia-della-convenzione-di-istanbul-il-lavoro-ancora-da-fare> accessed 15 April 2022.

Cicerone, P. E., 'Violenza sessuale ai danni di due studentesse americane: il caso di Firenze' [11 March 2020] <http://dirittopenaleuomo.org> accessed 15 April 2022.

Corn, E., 'Il femminicidio come reato. Spunti per un dibattito italiano alla luce della dell'esperienza cilena' [14 September 2013] Diritto penale contemporaneo 16.

———, 'Il femminicidio come fattispecie penale' [2017] in *Collana della facoltà di giurisprudenza—Università di Trento* 113 ff.

Delpino, L., *Diritto Penale Parte Speciale* (14th edn, Ed. Giuridiche Simone, 2004) 580 ff.

Filice, F., 'Diritto penale e genere' [11 September 2019] 9 Diritto penale e uomo 11 ff.

Goisis, L., 'La violenza sessuale: profili storici e criminologici. Una storia di "genere"' [2012] Diritto penale contemporaneo 1–28.

Mantovani, F., *Diritto penale. Parte speciale I. I delitti contro la persona* (Cedam 2014) 441 ff.

Maugeri, A. M., 'Le 'aggravanti' nei confronti degli uomini autori di 'violenza di genere' nella disciplina spagnola: possibile strategia politico criminale o strumento di una politica della 'sicurezza' discriminatoria?' [2016] Rivista di filosofia del diritto internazionale e della politica globale http://www.juragentium.org/forum/violenzadonne/it/maugeri.html accessed 15 April 2022.

Merli, A., 'Violenza di genere e femminicidio' [2015] 1 Diritto penale contemporaneo—Rivista trimestrale 436.

Nicosia, E., *Convenzione europea dei diritti dell'uomo e diritto penale* (Giappichelli 2006) 62 f.

Padovani, T., Luigi Stortoni, *Diritto penale e fattispecie criminose* (Il Mulino 1991) 49 ff.

Parlato, L., *Il contributo della vittima tra azione e prova* (Torri del Vento 2012) 25 f.

———, 'Vulnerabilità e processo penale,' in Antonella Marandola and Giorgio Spangher (eds.), *La fragilità della persona nel processo penale* (Giappichelli 2021) 427 ff.

Pavisic, B and Bertaccini, D., *The Other Criminal Procedures. Transitions in criminal procedural systems* I (Giappichelli 2002) 305.

Pecorella, C., 'Violenza di genere e sistema penale' (2019) 9 Diritto penale e processo 1181.

Pecorella, C. and Farina, P., 'La risposta penale alla violenza domestica: un'indagine sulla prassi del tribunale di Milano in materia di maltrattamenti contro familiari e conviventi (art. 572 c.p.)' [2018] Diritto penale contemporaneo 1–26.

Pilla, E., 'L'incidente probatorio e l'audizione protetta' [13 January 2019] www.giustiziainsieme.it.

Pinna, A. N., 'Violenza sessuale e ricerca del dissenso della vittima: la difficoltà dei giudici di merito a recepire gli insegnamenti della Corte di Cassazione' [8 March 2022] Sistema Penale, 5.

Rocco, A., 'Relazione a S.M. il Re del Ministro Guardasigilli Rocco, per l'approvazione del testo definitivo del Codice penale' in *Lavori preparatori del codice penale e del codice di procedura penale* IV [1929] 9 f.

Sacco, M. A, and others, 'The impact of the Covid-19 pandemic on domestic violence: The dark side of home isolation during quarantine' [2020] 88(2) Medico-Legal Journal 71.

Spanò, S., 'Il problema penale del Femminicidio. Analisi di un fenomeno' [March 2021] De Iustitia.

Travaglini, P D N, 'Trib. Roma, Sez. V, sent. 4 ottobre 2021 (dep. 23 novembre 2021), n. 11019' [11 January 2022] Sistema penale 1–15.

Venturoli, M., 'La protezione della vittima del reato quale autonomo scopo del diritto penale' in *Sistema penale e tutela delle vittime tra diritto e giustizia* (2015) 11.

Virgilio, M., 'Corpo di donna e legge penale. Ancora sulla legge sulla violenza sessuale?!' [1996] 1 Democrazia e diritto 166.

7

Between Challenges and Appropriate Responses to Sexual Violence

The Example of Bosnia and Herzegovina

Ena Kazić-Çakar

On a July summer evening in 2022, the public was taken aback by media information that a young girl in Sarajevo had reported being raped by a taxi driver who was driving her.[1] Not long before that, the public was appalled by the information about a high school sports teacher who committed indecent acts on his female juvenile student in the sports hall in front of her friends and had been indicted.[2] With a combination of these and many other cases and their frequency, it can be said that Bosnia and Herzegovina seems to be struggling with the prevention of sexual violence. That is partially confirmed by the newest research from the Organization for Security and Co-operation in Europe[3] regarding the *well-being of women in Bosnia Herzegovina* indicates that 84 percent of sexual violence remains unreported in Bosnia Herzegovina. That comprehensive research included 2321 women and resulted in the conclusion that four out of 10 women (38 percent) have experienced psychological or sexual violence; 28 of them have experienced harassment from the age of 15, and 1 out of 20 were harassed overall.[4]

Bosnia and Herzegovina, just like most countries in the world, aims to prevent sexual violence. One of the most important approaches to this task has been established through the criminal law system in a way that the State prescribes negative social phenomena as criminal acts and prescribes sanctions for their perpetrators. In this paper, the author approaches the subject from a critical aspect and presents both the advantages and challenges offered by the positive criminal law framework related to sexual violence in Bosnia and Herzegovina. The analysis is also comparative, given that due to its specific constitutional organization, the criminal regulation in Bosnia and Herzegovina had been established through four codes, which opens space for the question of harmonization of legal regulation on this topic between them.

It aims to determine the advantages, and challenges, but also the space for improvement of the substantive legal regulation of this specific topic in that country, for the preventive aim to be more likely achieved.

The paper falls into three parts. The first part provides an introduction that delivers the general idea about sexual violence, its legal nature, and responses to it. The second part represents the positive law provisions on sexual violence in Bosnia and Herzegovina and a comparative analysis of its quality among three applicable positive Criminal Codes in the same country, including topics of state in practice and sex offender registries. As for the third part, it offers critical assessments, such as, concluding observation of the existing regulation of this matter.

UNDERSTANDING SEXUAL VIOLENCE AS A GLOBAL PHENOMENON

Before approaching the positive criminal law of Bosnia and Herzegovina and detecting its challenges on the path of the fight against sexual violence, it is crucial to understand it as a phenomenon with its consequences, and theoretical preventing mechanisms used worldwide.

Although sexual violence is an example of the metamorphosis of the legal approach towards such negative social phenomenon through the years, as proofs of its existence and legal regulation are traceable in the far history,[5] it still exists as it remained unextinct parallel with national and international efforts to prevent it. Just as *Carmody and Carrington* note correctly, "the fact that the incidence of sexual violence is not declining, suggests we have not yet found a way to stop it."[6] Many agree on it as a phenomenon "difficult to detect, deter and to punish."[7] However, just as *Berlo and Ploem* emphasized once,[8] "it is a global problem and serious breach of human rights." It is a burning challenge for all legislation to recognize the most effective way to prevent it. Further, this aim went beyond the national, and it became an international burning matter to be solved.

As criminal law is primarily national law, the definition of sexual violence differs from one country to another and it is determined by the way how sexual violence is defined in the national criminal law. This fact confirms its particular quantitative and temporal nature since what an act of sexual violence is in one country does not necessarily have to be an act of sexual violence in another country. Further, what had been determined to be a sexual act in one country in one period, may have been decriminalized or new actions have been criminalized. However, many international documents, with an aim to overcome this potentially aggravating circumstance in a successful fight against sexual violence, recommend member states which actions to prescribe as sexual violence acts and offer definitions to be as comprehensive as possible, to bring one more universal definition on what sexual violence is. One of the definitions is offered by the United Nations High Commissioner which defines sexual violence as:

> A form of gender-based violence and encompasses any sexual act, attempt to obtain a sexual act, unwanted sexual comments, or advances, or acts to traffic, or otherwise directed against a person's sexuality using coercion, by any person regardless of their relationship to the victim, in any setting.[9]

World Health Organization (WHO) defines it as:

> Any sexual act, attempt to obtain a sexual act, or other act directed against a person's sexuality using coercion, by any person regardless of their relationship to the victim, in any setting. It includes rape, defined as the physically forced or otherwise coerced penetration of 3 the vulva or anus with a penis, other body part or object, attempted rape, unwanted sexual touching, and other non-contact forms.[10]

Antonio Gutierrez defined it "as a threat to every individual's right to a life of dignity and to humanity's collective peace and security."[11] The Hague principles on sexual violence note sexual violence as "encompassing all violations of sexual autonomy and sexual identity," and correctly notices that "sexual violence involves singular, multiple, continuous or intermittent acts which in the context are perceived by the victim, the perpetrator and/or their perspective community as sexual in nature."[12]

International documents offer us a list of potential acts that can be understood as sexual. For instance, the United Nations human rights High Commissioner names "rape, sexual abuse, forced pregnancy, forced sterilization, forced abortion, forced prostitution, trafficking, sexual enslavement, forced castration and forced nudity" as sexual violence acts.[13] On that line, *Berlo and Ploem*[14] confirm that "sexual violence can occur in different activities: from unwanted sexual behavior to assault and rape." According to them those actions also can be gender-based violence, rape, sexual abuse, sexual harassment, domestic violence, intimate partner violence, female genital mutilation, human trafficking, corrective rapes, conflict-based sexual violence and many others.[15] Regardless of which definition we observe, or action find prescribed as sexual violence in national law, it can be said that those acts can be committed by and against any person regardless of their age sex or gender,[16] at any time,[17] and in any environment including martial familiar and intimate relations.[18] Although there is still no universal definition of sexual violence or a list of its actions, these abovementioned definitions and lists are useful for the national legislator so that we can follow the idea and/or recommendations and consider their regulation within the national law.

Sexual violence in any of its forms has far-reaching consequences on the individual (psychological and physical) and community levels[19] for their victim. It always brings individual consequences and like no other criminal offense correlates potential community-level consequences to the level of maturity of the society the victim belongs to. Not only does it affect the image the victim has about themselves but also the image the victim has in their closer community among family, friends and colleagues. It brings economic consequences, isolation, and stigmatization for the victim. In addition to all these, it leaves deep psychological consequences such as fear, anxiety, and depression.[20] The feelings of shame and guilt[21] remain with the victim for as long as they live.[22] We can say that it changes (the quality of) life for a victim, deep to its roots.

Having in mind the gravity of its consequences, it is undisputed that (more effective) mechanisms of prevention of sexual violence that will provide effective outcomes must be brought. However, to *Carmody and Carrington*, "combating sexual violence is disagreeable to easy quick fit solutions so popular among politicians and crime prevention specialists."[23] Combating process is very challenging due to various factors. The most notorious ones include the particular nature of sexual violence commonly seen through its deep and close relationship to national legislation that may reflect traditional societies' approach to victimization; and the fact that sexual violence-related criminal offenses are part of the dark figure of crime as very often they remain unreported, which makes them be difficult to be measured.[24] The first element of its nature requires long-term solutions, that incorporate social reforms and shifts in gender roles in society and rising the awareness of negativity of any kind of violence including sexual violence and the requirement for its punishment. The second element of its nature is a byproduct of the first, as victims usually decide not to report sexual violence due to "inadequate support system, shame, fear of the risk of being retaliated, fear and risk of being blamed, fear and risk of not being believed, fear or risk of being mistreated."[25]

As sexual violence has been identified as a criminal offense from distant history, to nowadays, it is understandable that various mechanisms of its prevention[26] (including recidivism[27]) exist. According to *Carmody and Carrington*, mechanisms include, but are not exhausted in "law reforms, development of support services, the introduction of school education, videos, files, pamphlets, stickers, posters, billboards, journal articles, conferences, TV interviews, announcements, soap operas, training of professional staff and students, direct acts, public shaming, tree planting ceremonies."[28]

Consequently, in the theory and practice of law, five approaches to fighting against sexual violence have been developed so far: the feminist approach, human rights approach, criminal justice approach, medico-legal approach and public health approach.[29] While the feminist approach streams towards the examination of power relations and issues of patriarchy, the human rights approach sees sexual violence as a violation of human rights. As for the criminal justice approach, it is consumed in response by enforcing laws, while the last two correlate fight against sexual violence as a major goal for benefit of health as an aim of a global society.

Sexual violence, which is obviously a universal phenomenon, is a challenging issue in Bosnia and Herzegovina's reality. This country, just like the others, is decisive in detecting the best approach in the fight against sexual violence. Having in mind the idea of the above-mentioned criminal justice approach in the fight against sexual violence, this paper aims to critically inspect the positive criminal substantive law-legislative response against sexual violence in this country. The goal is to detect the potential weaknesses in the positive law legislation and to offer proposals of potential modification of *legi ferenda*, to achieve more effective prevention goals.

THE UNIQUE CASE OF BOSNIA AND HERZEGOVINA IN REACTION TO CRIME AND ITS IMPLICATIONS IN THE REGULATION OF SEXUAL VIOLENCE

According to the data from the Agency for Statistics of Bosnia and Herzegovina, for the last five years (2017–2021), the rates of sexual violence in Bosnia Herzegovina are moving variably. From 2017 until 2020 the rates were continuously growing. For example, in 2017 there were 156 cases, in 2018 157 cases, and in 2019 194 cases. In 2020 the rates dropped to 155 cases,[30] but in 2021 they increased to 210 cases of sexual violence in Bosnia and Herzegovina.[31]

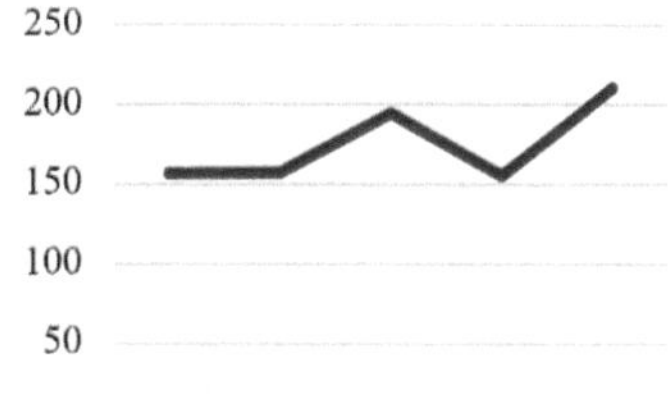

	2017	2018	2019	2020	2021
The number of cases of sexual violence in Bosnia and Herzegovina	156	157	194	155	210

Figure 7.1. The number of cases of sexual violence in Bosnia and Herzegovina. *Source*: Figure 7.1 is created by the Author, with the data from Agency for Statistics BH, Yearbook, 2022.

In all these cases, most perpetrators were adults.[32] The rates are visible in the figure below.[33]

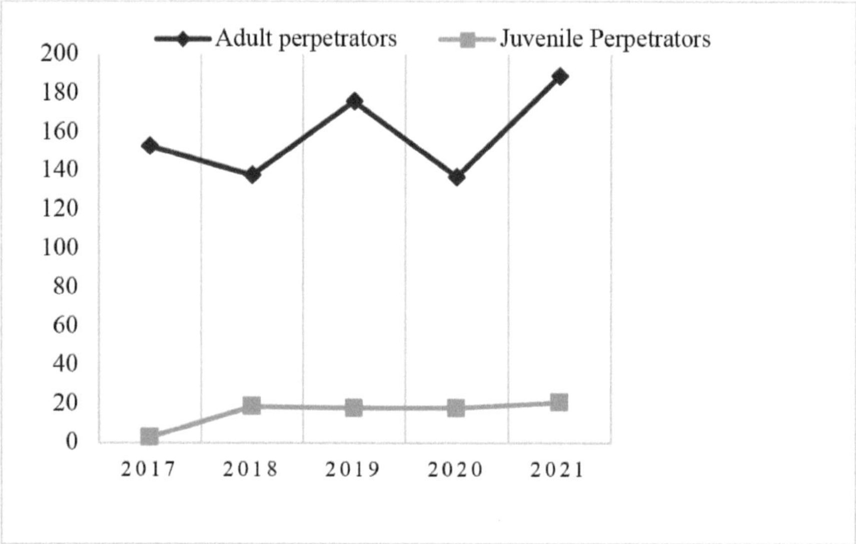

Figure 7.2. Age differentiation of perpetrators. *Source*: Figure 7.2 is created by the Author, with the data of the Agency for Statistics BH, Yearbook, 2022.

The abovementioned decrease in the rates for one year occurred during the Covid 19 pandemic. That may coincide with the fact that many of the crime opportunity factors of sex offenses were restricted or observed at that time, particularly with the lockdown. However, new growth indicates that the drop was only in appearance, and that still the prevention goals are not being achieved.

When compared with the general rates of crime in Bosnia and Herzegovina, based on the retrieved statistical data, it can be concluded that sexual violence is not a dominant type of crime, as its contribution to the crime rates does not go above 1 percent. More particularly, the rate of sexual violence within the general crime in Bosnia and Herzegovina retrospectively: in 2017 represented 0.61 percent of the general crime rate, in 2018 represented 0.69 percent of the general crime rate, in 2019 represented 0.88 percent of the general crime rate, in 2020 represented 0.83 percent, and in 2021 was 0.96 percent of the general crime rate.[34] The concern, however, exists, as its contribution to overall crime evidently rises with the years, as a reflex of the tendency of the increase of sexual violence cases overall. In addition to that, the dark number of crimes is still a burning question of sexual violence, so it can be estimated that the real rates are much higher.

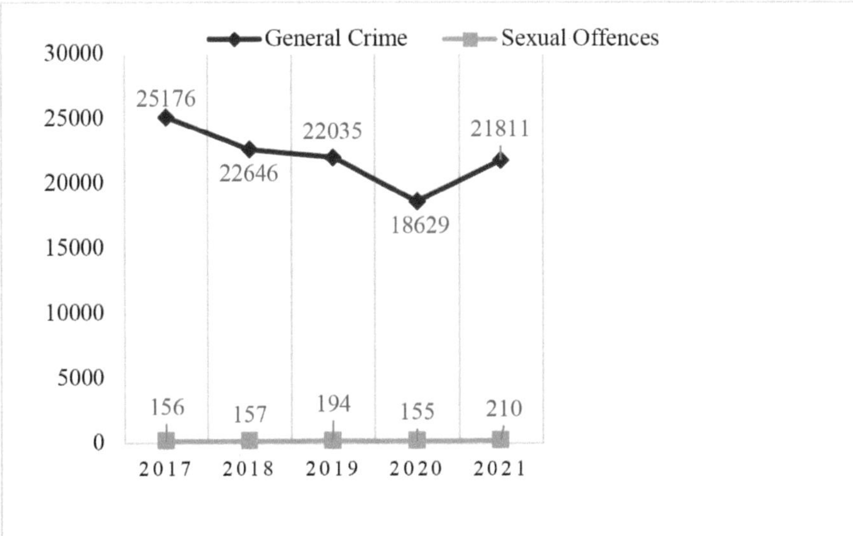

Figure 7.3. Correlation of general crime and sexual violence in Bosnia and Herzegovina (period 2017–2021). ***Source*: Figure 7.3 is created by the Author with the data from the Agency for Statistics BH, Yearbook, 2022.**

It can be concluded, from the statistical data offered, that although not the dominant type of crime in the general crime system in Bosnia and Herzegovina, sex offenses pose a worrying legal challenge, as their rates show a tendency to grow. Hence, it is necessary to inspect the state's approach towards this group of offenses and to establish if the approach may result in prevention.

LEGAL FRAMEWORK OF SEXUAL VIOLENCE: TWO SIDES OF A COIN

These figures confirm that the challenging process of finding the best response to sexual violence and overcoming the existing barriers on that path is present in Bosnia and Herzegovina, and it includes but is not limited to the issues of dealing with a high number of non-reported cases and the rise of rates of sexual violence in the last year. What is the cause of that situation, and does Bosnia and Herzegovina have a proper legislative response to it?

The specific state organization of Bosnia and Herzegovina that sources in Annex IV of the Peace Agreement (Constitution of Bosnia and Herzegovina) and the distribution of competencies between the State of Bosnia and

Herzegovina, two entities: the Federation of Bosnia and Herzegovina and Republika Srpska, and the Brčko District have been reflected on the criminal law legislation, given that there are four criminal (substantive) codes in force in Bosnia and Herzegovina. Those are: "Criminal Code of Bosnia and Herzegovina,"[35] "Criminal Code of Federation of Bosnia and Herzegovina,"[36] "Criminal Code of Republika Srpska,"[37] "Criminal Code of Brčko District BH."[38] Following the systematic interpretation of the way criminal law is regulated in Bosnia and Herzegovina, and the jurisdictions of the state, entity and district, the topic of sexual violence (crimes against sexual freedom and morality), is regulated through the entity and district criminal codes.[39] All three codes have similarities and differences in regulation of the same topic and further in the text, we will discuss them.

Prescribed Sex Offenses

The Criminal Code of the Federation of Bosnia and Herzegovina sexual offenses in Chapter XIX named "criminal offenses against sexual freedoms and dignity." These appear as rape, sexual intercourse with a helpless person, sexual intercourse with abuse of position, coercion to sexual intercourse, sexual intercourse with a child, indecent activities, the satisfaction of lust in front of a child or minor, inducing prostitution, exploiting a child or minor for pornography, introducing a child to pornography, trafficking in human beings, incest.[40] A similar list of offenses is offered within Chapter 15 (offenses against sexual liberty and moral) of the Criminal Code of Brčko District, as it prescribes: "rape, sexual intercourse with a helpless person, sexual intercourse by abuse of position, coercion to sexual intercourse, sexual intercourse with a child, indecent acts, the gratification of lust in front of a child or a minor for cutting inducing prostitution, exploitation of a child and minor for pornography,"[41] introducing a child to pornography, incest, human trafficking and organized human trafficking.[42]

The Criminal Code of Republika Srpska differs regarding passive subjects when prescribing these offenses and prescribes them in two chapters: as offenses against sexual integrity (referring to adults as passive subjects)[43] and offenses of sexual exploitation and abuse of a child. When it comes to situations in which the adults are potential passive subjects, offenses rape, sexual blackmail, sexual harassment, abuse of a vulnerable person, abuse of position, solicitation of prostitution, and indecent acts are prescribed. Finally, Chapter 15[44] describes sexual intercourse with a child under the age of 15, sexual abuse of a child over the age of 15, inveiglement of a child to attend sexual activities, exploiting children to pornography, exploiting children to pornographic performances, introducing a child to pornography inducing prostitution, satisfying the sexual needs in front of children, using a computer network or communication by other technical means to commit criminal acts of sexual abuse or exploitation of a child, as a set of offenses that may be perpetrated against children.

Systematically observed, the approach of all three codes to separate these criminal offenses into a particular group illustrates their recognized importance. It is an even better solution in Republika Srpska to further split these offenses regarding potential passive subjects, which makes space for more comprehensive legislative work. If critically observed, decentralization and split jurisdiction in criminal affairs may not be the best approach for one state, as it may lead to different legislative solutions within each part of the state, which is the subject of our interest in the further text.

Differences in the Criminalization

From the given list of offenses that had been prescribed in Bosnia and Herzegovina, it is visible that some criminal offenses are common in the entire territory. However, the list also demonstrates that some actions are criminalized only in one part of the territory, while others are not criminal offenses. Sexual harassment, for example, is criminalized only in Republika Srpska, but not in the Federation of Bosnia and Herzegovina and Brčko District BH. Many international sources of law, including the *Council of Europe Convention on preventing and combating violence against women and domestic violence* (Istanbul Convention), define sexual harassment and recommend member states to prescribe it within their national criminal law as a criminal offense.[45] Bosnia and Herzegovina is a state which has ratified the Istanbul Convention, and so far, this act has been criminalized only partially in one part of the State. Knowing the deep consequences of sexual harassment and the fact that it is commonly present in an everyday life, it is necessary that Federal and District legislators follow the recommendation about criminalization of that act as a criminal offense, as well.[46]

Sexual harassment, which is a new offense in the criminal law in Bosnia and Herzegovina, according to the Criminal Code of Republika Srpska is defined as "sexual harassment of another person who is in a relationship of subordination or dependence or who is particularly vulnerable due to age, illness, disability, addiction, pregnancy, or has severe physical or mental disabilities."[47]According to Šikman, "The criminal-political goal of this incrimination is to sanction and to prevent sexual activity harassment aimed at violating the dignity of the person in the sphere of sexual life, and which causes fear or creates a hostile, humiliating or offensive environment."[48] The essential elements of the body of this crime are a particular relationship between the perpetrator and victim, in which the perpetrator is in a superior position compared to the passive subject or a particular condition of the passive subject (due to its age or health condition). Consequently, it can be concluded that the perpetrator may be only a person who is superior to the passive subject and the passive subject may be only the person who is subordinated to the perpetrator or who carries the above-mentioned conditions that make them be in a relationship of dependence with the perpetrator. The act of harassment can be performed verbally, physically and non-verbally.[49] The criminal sanction prescribed for this criminal offense is imprisonment for up to two years.[50]

Another offense that *per nomen* is missing in the Federal and District codes but is present in the Republika Srpska Code is sexual blackmail.[51] It consists of "coercion to sexual intercourse or equal sexual activity by threatening to reveal something about the person or their close ones, that would damage their honor or reputation or threat of some other grave evil."[52] When compared to the offense *coercion to sexual intercourse* in the Federal and District Codes[53], it is obvious that the actions are similar, but sexual blackmail is prescribed in a more precise and wider manner, in a sense that it does not include only the threat with the grave evil, but emphasizes the potential in damaging the honor or reputation of the passive subjects.[54] So, that means, the same/similar action is prescribed by all three codes, but under different names and the latter one is prescribed in the wider sense which should be affirmatively noted as it incorporates wider grounds of incrimination. According to *Adžajlić-Dedović and others,* that harmonization would better lead to the full harmonization with international standards and primarily with the Istanbul Convention.[55]

The fact that some offenses cannot be identified by their name in all three codes, but there is a need for them to be deeply analyzed and so that their similarities may be noted is confirmed by the decision of the legislator of Republika Srpska to separate sexual offenses against children and juveniles into a special chapter. Systematically observed, this motion emphasized as below:

> The importance of protection of this vulnerable group from sexual violence, as they were singled out as the subject of protection of the entire chapter of the Code; dedication of the whole chapter of the Code only to those crimes of sexual violence, in which the potential victims might be children (and minors), from the nomo-technical point of view, provided sufficient opportunity for more detailed prescription of the acts of those crimes; positive examples of comparative law have been followed.[56]

However, when comparing the *lex priori* in Republika Srpska and the other positive criminal substantive codes in Bosnia and Herzegovina, only two new offenses prescribed within this chapter appear, while other criminal offenses already existed in other codes, but the aggravating circumstances due to the age of passive subject (children or juveniles) are extracted as separate offenses with new titles, leaving the ones prescribed with adult passive subjects in the form and the chapter they already were. Therefore, substantially new criminal offenses prescribed by the Criminal Code of Republika Srpska, which are not prescribed by the other two positive criminal codes are *inveiglement of a child to attend sexual activities*[57] and *exploitation of a computer network or communicating with other technical means for committing crimes of sexual abuse or exploitation of a child.*[58]

While *inveiglement of a child to attend sexual activities* incriminates engagement of a child to attend a rape, sexual intercourse or equivalent sexual activity, and its prescription was made to protect children from moral and mental corruption, the second offense has been prescribed as a result of the worldwide motion of prevention of online grooming, an offense which became an issue of concern due to its increased frequency.[59] Many international documents which have been ratified by Bosnia and Herzegovina, including the *Council of Europe's Convention on the Protection of Children against Sexual Exploitation and Sexual Abuse,* briefly known as the Lanzarote Convention, in Chapter VI, and the *Convention on Cybercrime* (2007) recommend criminalization of that action. Obviously, by incriminating it only in Republika Srpska, it can be inferred that that recommendation has been fulfilled only partially in the territory of Bosnia and Herzegovina. This criminal offense, according to Art. 178 of the Criminal Code of Republika Srpska, is prescribed in its basic and aggravated form.[60] The basic form consists of two-act action: "arranging a meeting with a child over the age of fifteen, by a computer network or communication or other technical means, to perform a sexual intercourse or to produce pornographic material or other forms of sexual exploitation and appears at an agreed location for a meeting."[61] "The essential element of the body of this crime is its motive: sexual intercourse or with it equalized sexual act or production of pornography."[62] Perpetrators may be punished by imprisonment from one to five years. According to paragraph 2 of the same Article, the aggravated form of this criminal offense would exist in the case that the same above-mentioned action would be perpetrated against a child who is younger than 15 years of age. Consequently, the sanction is harder for this form, and it is imprisonment from two to eight years.

What's more, from the comparative analysis of the relevant chapter on positive criminal codes in Bosnia and Herzegovina, it is visible that the Federal and District criminal codes categorized incest as an offense against sexual dignity and morals. The Republic Criminal Code categorizes it as an offense against the family. It can be said that it is prescribed by all three criminal codes, but the object of protection is differently valued as the two codes find the prevailing value to be sexual dignity and morality, and the latter to be the family. Similarly, the offense of trafficking in human beings fits into the section of crimes against sexual dignity and morality in both Federation of Bosnia and Herzegovina and Brčko District of Bosnia and Herzegovina, while it is part of a different chapter in Republika Srpska named Crimes against liberties and rights of citizens.[63] The first two found the motive as a value, which has sexual nature, as the prevailing one to fit into this group of offenses, while the latter code finds the consequence that is mirrored in violation of humans' liberty as the prevailing value to be protected.

A Few Remarks about the Nature of Prescription of the Sexual Offenses in Bosnia and Herzegovina

Regardless of their differences in the criminalization of sexual violence, all three positive criminal codes have the same or similar approach to the nature of sexual offenses.[64]

- All sexual offenses prescribed in them are stipulated as unisexual per their nature, which means that they may be perpetrated by any person, regardless of their gender, and they may be perpetrated against any person, regardless of their gender. Further, excluding the offenses where the relationship between the active and passive subject is an essential element of the body of criminal offense (for example sexual intercourse with the use of power, sexual blackmail, etc.), the nature of the relationship does not exclude the punitivity of the action, moreover, it qualifies it. These two facts are of a newer history of criminal thought in Bosnia and Herzegovina, taken that the last criminal code of the Socialist Republic of Bosnia and Herzegovina (1977), which was brought before the reformer criminal codes (from 1998 and onwards), clearly prescribed that rape could have been perpetrated only against female with whom the perpetrator is not married.[65] That implied that men could not be victims of rape, and that rape could not be committed in marriage. Since the reality confirmed otherwise, and the international motion of unisexualization of sexual violence made its results, we can now testify to the existence of the unisexual provision in the Bosnian and Herzegovinian positive criminal law.[66] So, through time, something that was "considered to be a private issue, became a public issue."[67]
- Most sexual offenses are prescribed through their basic and aggravated forms. Aggravating circumstances are mostly the age of the passive subject (child under 14/15 years of age, child over 14 years of age), motive

(hate), aggravating *modus operandi* (multiply perpetrated action against the same passive subject or by humiliating the victim, or by violating the relationship of trust, etc.), the relationship between perpetrator and victim (dependence), aggravating consequences (death, bodily injuries).[68]

- When it comes to crime policy, it is known that *poenalia sunt restriguenda,* therefore, the recommendable comparison of criminal sanctions should be criminal offense *per* offense. However, from a more general approach, it can be said that the prevailing type of criminal sanction is imprisonment. The heavier criminal sanctions overall are being prescribed by the Criminal Code of Republika Srpska in a dual sense: not only does it prescribe a longer term of imprisonment than the other two codes, but also very often cumulatively prescribes imprisonment and monetary fine as sanctions for particular criminal offenses. The Federal and the District criminal codes are more harmonized in criminal politics.

Diversity of Approaches in the Establishment of Sexual Registries in Bosnia and Herzegovina

Apart from the prescription of sexual criminal offenses, the establishment of sex offender registries takes an important part in the discourse about the prevention of sexual violence and the challenges that many countries face within that context. The idea of prevention of the crime of its repetition and the favorable approach of the victim who wishes to know if the sex offender is near them, as the two most notorious arguments for their establishment,[69] sex offender registries have been established in many countries in the world.[70] Furthermore, many international documents, such are *Resolution 1733/10 of the European Parliament on Reinforcing Measures Against Sex Offenders, Directive 2011/92/EU on Combating Sexual Abuse of Children and Child Exploitation and Child Pornography and the Convention of Council of Europe on the Protection of Children from Sexual Exploitation and Sexual Abuse*, Recommendation CM/Rec (2021) 6 of the Committee of Ministers to member States regarding the assessment, management and reintegration of persons accused or convicted of a sexual offense, recommend their establishment.[71]

Sex offender registries have been established only partially in Bosnia and Herzegovina, since they have been established only through the *Code on the Special Registry of Convicted Persons for Sexual Abuse and Exploitation of Children*[72] in 2018, but not through the *legispeciali* of other levels of authority in Bosnia and Herzegovina. Federation of Bosnia and Herzegovina and Brčko District do not have a special code that establishes a particular sex offenders registry, thus, the general provisions of the applicable criminal codes related to the universal criminal registries of all offenses, whose entries are erasable with the flow of the time (*ex offo*), are the one that is being applied.[73] However, with the establishment of the sex offender registry in Republika Srpska[74] and with the impact of the international community, the awareness about the benefit of such a register has been raised,[75] so the draft of the same-named code has been adopted by the parliament, but the proposal of the Code has been adopted only by one of the houses of the Parliament of Federation of Bosnia and Herzegovina. Until it is accepted by the other house of the Parliament, the establishment of the registry is still on standby status for the Federation of Bosnia and Herzegovina and remains unregulated.[76]

The republic *Code on the Special Registry of Convicted Persons for Sexual Abuse and Exploitation of Children* has been brought with the aim "to protect children from sexual abuse and exploitation and to protect convicted people from recidivism."[77] The data that is being obtained by the Ministry of Internal Affairs, based on this code, are permanent and they store the data about all sex offenders who were convicted of criminal offenses from Chapter XV of the Criminal Code of Republika Srpska.[78] Although established with the purpose to achieve the flow of information about sexual offenses so that in future they may be prevented, this Code has a "middle path" approach, as it allows access to this data only to relevant institutions, not to a wider public, as some sex offender registries throughout the world do.[79]

It is important to wonder if the purpose and the idea of establishing sex offender registries, which can be technically achieved with the flow of information about sex offenders in one country was achieved with the establishment of such a registry within only part of its territory. Sex offenders from the Federation of Bosnia and Herzegovina and Brčko District would not be part of it. Alternatively, in the international environment, sharing information about sex offenders as a part of legal aid, only for part of the territory of one state does not achieve the purpose of such collaboration as the data are not full. For the purpose of achieving its aim, it is necessary to bring sex offender registry at the Federal and District levels, as the optimum solution of the State Sex Offenders Registry is unachievable due to the particular distribution of jurisdiction among the state and entities in the criminal matters.

CONCLUSION

This paper confirms that Bosnia and Herzegovina approached most responsibly in the fight against sexual violence, its legislative endeavors within the criminal justice system illustrate that it has recognized certain behaviors as criminal offenses and has prescribed criminal sanctions for them. The state in practice has justified it, as the statistics show the tendency of the rise of sex offenses committed dominantly by adults, which however are not a dominant type of offenses in the system of crime in Bosnia and Herzegovina. The severity of the approach is confirmed by the fact that Bosnia and Herzegovina has ratified the most important international sources that are related to the fight against sexual violence. However, when analyzing the legislative and overall criminal law approach, it is visible that one of the most notorious challenges that prevent the efficient fight against sexual violence is the specific distribution of criminal law jurisdiction in the state and the *lack of harmonization* in regulation among the positive criminal laws.

Lack of the harmonization is visible on several levels. First, an unharmonized incrimination of actions as offenses exists. Although that lack of harmonization is not present between the Federal and District Criminal Codes, it is evident between them on one hand, and the Criminal Code of Republika Srpska. Not only has it prescribed completely new offenses, just in accordance with the ratified international documents and contemporary criminal law motions but it approaches the juvenile victims of sexual offenses carefully and prescribes sexual criminal offenses perpetrated against them in a separate chapter.

Having certain actions prescribed to be criminal offenses only in one part of the territory of the same country sends a controversial message to both potential perpetrators and victims. Potential victims are not being protected as the act is not criminalized to be prevented. Further, that refers only to part of the citizens of the same country—the ones in the territory of the Federation of Bosnia and Herzegovina and Brčko District BH. The ones in the territory of Republika Srpska are protected as the basis of prevention exists with the positive code. Alternatively, the same rules for the potential perpetrators. Just for being from Republika Srpska, the act is punishable, while if being from the Federation of Bosnia and Herzegovina and Brčko District, there is no punishability for the same action as the other two codes are applicable, and they do not prescribe certain acts as criminal. That brings discrimination among citizens of the same state and brings legal uncertainty. Similarly, the lack of harmonization among those three criminal codes is visible in crime policies, as it is stricter in Republika Srpska. Consequently, although in that case the acts are both criminalized and are similar, criminal sanctions are different.

Finally, when it comes to the sex offender registry, the lack of harmonization of the approach is visible here as well. It must be brought urgently at the Federal and District level, following the example of the Code of Republika Srpska. Without those two, the purpose of each one of them individually cannot be accomplished and the potential for criminal prevention of this group of criminal offenses cannot be achieved in its full capacity.

NOTES

1. '"He Took Her to the Parking . . ." An Interview with a Mother of a Teenage Girl, Telling Us the Horrifying Details' *Avaz* (7 May 2022) <https://vecernjenovosti.ba/70402/hronika/detalji-silovanje-sarajevo-tinejdzerka-najnovije-vijesti/> accessed November 2, 2022.

2. *T04 0 KT 0047277 21, Indictment* (Prosecutorial Office of Zenica).

3. Hereinafter OSCE.

4. *Well-being and safety of women OSCE-led survey on violence against women: Bosnia and Herzegovina - results report* (OSCE 2019) iii.

5. Example of the state's approach to fighting sexual violence is detectable even in Hammurabi's Code (named after ruler Hammurabi 1792–1750 B.C), which prescribed death punishment for an individual who would commit sexual violence over a female in her father's house. See more: Ena Kazić, *Seksualnonasilje u savremenomkrivičnompravu* (International University of Sarajevo 2020) 67.

6. Moira Carmody and Kerry Carrington, 'Preventing Sexual Violence?' (2000) 33 (3) Australian and New Zealand Journal of Criminology341, 346; World Health Organization established that one in three women experienced sexual violence during their life. That means that 30 percent of women in the world experience sexual violence. See: 'Violence against Women' (*World Health Organization*) <Violence against women, https://www.who.int/news-room/fact-sheets/detail/violence-against-women#:~:text=Estimates%20published%20by%20WHO%20indicate,violence%20is%20intimate%20partner%20violence.> accessed February 9, 2022. However, in this discourse, it is important to remember that men can be victims as well, as this group of criminal offenses is unisexual.

7. Lana Wells and others, *Primary Prevention of Sexual Violence: Preliminary Research to Support a Provincial Action Plan* (Shift, The University of Calgary 2012) 7.

8. Willy Van Berlo and Rachel Ploem, *Sexual Violence-Knowledge File* (Rutgers 2018) 3.

9. 'Sexual and Gender-Based Violence in the Context of Transitional Justice.'

10. 'Violence against Women' (*World Health Organization*) <Violence against women, https://www.who.int/news-room/fact-sheets/detail/violence-against-women#:~:text=Estimates%20published%20by%20WHO%20indicate,violence%20is%20intimate%20partner%20violence.> accessed February 9, 2022.

11. Antonio Gutierrez, 'Antonio Gutierrez on Sexual Violence' (*United Nations*, 19 March 2017) <https://www.un.org/sg/en>accessed January 6, 2022.

12. 'The Hague Principles on Sexual Violence' <https://4genderjustice.org/ftp-files/publications/The-Hague-Principles-on-Sexual-Violence.pdf> accessed June 25, 2022 5–8.

13. 'Sexual and Gender-Based Violence in the Context of Transitional Justice' 1.

14. Van Berlo and Ploem(n 8)3.

15. Van Berlo and Ploem(n 8)4–5.

16. 'THE HAGUE PRINCIPLES ON SEXUAL VIOLENCE' <https://4genderjustice.org/ftp-files/publications/The-Hague-Principles-on-Sexual-Violence.pdf> ac-

cessed June 25, 2022 8, and Ena Kazić, *Seksualnonasilje u savremenomkrivičnompravu* (International University of Sarajevo 2020) 26.

17. Ibid 8.

18. Ibid 8.

19. Van Berlo and Ploem (n 8) 3.

20. Evelyne Josse, 'They Came with Two Guns.: The Consequences of Sexual Violence for the Mental Health of Women in Armed Conflicts' (2010) 182–187.

21. Imran Zafarzai and Aimal Amiri, 'Clinical and Psychological Consequences of Sexual Assault' (2021) 11 International Journal of Academic Research in Business and Social Sciences 433, 437–438.

22. Josse (n 20) 177–187; 'Violence against Women' (*World Health Organization*) <Violence against women, https://www.who.int/news-room/fact-sheets/detail/violence-against-women#:~:text=Estimates%20published%20by%20WHO%20indicate,violence%20is%20intimate%20partner%20violence.> accessed February 9, 2022.

23. Carmody and Carrington (n 6) 344.

24. Wells and others (n 7) 12.

25. Claudia Gracia Moreno, Alessandra Guedes and Wendy Knerr, 'Understanding and Addressing Violence against Women' <https://apps.who.int/iris/handle/10665/77432>accessed June 25, 2022 1.

26. There are three types of prevention of sexual violence: primary prevention, secondary prevention and tertiary prevention. While primary prevention refers to all actions and mechanisms of prevention of critical event to happen in the first place (which includes education about sexual violence, impact of gender roles, healthy relationships), secondary prevention is the response upon the critical event. The tertiary prevention refers to a long-term care in the wake of the violence. See more Wells and others (n 7)10–18.

27. Natalija Lukić, 'Empirijska Analiza Recidivizma Seksualnih Prestupnika' (2015) LXIII Anali Pravnog fakulteta u Beogradu 174, 175.

28. Carmody and Carrington (n 6) 346.

29. Wells and others (n 7) 28–30.

30. The decrease in the number of cases may coincide with the Covid Pandemics.

31. 'Demography and Social Statistics' (Agency for Statistics of Bosnia and Herzegovina 2021) Priopćenje X <https://bhas.gov.ba/> 3.

32. Ibid. 2.

33. Although juveniles do not incline to be the dominant sex offender group in Bosnia and Herzegovina, cases of their perpetration do happen. In practice, a liberating verdict in a case in which three juveniles had been accused of raping a juvenile female is particularly interesting for its reasoning part. Allegedly, they raped her in an apartment and took photos of her during the act, and afterward threatened her they would share it with her acquaintances. After the evidential stage of the criminal procedure was terminated, the court was not convinced beyond a reasonable doubt of the existence of coercion during the intercourse. The court did not find "pulling her hand" as an act of coercion and in addition to that, has established that she blamed the three defendants for rape when she heard they had her photos, and not before that.

The court found that fact as a reason to doubt the allegations of the passive subject and set the defendants free. *65 0 Km 430959 14 Km Verdict* (Municipality Court of Sarajevo, dated from 04/12/2014)

34. 'Demography and Social Statistics' (n 31) 1–3.

35. Criminal code of Bosnia and Herzegovina [3/03, 32/03, 37/03, 54/04, 61/04, 30/05, 53/06, 55/06, 32/07, 8/10] 74.

36. Criminal Code of Federation of Bosnia and Herzegovina [36/2003, 21/2004 -ispr.69/2004, 18/2005, 42/2010, 42/2011, 59/2014, 76/2014, 46/2016, 75/2017].

37. Criminal Code of Republika Srpska [64/2017, 104/2018, 15/21, 89/21].

38. Criminal Code of Brčko District of Bosnia and Herzegovina [6/05, 21/10, 9/13, 26/16, 13/17, 50/18, 19/20].

39. Ena Kazić- Çakar, 'A Brief Discourse About the Need For Criminalization of Online Grooming in Bosnia And Herzegovina' (2021) 18 Balkan Social Science Review 167, 171.

40. Criminal Code of Federation of Bosnia and Herzegovina (n 36) Arts. 203–213.

41. One of the most notorious *modiopperandi* of the offense "exploitation of a child and minor for pornography" is the use of the internet. In case 65 0 K 189121 12 K, P.S. was found guilty of committing this offense, based on the search of his laptop. In verdict number 65 0 K 189121 12 K of the Municipality Court of Sarajevo, dated October 13, 2013, it is stated that based on the laptop inspection it was established that "he accessed the website "buildarecipe.co.uk," where were photos of children with pornographic content, on which he recorded (downloaded) said photos, obtained them, i.e. according to the findings and opinion of the forensic expert from August 10, 2012., it follows that in the photographs number 8.T1.1.1 to 8.T1.1.41, content depicting persons of minor age in erotic contexts can be seen, and under number 8.T1.1.53, a digital video recording of pornographic content of an underage female actor and a dog." *65 0 K 189121 12 K, Verdicit* (Municipality Court of Sarajevo, dated October 13, 2013).

42. Criminal Code of Brčko District BH (n 38) Arts. 200–210.

43. Criminal Code of Republika Srpska (n 37) Arts.165–172.

44. Criminal Code of Republika Srpska (n 37) Arts. 172–181.

45. 'Council of Europe Convention on Preventing and Combating Violence Against Women and Domestic Violence' <https://primarysources.brillonline.com/browse/human-rights-documents-online/council-of-europe-convention-on-preventing-and-combating-violence-against-women-and-domestic-violence;hrdhrd99532014005> accessed September 25, 2022, Art. 40.

46. *Čengić and others* also highly recommend this offense to be incriminated in the other two criminal codes in Bosnia and Herzegovina, Nejra Čengić and others, *Krivična Djela Silovanja i Ostalog Seksualnog Nasilja u Bosni i Hercegovini* (First ed, Sarajevski otvoreni centar 2017) 27, 45.

47. Criminal Code of Republika Srpska (n 37) Art 170 (1).

48. Mile Šikman, 'Analiza Usklađenosti Zakona i Politika Republike Srpske s Međunarodnim Standardima u Vezi Sa Seksualnim Uznemiravanjem' (Fondacija Udružene žene 2021) 5, 18.

49. Ibid. 6.

50. Criminal Code of Republika Srpska (n 37) Art 170 (1).

51. Ibid. Art. 166.

52. Ibid.

53. Criminal offense Coercion to sexual intercourse, article 206 of the Criminal Code of Federation of Bosnia and Herzegovina reads: „Whoever forces another person to have sexual intercourse or a serious sexual act equated with it by threatening some serious evil, will be punished by imprisonment from six months to five years."

54. A case of sexual blackmail has been reported to the Ministry of Internal Affairs of Doboj (Republika Srpska) in September 2022. The resident of Doboj agreed to meet with an unknown woman from Ivory Coast. When they established a video connection, they agreed to be naked in front of cameras and to show genitalia. After the meeting, the resident of Doboj received a message from the woman that she recorded a video of him and required him to pay her 500 Euros so that she would not send the video to his family. See: https://www.rtvbn.com/4032075/ubijedila-ga-da-pokaze-polni-organ-onda-ga-ucjenjivala accessed November 2, 2022.

55. Azra AdžajlićDedović and ŠejlaDrpljanin, 'Priručnik Za Postupanje u SlučajevimaRodnozasnovanog I SeksualnogNasiljaNadŽenamaiDjecom -Za Policiju, TužiteljeiSudije' (Udruženje 'Zemljadjece u BiH' 2018) 52.

56. Ena Kazić, 'Brief Overview of Novelties Within the New Criminal Code of Republika Srpska Regarding Legal Protection of Children and Juveniles from Sexual Violence' (2020) 1 Iliria International Review 193.

57. Criminal Code of Republika Srpska (n 37) Art 174.

58. Ibid, Art. 178.

59. World Health Organization estimates there are "200 million children that are being sexually abused online" in 'Child Online Safety Report' (2011) UNESCO 2.

60. According to the statistics of the Government of Republika Srpska, in the previous year, one offense was reported. The Government recommends parents to pair with their childrens smartphones and computers and to always have an insight in their online activities. See more: https://mup.vladars.net/lat/index.php?vijest=vtk&id=28245&vrsta=aktuelnosti.

61. Ibid.

62. Kazić- Çakar (n 39) 172.

63. Criminal Code of Republika Srpska (n 37) Art. 145.

64. Čengić and others (n46) 45 also agree about the fact that the Criminal Code of Republika Srpska has differences when compared with the Federal and District Criminal codes. They find the harmonization to be crucial in further legislative modifications.

65. Kazić (n 5) 95.

66. However, *Čengić and others* criticizes the existing regulation which silently includes spouses into the group of potential passive subjects. According to her, that should be specified. See Čengić and others (n 46) 42.

67. Carmody and Carrington (n 6) 342.

68. Zvonimir Tomić, *Krivično pravo II—posebni dio (Criminal Law II—special part)* (University of Sarajevo 2007) 110.

69. Opposite arguments, against their establishment, involve the labeling theories, isolation, negative economic, social, and psychological impact on the ex-convict, and the never-ending question of why a person should be labeled for life if they have already paid their debt to society by being punished for that criminal offense. Elizabeth J Letourneau and others, 'Evaluating the Effectiveness of Sex Offender Registration and Notification Policies for Reducing Sexual Violence against Women' 9.

70. Most of the sex offender's registries laws were initially brought as a result of cruel sexual offenses that had been perpetrated in those countries. The public exerted pressure on the authorities to change the attitude toward sex offenders, and to take more decisive measures to prevent such crimes. The USA is one of the pioneer countries establishing such a registry through *Jacob Wetterling Crimes Against Children and Sexually Violent Registry Act* in 1994. The Act was named after a child Jacob Wetterling who was a victim of such a crime. Many federal codes were brought by the time with the same aim. Well known is *Californian Megan's Law*, which brought the obligation of public notification of perpetrators of sexual offenses. See more: California Megan's Law Website. In: California Megan's Law Website. Similarly, the Serbian *Marija's Code* was grounds for the establishment of sex offender registries. Afterward, positive outcomes of already established sex offender registries resulted in international and regional documents recommending the establishment of such registries, particularly in order to protect children. See more: Elizabeth J Letourneau and others, 'Evaluating the Effectiveness of Sex Offender Registration and Notification Policies for Reducing Sexual Violence against Women' 9 and Tom Condon, 'Sex Offender registry: More harm than good?,' The CT Mirror [online]. (2018) <https://ctmirror.org/2018/05/21/sex-offender-registry-harm-good/> accessed December 12, 2020.

71. See more: Ena Kazić, 'Yes or no to Sex Offender Registries? Lessons for Bosnia and Herzegovina' (2021) The Lawyer Quarterly 440, 447.

72. The Code of Republika Srpska on the Special Registry of Convicted Persons for Sexual Abuse and Exploitation of Children [31/18].

73. Criminal Code of Federation of Bosnia and Herzegovina (n 36) Art. 125.

74. The Office of Ombudsperson for children of Republika Srpska acknowledges the importance of this code for the protection of children from sexual violence. However, it stated that this is only one of many other steps in their prevention. The office finds education and the rise of awareness about the problem to be equally important mechanisms in the prevention of this crime and in the protection of children. <https://www.etrafika.net/djeca-imaju-pravo/72345/registar-pedofila-bitan-ali-tu-ne-treba-stati/> accessed November 2, 2022.

75. For example, the Ministry of Internal Affairs of Republika Srpska periodically organizes educational sessions on this topic, visiting schools where the topic is being discussed. Novosti https://mup.vladars.net/index.php?vijest=informisanje_javnosti&vrsta=novosti accessed November 2, 2022.

76. The cases from the practice in the Federation indicate the need for the establishment of such registries. Recidivism and the young age of victims of sex offenses should be the most important arguments for their establishment in this part of Bosnia and Herzegovina. To illustrate, according to the municipality court verdict number

65 0 K 128387 10 K (July 8, 2010), a prior convict P.B. was found guilty of offense indecent activities that had been perpetrated in real concurrence. Namely, only in 10 days, he had approached with his car to 4 elementary schools, through the window of his car invited children passing by to see something in his car, and then showed them his genitalia. He was convicted of one year of imprisonment. Prohibiting such individuals' approach to educational institutions and keeping them in the records, would without any doubt increase their observance of them and decrease the potential for recidivism.*65 0 K 128387 10 K, Verdict* (Municipality Court of Sarajevo, dated 08.07.2010).

77. Ibid Art. 2.

78. Ibid Arts. 7–9.

79. For example, in the United States of America, the *Dru Sjodın national sex offender public website* offers data about sex offenders by a simple query. That, in other words, means that the data about the offenders are available to the wider public. That is what criticists of sex offender registry usually name as an argument against their establishment, as the data may be easily misused and also question why a person who has been punished and thus paid their debt to society, need to be tagged by their social environment and carries the burden of their act for life. See more in: Kazić (n 71) 440–458; Tom Condon, 'Sex Offender Registry: More Harm than Good?' CT Mirror <https://ctmirror.org/2018/05/21/sex-offender-registry-harm-good> accessed January 12, 2020.

BIBLIOGRAPHY

Adžajlić Dedović A and Drpljanin Š, 'Priručnik Za Postupanje u Slučajevima Rodno zasnovanog I Seksualnog Nasilja Nad Ženama I Djecom -Za Policiju, Tužitelje I Sudije' (Udruženje 'Zemlja djece u BiH' 2018)

Agency for Statistics of Bosnia and Herzegovina, *Demography and Social Statistics* (2021) <https://bhas.gov.ba/> accessed February 9, 2022.

Carmody M and Carrington K, 'Preventing Sexual Violence?' (2000) Australian and New Zealand Journal of Criminology 35.

Čengić N and others, *Krivična Djela Silovanja I Ostalog Seksualnog Nasilja u BosniiHercegovini* (First ed, Sarajevski otvoreni centar 2017).

Condon T, 'Sex Offender Registry: More Harm than Good?' CT Mirror <https://ctmirror.org/2018/05/21/sex-offender-registry-harm-good> accessed January 12, 2020.

Condon T, 'Sex Offender registry: More harm than good?' The CT Mirror [online] (2018) <https://ctmirror.org/2018/05/21/sex-offender-registry-harm-good/> accessed December 12, 2020.

Dobrobit i Blagostanje Žena. Bosna i Hercegovina-Izvješće Sa Rezultatima (OSCE 2019).

Gracia Moreno C, Guedes A and Knerr W, 'Understanding and Addressing Violence against Women' <https://apps.who.int/iris/handle/10665/77432> accessed June 25, 2022;

Gutierrez A, 'Antonio Gutierrez on Sexual Violence' (*United Nations*, 19 March 2017) <https://www.un.org/sg/en>accessed January 6, 2022.

'He Took Her to the Parking . . .—An Interview with a Mother of a Teenage Girl, Telling Us the Horrifying Details' *Avaz* (Sarajevo, 7 May 2022) <https://vecernjenovosti.ba/70402/hronika/detalji-silovanje-sarajevo-tinejdzerka-najnovije-vijesti/> accessed November 2, 2022.

Josse E, 'They Came with Two Guns: The Consequences of Sexual Violence for the Mental Health of Women in Armed Conflicts' (2010) 92 *International Review of the Red Cross* 19.

Kazić- Çakar E, 'A Brief Discourse About the Need For Criminalization of Online Grooming in Bosnia And Herzegovina' (2021) 18 Balkan Social Science Review 167.

Kazić E, '"Brief Overview of Novelties Within the New Criminal Code of Republika Srpska Regarding Legal Protection of Children and Juveniles from Sexual Violence"' (2020) 1 Iliria International Review 189.

Kazić E, 'Yes or No to Sex Offender Registries? Lessons for Bosnia and Herzegovina' (2021) The Lawyer Quarterly 19.

Kazić E, *Seksualno nasilje u savremenom krivičnom pravu* (International University of Sarajevo 2020).

Letourneau EJ and others, 'Evaluating the Effectiveness of Sex Offender Registration and Notification Policies for Reducing Sexual Violence against Women' 77.

Lukić N, 'EmpirijskaAnalizaRecidivizmaSeksualnihPrestupnika' (2015) LXIII AnaliPravnogfakulteta u Beogradu 174.

Muehlenhard C and Peterson Z, 'Conceptualizing Sexual Violence: Socially Acceptable Coercion and Other Controversies,' *The social psychology of good and evil* (AG Miller, Guilford 2004).

Research to Support a Provincial Action Plan (Shift, The University of Calgary 2012)

Šikman M, 'Analiza Usklađenosti Zakona I PolitikaRepublike Srpske s Međunarodnim Standardima u Vezi sa Seksualnim Uznemiravanjem' (Fondacija Udružene žene 2021).

Tomić Z, *Krivično pravo II—posebni dio (Criminal Law II—special part)* (University of Sarajevo 2007) 534.

UN Human Rights Office of High Commissionaire, *Sexual and Gender-Based Violence in the Context of Transitional Justice* (2014) 1.

UNESCO, *Child Online Safety Report* (2019) 84.

Van Berlo W and Ploem R, 'Sexual Violence-Knowledge File' (Rutgers 2018).

Wells L and others, *Primary Prevention of Sexual Violence: Preliminary Research to Support a Provincial Action Plan* (Shift, The University of Calgary 2012).

World Health Organization, *Violence against Women* <Violence against women, https://www.who.int/news-room/fact-sheets/detail/violence-against-women#:~:text=Estimates%20published%20by%20WHO%20indicate,violence%20is%20intimate%20partner%20violence.> accessed February 9, 2022.

Zafarzai I and Amiri A, 'Clinical and Psychological Consequences of Sexual Assault (2021) 11 International Journal of Academic Research in Business and Social Sciences 433.

8

Attrition in Sexual Offenses with Evidentiary Challenges

The Example of Türkiye

Rahime Erbaş, Neslihan Can, Ahsen Akdemir, and Selen Çakırhan

Consider the following case: A woman went to a beauty salon and had her hair cut by a hairdresser. The day after, she, with her two children, revisited the salon and told the hairdresser that his work made her unhappy since it was overcut contrary to her wish. He expressed that he would like to make up for this mistake by providing a hair mask and skin care, free of charge. She accepted the offer. Regarding her claim, she stated that while he was performing skin care on her face, he got too close to her face which irritated her, thus she warned him of staying not so close. He responded that he could only recognize the black spots in her face through such a close look, and suddenly, he kissed her on the lips. In the meantime, her children, who were in another room watching TV, did neither see them nor hear anything about the accident. Six days later, she filed a complaint with the criminal court. The hairdresser constantly denied the accusation.[1]

The central question of this case—through its journey from the first instance to the last instance court—was, whether the sexual assault had occurred or not, i.e., proving the incident's occurrence. The court of first instance sentenced the hairdresser to two years of imprisonment. Despite the defendant's denial, the court accepted the victim's statements as credible since her statements were made in a consistent manner throughout the entire proceeding, and it was observed that there is no reason for the victim to slander the defendant. The Court of Cassation (The Revision Court), *Yargıtay,* approved the conviction.[2] However, this reasoning did not clear all doubt for some of the judges. As such, the dissenting opinion argues that:

> Although the victim's statement represents the very key piece of evidence in proving sexual offenses, it is not sufficient to prove a point by itself. The defendant neutralizes the absence of a case in which the victim claims to exist, by claiming that it was not committed. In these cases, supporting (i.e., corroborating) evidence that confirms the victim's statement and increases the suitability of proof should be applied. If any indirect evidence could not be obtained despite all the best efforts, this time the victim's statement should be tested for its credibility and reliability. The conclusion should be reached by evaluating the statement evidence according to various criteria including logic, consistency, details, any previous hostility between the victim and the defendant, mode of delivery, and time of complaint.[3]

This is a very typical case of when a "he said—she said"[4] situation arises in proving processes.[5] The criminal justice authorities have to tread a fine line: If the victim's statement is taken into consideration, the authorities run the risk of violating *the presumption of innocence*, whereas if the defendant's statement is taken into consideration, they risk *an attrition,* which leads to the impunity of perpetrators in sexual offenses. Indeed, the Turkish Court of Cassation draws attention to the difficulty of proving sexual offenses as: "Sexual offenses are one of the most difficult crimes to prove in our criminal jurisdiction. The proof of these crimes is achieved through the reports and statements of the parties as well as the impression obtained during the hearings."[6]

Attrition in sexual offenses, as *a phenomenon,*[7] literally refers to the losses occurred at any stage from the reported/known point to the point of finalization. As aptly put by *Jehle*, attrition is "the 'loss' of cases within the criminal justice chain."[8] A loss from one stage to another within the entire system.[9] This chapter conceptualizes these losses as *case erosion in sexual offenses*, from police investigation to the pre-trial and from pre-trial to trial stage for a variety of the following reasons.[10] Difficulties in proving are among the reasons. The quality of evidence, in this respect, impacts the decisions of the public prosecutors to commence the investigation and the judgment of the court in finalizing the case. Because the discretionary power of the public prosecutor over whether to prosecute in Turkish criminal law is rare by virtue of the strong legality principle.

This chapter aims to demonstrate the Turkish law approach and solutions on difficulties of proving sexual offenses, particularly in situations, where the sole evidence is the statement by the victim. To analyze the current Turkish case-law on the matter, the chapter first shows the necessity of dismantling rape myths' impact on the necessity of proving as an unspoken impediment. Before proceeding further, it is required to provide an overview from Turkish evidence law. Then it questions the necessity of resistance, where consent turns into an object of proof. Because "most rape cases usually turn upon the issue of consent."[11] The chapter does not cover all types of sexual offenses, as defined in the Penal Code, but addresses only sexual assault against adults, including bodily sexual contact on the level of both touching (basic form) and organ penetration (aggravated form) as stipulated in Art. 102.

The chapter highlights the significance of corroborating the evidence. Corroboration may be found in many ways. But it has four main examples applied in a cumulative manner by the Turkish case-law. These are: modus operandi and time period for filing a complaint (1); whether the victim's statements are consistent throughout the process (2); natural flow of life: no previous hostility between the victim and the defendant (3); and finally, whether there is any reason for the victim to slander the defendant (4). To reach a judgment, satisfying only one of the elements is not sufficient, they only serve the function cumulatively. Then, the chapter offers some recently collected data from judicial statistics, covering the period of the last five years. Finally, it provides a set of concluding remarks as avenues for prospective studies.

THE IMPACT OF COMMON MYTHS ON SEXUAL OFFENSES ON PROVING

Common myths on sexual offenses, well-known as *rape myths*, were defined initially by *Burt* as "prejudicial, stereotyped, or false beliefs about rape, rape victims, and rapists,"[12] are of consequence in every-day life. People have faced them as they are handed down for generations as stubbornly persistent misconceptions. To illustrate, some well-known examples of these myths are, "women routinely lie about rape,"[13] "only certain women get raped"[14] and "all sexual assault victims report the crime immediately to the police." If they do not report it instantly or there is a delay in reporting it, then, the assumption being, they must have either changed their minds after it happened, want revenge, or do not want to look at as if they were sexually active.[15] According to *Leverick,* one can conceptually distinguish the constitutive elements of these myths into the following four main categories: as the beliefs blaming the victim, casting doubt on allegations, excusing the accused, and regarding what 'real rape' looks like.[16]

It is possible to observe these myths perpetuated in society such as media outlets, movies, and television shows, and in advertisements as well.[17] These all may have detrimental effects to some extent; however, when these victim blaming and perpetrator excusing myths have influence over the judiciary, this represents a serious impediment to the delivery of justice.[18] In their research, *Ellison and Munro* conclude that "any suggestion that jurors in rape cases can leave their personal prejudices and stereotypical preconceptions behind when they enter the courtroom" [19] is false. However, *Leverick* draws attention to overwhelming evidence that jurors take these myths into the court room.[20] It should be noted that in Turkish criminal justice system, there are no juries, no lay participation, and, thus, only legal professionals have the competence to participate in the legal proceedings of delivering justice. *Albeit* this does not mean that the traces of such common myths or misconceptions cannot be found in the courtroom.

To illustrate, the following case exhausted all legal remedies nationally and ended up before the Court of Cassation. The court of first instance noted that "considering the fact that the woman, only 18 years old, consumed alcohol excessively, was in a house with three men and the sincere confessions of the defendants that they had consensual sex with her, the fact that the victim's responsive behaviors started out of nowhere, starting to shout in a manner that could not be explained by the defendants *does not mean* that the act was carried out by force. The victim was excessively intoxicated. There may be dozens of reasons why someone who is so drunk may shout and react. As can be seen in ordinary life, someone who is drunk may swear at a passer-by for no reason, yell, make strange words. In a situation where brain functions stop under the influence of alcohol, abnormal behaviors are attributed to a certain reason. It cannot be expected, and it is normal for the accused to not be able to explain the responsive behavior of the victim. For this reason alone, it cannot be accepted that the defendants committed sexual assaults."[21]

The Court of Cassation, however, overruled the judgment by arguing that the existence of the consent cannot be proven through these presumptions, by referring to the Penal Code's definitions. This, indeed, can be considered as a success of the new penal code after 2005.[22] As a matter of fact, the sexual assault provision has no wording such as "non-consensual," "coercively" or "under force," and is, rather, defined as the act of "violating someone's bodily integrity through sex acts"[23] in Art. 102 of Penal Code.[24] This means that the existence of consent leads to the acquittal of the defendant. One can note that the change in the wording of the provision regarding sexual offenses, e.g., avoiding resistance and categorizing these crimes against individuals, rather than public morality, as a result of a paradigm shift in Turkish law in 2005, demonstrates how the influence of rape myths were lessened in comparison with the Penal Code.[25]

EVIDENCE LAW AND SEXUAL OFFENSES: AN OVERVIEW

A recent directive of the Ministry of Justice, dated 31 October 2022, titled *Criminal Investigations on Sexual Offenses* ranges the types of evidence in criminal investigations on sexual offenses for the judicial authorities to take into consideration "how and when the incident is to be reported to judicial authorities, with whom the incident is to be shared for the first time and how, in which physical and mental state the victim was for the first time he/she shared the incident with others, incident reports and records about arrest without warrant, medical reports, consistency among statements of victim, defendant, and witnesses, expert reports, whether there is hostility between the victim and defendant or not, the evidence collected from the house or workplace of defendant or victim, the images and messages collected from mobile phone or computer."[26]

Sexual offenses, especially in the form of sexual intercourse, are often committed within the closed or secluded places. As a consequence, in a wide range of cases, only the statements of the victim and the perpetrator appear as primary sources for criminal investigation authorities. Biological evidence, such as medical evidence that holds a high probative value,[27] does not always exist. As a matter of fact, once it becomes known by the people around the victim that a sexual offense has been committed, they may show a tendency to obscure it by the virtue of cultural factors and prevailing myths in that society. As a case point, when information—such as being a victim of sexual offenses—spreads, this may have the consequence for the victim to be revictimized.[28] Therefore, to find a direct witness in some cases will be a barely likely scenario. Particularly, providing evidence in sexual offenses, where the perpetrator is well-known by the victim, such as when it involves a spouse, partner or a relative is relatively more problematic.[29] The core problems in proving sexual offenses in Turkish law can be mainly divided into five categories as:

- Lack or insufficiency of biological (e.g., medical) evidence
- Lack or insufficiency of (direct) eyewitnesses
- Over-reliance on victim statement
- Consent as a subject of prove: resistance
- Proving sexual acts by differentiating sexual acts with/without contact

Despite the challenges in proving sexual offenses, the standard of proof does not change. In other words, there is no discrimination as to the type of crime regarding the application of *rules of evidence* and principles in Turkish criminal law. That being said, in criminal procedural law it is held that, *unus testis, nullus testis*,[30] a Latin expression for one witness is no witness at all, that therefore requires the corroboration of testimony in continental criminal procedural laws, which, as such, is susceptible to resulting in acquittals.[31] In Turkish criminal procedural law, this implies not only the corroboration of testimony, but also for all sort of evidence in reaching the judgment. That is to say, every corroborating and supporting evidence is to be sought, as such, there is a mandatory requirement for corroboration. Art. 217 of the Penal Procedure Code in 2005 reads:

- The judge is allowed to give a judgment only by basing the evidence that is brought to the hearing and discussed in his/her presence. These pieces of evidence are assessed by the judge based on his/her *free conscience.*[32]
- The charged crime shall be proved through any kind of legally obtained evidence.

Furthermore, where there is no other evidence but victim statement, the defendant is to be acquitted by virtue of the principle, *in dubio pro reo,* a Latin expression for in favor of the defendant in case of doubt as an outcome of *the presumption of innocence* that is enshrined in the Constitution, Art. 38.[33] The burden of proof is the obligation of the State, not the victim nor the defendant's duty. The Court of Cassation's argument as "absence of any reason for the victim to slander the defendant" in sexual offenses is criticized as it reverses the burden of proof, which is inconsistent with rules of evidence and principles in Turkish criminal law.[34] The problem of the high attrition rate in sexual offenses—in particular where the authorities fail to obtain evidence due to the ineffective criminal investigation—is 'resolved' by resorting to the principle of *in dubio pro reo* and, consequently, acquitting the defendant.[35]

Furthermore, the exclusionary rule in evidence law has been adopted in Turkish law in 2005 in both the Constitution (Art. 38/6) and the Penal Procedure Code (Arts. 217, 206, and 289).[36] As such, only the legally obtained evidence can be used in reaching the judgment, and any assessments to weigh the importance of the case in using an illegally obtained evidence is prohibited. This was an outcome reached by the ECtHR. Indeed, Turkish law of evidence has been radically altered by the case-law of the ECtHR.[37] To exemplify, when there is no medical evidence, the victim may look for methods to prove her victimization by recording the phone call, thereby violating the confidentiality of communication with the defendant, and then submitting it publicly to judicial authorities, which is prescribed as an offense in Art. 132/3 of the Penal Code. Because of the aforementioned Articles, this illegal evidence shall be excluded. However, the Court of Cassation accepts this sort of evidence obtained illegally, on the specific condition that it occurred in a spontaneous way and there is no other possibility of proving that the act was committed.[38]

On the one hand, proving sexual offenses has many obstacles and difficulties, and a system involving a sexual assault nurse examiner to obtain and preserve evidence properly before the criminal justice authorities, briefly known as SANE, as in the U.S.A., does not exist yet in Türkiye. Just recently, since 2019, the criminal law stipulates that the statements of the sexual assault victims (Art. 102/2 of Penal Code) are to be taken in a specialized center (Art. 236/6 of the Penal Procedure Code) that has been originally designed for taking statements of the child victims, called Çocuk İzlem Merkezi, briefly known as ÇİM.[39] On the other hand, the punishments of sexual offenses are quite high in Türkiye, which is criticized by scholars.[40] Therefore, this chapter considers the risk for both violation of the presumption of innocence and impunity of perpetrators of sexual offenses.

CONSENT AS AN OBJECT OF PROVE: RESISTANCE?

Sexual offenses provisions in the penal code represents a paradigm shift in terms of defining sexual offenses to protect individual sexual freedom and integrity rather than public morality.[41] Further, the outdated concepts such as "pudicity," "honor," or "virginity" are excluded from the legal provisions. Instead, objective criteria were applied in formulating these offenses in the Penal Code in Arts. 102–105.[42] One of these criteria comes in form of the element of the consent, which serves as a decisive element in regulating sexual offenses for the adult victims.[43] Traditionally, many jurisdictions require the resistance of the victim, as an indicator of non-consensual sexual act[44] just as the Turkish law did before 2005. As a matter of fact, the ECtHR, in 2003, concluded that:

> . . . [A]ny rigid approach to the prosecution of sexual offenses, such as requiring proof of physical resistance in all circumstances, risks leaving certain types of rape unpunished and thus jeopardizing the effective protection of the individual's sexual autonomy. In accordance with contemporary standards and trends in that area, the member States' positive obligations under Articles 3 and 8 of the Convention must be seen as requiring the penalization and effective prosecution of any non-consensual sexual act, including in the absence of physical resistance by the victim.[45]

The resistance of the victim is neither an element of crime nor an indicator of non-consensual sexual act in Turkish law after 2005. Accordingly, all sexual offenses are regulated on the basis/presumption of lack of consent.[46] That means: ". . . [T]he judge does not seek whether the act is non-consensual (the will of the victim is defeated or affected) or not, rather they must seek for whether the victim consented or not (the act is consensual or not). Therefore, it can be inferred that the Turkish law is closer to the 'only yes-means-yes model.'"[47] Prior to 2005, when sexual offenses in the penal code were categorized as crimes against public morality, the resistance was kind of a reflection of social norms as an obligation of the victim towards public.[48] However, even if these offenses had been categorized in the penal code as crimes against individual sexual freedom and integrity, the courts still sought the victim's resistance as an indicator of non-consensual sexual act. Consider, for example, the case below:

"The 24-year-old victim was allegedly sexually assaulted through the insertion of the male organ by a gynecologist to whom she went for a check up. The victim first reported the incident to her friend and then to the police on the same day. The defendant's sperm was found in the victim's vagina. Before this evidence was obtained, the defendant denied the rape allegations and then claimed that the victim had consented to intercourse. The final verdict was acquittal. Although the victim gave the statement before the prosecutor by saying that the action took place within her consent, which she later contradicted in the court by stating that she gave testimony in this direction because her family received 'hush-money' from the defendant. On the other hand, at the time of the incident, there were employees and other patients in the clinic including the mother of the victim, therefore, if she had shouted, she could have been heard. However, the victim did not show any reaction and made contradictory narratives about not shouting at different stages of the prosecution. To the Turkish Court of Cassation, when the defense and the entire scope of the case are taken into consideration, it is sufficient to acquit the defendant based on the lack of evidence that he had sexual intercourse by using force and threat on the day of the incident, instead of a verdict of conviction given by the court of the first instance."[49] One judge dissented by arguing that;

> . . . [R]emaining silent or not showing any resistance to the perpetrator cannot be considered as a consent alone. In other words, the fact that the victim does not show active resistance cannot be interpreted as consenting to sexual intercourse. The victim has no previous intimacy or romantic relation with the defendant, indeed. It is not a natural and an expected life experience for the victim, who cannot have any relationship other than the patient-doctor relationship with the defendant, to perform the sexual intercourse willingly during the medical examination on the treatment chair in the private clinic where she comes for control. If the sexual intercourse is consensual, it is naturally expected that the victim does not immediately blame the defendant.[50]

Notwithstanding, that a court seeks a resistance as an indicator of non-consensual sexual act may be inevitable, especially in cases in which the victim's mind changes during the sexual contacts. Although she/he may consent to it, in the latter moment they may want to withdraw, which requires certain active actions indicating consent is not any more present.[51]

What is more, the victim may not have resisted, because he or she was afraid of being confronted with lethal force by the defendant,[52] or he or she may have been duped into believing that no sexual assault occurred. Further, the supposition "if there is no resistance against the defendant, there is no rape" is also a rape myth, accordingly, in the case where the woman resists or escapes and thus sexual assault did not occur.[53] The Court of Cassation applies the criteria of "surmountable resistance of the victim" in cases of the perpetrator attempts to sexual assault. Because of the voluntary abandonment provision (Art.36 of Penal Code), if the perpetrator begins to directly commit the offense and is able to complete the offense without any circumstances beyond his or her control other than the victim's surmountable resistance, the perpetrator is not subject to a sexual assault's penalty. The perpetrator is only punished for the act as long as it constitutes a separate offense.[54]

The severity of the victim's resistance, on the other hand, is critical in determining whether the courts apply the voluntary abandonment provision or an attempt at sexual offense. According to another case before the Court of Cassation,[55] the defendant intrudes on the victim's house, where she, who is both deaf and mute, lives alone, and starts to take off her pajamas while he, the defendant, half naked and wearing only an undershirt, rubs the victim's breasts. Then the victim wakes up and punches the defendant, and he expresses himself in sign language since she is deaf, symbolizing a wedding ring and pregnancy. The victim grabs a knife and kicks the defendant out of the house. In this case, the Court of Cassation does not apply the voluntary abandonment provision since the defendant is naked, symbolizing pregnancy, which points out *mens rea* for sexual assault; however, he is incapable of completing the offense owing to the victim's active resistance.

THE SIGNIFICANCE OF CORROBORATION

To the claim of victim, she met the defendant on a dating website at 1:00 p.m. and at 3:00 p.m. on the same day, that they went to the defendant's house together with beer and cigarettes from the market after the defendant told her that he must drop by his house. The victim entered the house upon the insistence of the defendant, where the defendant attacked the victim by using force and threats inside the house and raped her anally, orally and vaginally for about two hours; that she was photographed against her will; and she then left and went to her home. The next day, the defendant persistently called her on the phone and sent her messages, after which she went to the police station, about 23 hours after the incident, and filed a complaint.[56] The data contained in the medical reports were limited, however. The defendant alleged that this was a consensual sexual intercourse. Notwithstanding this, the court of first instance convicted the defendant, and the Court of Cassation, first section and the assembly, respectively approved the conviction by stating that:

> It was determined that the victim gave detailed and consistent statements at all stages in a way that did not change in substance. There were many pornographic images showing their relations in a way that confirms the statements of the victim in the mobile phone, seized as a result of a duly search of the defendant. There were also the threatening text messages sent by the defendant to the victim, which were found in the examination on the phone of the victim. Since the findings in the report prepared by the hospital are in accordance with the allegations of the victim, there is no reason for the victim to slander the defendant, despite the defendant's statement in his defense, that he said that the bruise on his hand was made by his wife; the defendant divorced his wife in 2007, so such a bruise would not last until the date of the crime. Considering the fact that it is not possible to maintain its existence for four years together; it is to be accepted that the defendant committed crimes of sexual assault and deprivation of liberty.[57]

As this case properly portrays the significance of corroboration among obtained evidence, as in *he said—she said* cases, the victims' allegations become neutralized in judges' view, when the defendant consistently claims innocence. Absent ancillary evidence to support the victims' claims, be it because of the time and place of the incident or the fact that the victim waited too long to report, and thus all biological evidence was lost, the victim's claims are the only arrows pointing at the defendant. Therefore, the evidence at hand has to be concise, sincere, and corroborated. Corroborating evidence is evidence that strengthens or confirms the existence and veracity of already existing evidence.[58] It requires all evidence to be presented and discussed by all subjects of the case.[59] In sexual offense cases where there can be very limited evidence, the court is held to examine other aspects of the case more attentively to determine if the accusations are true. In this context, we will examine different sets of criteria the Turkish penal courts have adopted over the years and discuss whether they create a deeper problem within the evidentiary challenges these cases already exhibit.

Modus Operandi and Time Period for Filing a Complaint

Most commonly occurring behind closed doors, sexual assault cases often lack witness testimonies as evidence, as we discussed above. Therefore, in addition to the statements of the victim and the defendant, biological evidence plays a highly crucial role. However, when the victim defers in filing of an official complaint long enough, such that the gathering of samples of biological evidence becomes hopeless, then the court usually seeks a justified reason for the delay. Otherwise, it is deemed unreasonable in favor of the defendant. In one case where the victim had waited 23 hours after the alleged incident to file a complaint was deemed unacceptable because she was an educated and cultured woman.[60]

It affects the credibility of the victim's statement if there is a sustained period of time between the moment sexual assault occurs, and the moment the victim files a complaint about sexual assault with judicial authorities. In a case heard before the Court of Cassation, the victim was a college student, and according to her statement, the defendant raped her a couple of times between 1999 and 2013. The Court evaluates her statement as contrary to the natural flow of life since she, as a college student without any physical or mental disadvantage, is not incapable of appreciating the meaning of rape and resisting it. Although she gets rid of the possible pressure on the defendant following her move from France to Türkiye, she did not file any complaints against him for years.[61] However, this alone should not result in disregarding the victim's statement. Because the victim may be too afraid or ashamed to come forward as a "rape victim" in society,[62] or he or she may be too traumatized to realize the meaning of rape.[63]

In another case, however, the victim abstained from filing a complaint about the incident until her pregnancy became visible. The Court held by stating: ". . . On the other hand, the fact that the victim did not mention the rape incident to her family until her pregnancy was discovered does not indicate that the sexual intercourse was consensual. The fact that the victim's grandmother attacked her in front of the law enforcement officers after the victim's explanation of the incident, then the victim was pressured and threatened by her uncle and other relatives to change her statement in her favor, and that the victim was unable to stay in the village and had to take shelter with her mother after the incident was revealed, proves the justification of her predictions, which were the reason for her previous silence."[64] However, in a similar incident where the victim was 22 weeks pregnant before she filed a complaint had resulted in an acquittance of the defendant as it was seen as an act to legitimize her pregnancy to her community.[65]

Whether the Victim's Statements Are Consistent throughout the Processes

The other cumulative criterion that the courts examine in sexual assault cases is, whether the victim has made consistent statements about the incident throughout the entire procedure. Especially in cases where it is the victim's words against the defendant's, whichever party has consistently defended their statements has the case resulting in their favor. In He Said-She Said cases where the victim lacks consistency, the defendant may be acquitted by virtue of the *in dubio pro reo* principle.[66] In contrast, if the defendant's statements are lacking in consistency rather than the victim's as in the introductory case to this chapter, this may serve as one of the grounds leading to conviction.

When the "unreliable" personality of the victim combines with the contradictory and inconsistent statements of the victim, the court will disregard the victim's statement on the grounds of inconsistency. In one case before the Court of Cassation, the court of first instance applied twice to the psychiatry department of a university hospital for a medical report that indicated the victim's mental state. The expert physician diagnosed that the victim's statement is not reliable in the first report, and according to the second report, the victim's statement can be taken into account for undetailed information, but not for the ability to appreciate things in detail. Following the expert report, the victim's mother testified and said that "her daughter said she was not deprived of her liberty; she told the defendants she had nowhere to go, and upon her request, she went to their apartment, and also the ones in the house kicked her out." While this testimony is considered in combination with other statements by the victim's mother that her daughter tells her how she hallucinates and escapes from the house every time the door is open, the court applies the principle of *in dubio pro reo*.[67]

The courts question the reliability of the victim's statements and whether he or she is being manipulated by someone else in cases where the victim has mental problems or retardation. In one case before the Court of Cassation, the victim is mentally retarded with a 65 IQ score and has lived with her mother and stepfather for a long time. There are financial problems among the spouses. The victim claims that her stepfather forced her to anal intercourse against her consent; however, there is no medical report about this. In contrast to the medical report that diagnosed her mental state, which suggests that statements can be trusted in principle for her, the psychologist, who accompanies her during the interview claims that she is susceptible to manipulation. Aside from that, according to the victim's statement, the moment the defendant raped her was after she came from school, which was Saturday, when the school is not in session. According to the witness' statements, the relationship between the victim and defendant is a typical father-daughter relationship, and there is a dispute between the defendant and his wife, for which he filed a complaint against her. Moreover, she filed a complaint about rape while in pursuit of his complaint. The Court of Cassation takes into account the hostility between the victim's mother and the defendant and evaluates the doubt in favor of the defendant, as he consistently denies the accusations.[68]

Natural Flow of Life: No Previous Hostility between the Victim and the Defendant

It is useful to prospect a recent case, dating from 2020 where the victim has been working as a nurse in a private hospital for about three months, while the defendant was a health care provider in the same hospital. Regarding the claims of the victim, after leaving the urology surgery on the day of the incident, while they were passing by the sterilization room, the defendant said to the victim "Girl, I will assign you here. You can wash tools here." The defendant then suddenly took the victim's face in his hands and kissed her on the lips and neck, while she could not react to the defendant and started to laugh because she was upset, then she found herself in the sterilization room, where the defendant kissed her on the lips and neck by caressing her breasts and hips, then her genitals. The defendant attacked her for about 30–40 seconds, she then struggled and reacted to the defendant, and shouted "What are you doing? Get out of here! Let me go!" The defendant stopped attacking her when he heard the footsteps coming from outside the door. After the incident, the victim left the hospital with a half-day leave for special reasons permitted by a witness, the operating room supervisor. She then came to the hospital the next day and told another witness, who was working as the hospital chief physician, that she could not work this way and submitted a resignation letter, claiming that she had applied to the judicial authorities on the same day.[69] As for the defendant, he denied all allegations by saying that throughout the last months he had helped the victim and another nurse with the preparation of the operating table and tried to raise/develop them professionally, while showing more interest in the other nurse, who developed slower than the victim in this process. When the victim came out of the urology surgery on the day of the incident, he stated that she wanted to talk to him about her deficiencies in the surgery, that they talked about this issue, and that the victim had said "You are always dealing with the other nurse." The victim informed him that she will resign for family and personal reasons. He claimed that he did not know why the victim made such an accusation.[70]

At the end of the trial, the court of first instance acquitted the defendant on the grounds that no evidence other than the victim's statement exists, which was not supported by the statements by the only two witnesses. To the Court, there was no fear, panic, shame and anger in the victim's face and movements in the video recordings showing the exit of the crime scene.[71] The Court of Cassation, however, overruled the judgment by holding the victims' statement reliable for the following reasons: the victim's consistent narratives at the all stages of prosecution, in terms of how the incident took place, her leaving the hospital with half a day's leave after the incident, and telling the chief physician about the incident, giving a resignation letter when she understood that the hospital authorities were not going to act on the incident and filing a complaint about the defendant by applying to the judicial authorities in the evening hours of the same day; and for there being no hostility between the victim and the defendant, as would be required for the satisfaction of the offense of slander. As for the defendant's statements, the Court held them to unreliable by stating that the defendant and the victim entered the sterilization room at 13.41.45, stayed there for one minute and three seconds, the victim leaving first at 13.42.48 with no visible expressions of fear, shame or anger to which the defendant was not able to give any plausible explanation as to what they were doing there for one minute only, and the lack of resolution of the footage not being able to display the exact facial expression of the victim.[72]

Another remarkable case, from 2019, is where the Court of Cassation considers the fact of not being acquainted, as constituting a ground for the victim not slandering the defendant. In one case before the Court of Cassation of frotteurism on a bus, the defendant touched the victim's hip, and since they were on a bus and she was embarrassed to yell, but scolded him by saying, "What are you doing?" Neither biological evidence nor a medical report existed. The Court of Cassation reaches the verdict that this is a "he said—she said" case, however, since there is no acquaintance between the victim and the defendant nor any hostility, it upheld the conviction.[73]

In some cases, even sexual intercourse rests on the consent of both parties, on the grounds of prostitution. After the intercourse, the parties may end up in a disputed state due to the amount of money, and this may lead to the situation where the prostitute claims that it was rape. Apart from the fact that duress or resistance may not have existed in these scenarios, text messages, voice recordings, and images can be used to prove guilt. In one case before the Court of Cassation, the medical report detects no bruises or signs of attack on the victim's body; however, according to the voice record on the defendant's mobile phone, the victim says the sexual intercourse lasted more than half an hour and the defendant must pay 500 Turkish liras. Taking the voice record into consideration, the court applies the principle of *in dubio pro reo* and overturns the defendant's conviction.[74]

The Absence of Any Possible Reason for the Victim to Slander the Defendant

To measure the reliability of the victim statement, referring the absence of any possible reason for the victim to slander the defendant in sexual offenses serves as an additional standpoint to the Case-law by the Court of Cassation.[75] In particular, when the victim is a child, the Court adopts the approach that it is not possible for a child victim to be hostile to or slander the defendant due to his/her age.[76] However, this approach faces harsh criticism in the doctrine as the child victim may be misused as a tool by the adult, the parents, to mislead justice.[77]

What's more, in some cases, the fact that claiming of being victim of sexual offenses may impair the victim's own chastity and dignity is taken into account by the Court. Therefore, the Court values the statement of the victim, who does not have any claim of hostility to the extent that she should slander the accused on a matter of her own chastity and dignity.[78] However, chastity and dignity are quite abstract values that vary from one person to another. Establishing the existence of a previous hostility between the victim and the defendant by alleging sexual offenses at the cost of impairing own chastity and dignity is a legally unfounded judgment. Put differently, the defendant faces punishment through the statement of victim, i.e., the value of the victim.[79] To illustrate, consider the case below where the sexual acts are not to a degree to leave biological evidence, but only kissing or touching level, and absent of any eyewitness:

"A 32-year-old woman claims that her chief progressively changed his attitude towards her, as he told her 'I like you' and 'I love you.' Despite her warnings, he intensified these behaviors. When they were alone, he hugs, cuddles, and kisses her body parts by coercing her. This lasted for seven months. She applied for a change of working place, but her chief prevented this. She alleged, that he continued to coercively kiss and cuddle her through. Because of this exposure, she experiences migraine attacks, psychological problems and feels shame for her family. To escape from his sexual acts, she lied that she had a fiancé, which did not help at all. Finally, she disclosed the case to the head of office. When he is out office, she managed to file a complaint. He denied all allegations by saying that this is a plot against him, and she is an underqualified worker, thus he had a lot of problems with working with her. The defendant was convicted."[80] This conviction was approved by the Court of Cassation by stating in this case on which any eyewitness does not exist, a single and young woman cannot lie to slander the defendant on a matter of her own chastity and dignity. The defendant's statement was only focused on denial of charge, not any other aims were addressed.[81]

The Court of Cassation's argument of "absence of any reason for the victim to slander the defendant" in sexual offenses is criticized as it reverses the burden of proof, which is inconsistent with rules of evidence and principles in Turkish criminal law.[82] It implies that the defendant would have to prove that the victim has a reason to slander. However, the Turkish criminal procedure system is closer to the inquisitorial system on the adversarial- inquisitorial spectrum.[83] As a matter of fact, in seeking out evidence to find out the material truth, which is deemed as "overriding goal of the inquisitorial paradigm,"[84] proving is the duty of the criminal justice authorities, *inter alia,* public prosecutor at the pre-trial stage; the court or judge at the trial stage, as Art. 160/2 of the Penal Procedure Code reads as:

> In order to find out the material truth and conduct a fair trial, the public prosecutor is under the obligation to collect and preserve the evidence, which is both in favor of and against the suspect, as well as to protect the rights of the suspect through the means of the judicial law enforcement officers under his/her command.

The Court of Cassation, thus, expects from the criminal justice authorities to determine whether any previous hostility between the victim and the defendant exists or not.[85] The Court overruled the judgment by stating "that the hostility claim is to be evaluated together with the evidence to be collected."[86]

RELEVANT STATISTICS ON SEXUAL OFFENSES IN TÜRKIYE

Official statistics pertaining to sexual offenses, which are publicly available in Türkiye, are primarily obtained from the Ministry of Justice, called judicial statistics. It should be noted that these statistical data are not time series data, the Ministry of Justice publishes them annually by classifying them based on various criteria, mainly the relevant articles of every crime types from the penal code and other penal related side codes, regions and cities of Türkiye, gender and age of the perpetrator, etc.[87] In this respect, judicial statistics are presented in a detailed manner,[88] but on the other hand, they suffer from some deficiencies,[89] for example, information regarding perpetrators such as civil status, education and job etc. are not provided. Further, information related to the victims is scarce. The relationship between the victims and perpetrators are not provided either, which is of a particular significance in sexual offenses. Indeed, it is pointed out by attrition studies that the characteristics of the victims are the determining factors for prosecutors to proceed the cases.[90]

In an attempt to gain clear insight into the attrition rate in sexual offenses in Türkiye, the chapter considers the data over the last five years from 2017 to 2021, since the data of 2022 has not been published yet. As such, the chapter counts the number of cases, not the persons suspected or stand accused, since a single person may face multiple charges that implies multiple cases as a rule.

According to the data of the Ministry of Justice, in the period from 2017 to 2021, the total number of sexual offenses, which includes sexual assault (Art.

102), sexual abuse of children (Art. 103), sexual intercourse with a minor (Art. 104) and sexual harassment (Art. 105), increased steadily from 2017 to 2019, except for a slight decrease from 2019 to 2020. It can be inferred that the drop in 2020 was atypical, because no substantial amendment regarding sexual offenses had been enacted. Notwithstanding, an upward trend is again observed in the year 2021, which amounts to the same number of offenses as in 2019, as can be gleaned from Figure 8.1 below.

Regarding the commenced and finalized case numbers, apart from the year of 2020, the number of the commenced cases of sexual offenses gradually increased in the period from 2017 to 2021. There is an insignificant decrease of commenced cases in all categories of sexual offenses in the year of 2020. In terms of the range between the commenced and finalized cases, finalized cases data is higher than commenced case in that year, because the number of finalized case covers the previous years. Although this makes it hard to discern how many of those finalized cases are from the previous year or the year they are commenced, Table 8.1 allows us to draw an inference that some sexual offenses related cases proceed through all stages of criminal justice system, whereas remarkable amount of them dropped from the system. Table 8.1 below compares the number of the commenced and finalized cases.

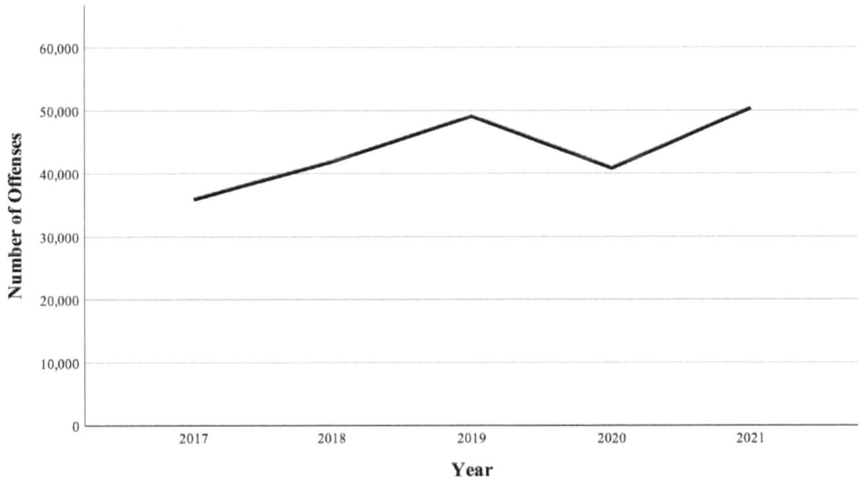

Figure 8.1. Line graph of total number of offenses in sexual crimes, by year. *Source*: Figure 8.1 is created by the Authors, with the data from Republic of Turkey, Ministry of Justice, General Directorate of Judicial Record and Statistics, Judicial Statistics (<https://adlisicil.adalet.gov.tr/Home/SayfaDetay/adalet-istatistikleri-yayin-arsivi> accessed December 18, 2022)

Table 8.1. Total number of crimes in commenced cases vs. total number of crimes in finalized cases, by year

	2017		*2018*		*2019*		*2020*		*2021*	
File status	*Commenced*	*Finalized*	*Commenced*	*Finalized*	*Commenced*	*Finalized*	*Commenced*	*Finalized*	*Commenced*	*Finalized*
Sexual assault (art. 102)	6621	7368	7602	8495	8896	9839	7553	8724	9341	9241
Sexual abuse of children (art. 103)	16348	18302	18290	20730	22689	25442	17948	19999	20459	19870
Sexual harassment (art. 104)	1295	1966	1520	3495	1630	2445	1211	3547	1738	1026
Sexual intercourse with a minor (art. 105)	11632	11228	14429	14143	15842	15310	14107	13748	18832	18218

Source: Table 8.1 was created by the Authors, with the data from Republic of Turkey, Ministry of Justice, General Directorate of Judicial Record and Statistics, Judicial Statistics (<https://adlisicil.adalet.gov.tr/Home/SayfaDetay/adalet-istatistikleri-yayin-arsivi> accessed December 28, 2022)

Table 8.2. Total number and types of decision/judgment, by year

YEAR	*Total Number of Decisions*	*Verdict of Non-prosecution*	*Filing of a Public Case*	*Conviction*	*Acquittal*	*Postponement of Announcing a Judgment*	*Lack of Venue—Lack of Jurisdiction*	*Other Decisions*
2017	89.725	40.169	32.687	23.742	8.600	3.928	16.855	9.192
2018	119.531	56.300	41.409	25.921	9.445	4.623	21.764	10.471
2019	138.527	64.972	48.044	29.892	12.473	5.804	25.501	12.812
2020	112.811	53.329	38.340	23.054	9.706	4.724	21.140	10.540
2021	127.297	59.268	43.015	36.016	14.803	7.666	25.008	13.674
Total	587.891	274.038	203.495	138.625	55.027	26.745	110.268	56.689

Source: Table 8.2 was created by the Authors, with the data from Republic of Turkey, Ministry of Justice, General Directorate of Judicial Record and Statistics, Judicial Statistics (<https://adlisicil.adalet.gov.tr/Home/SayfaDetay/adalet-istatistikleri-yayin-arsivi> accessed December 18, 2022)

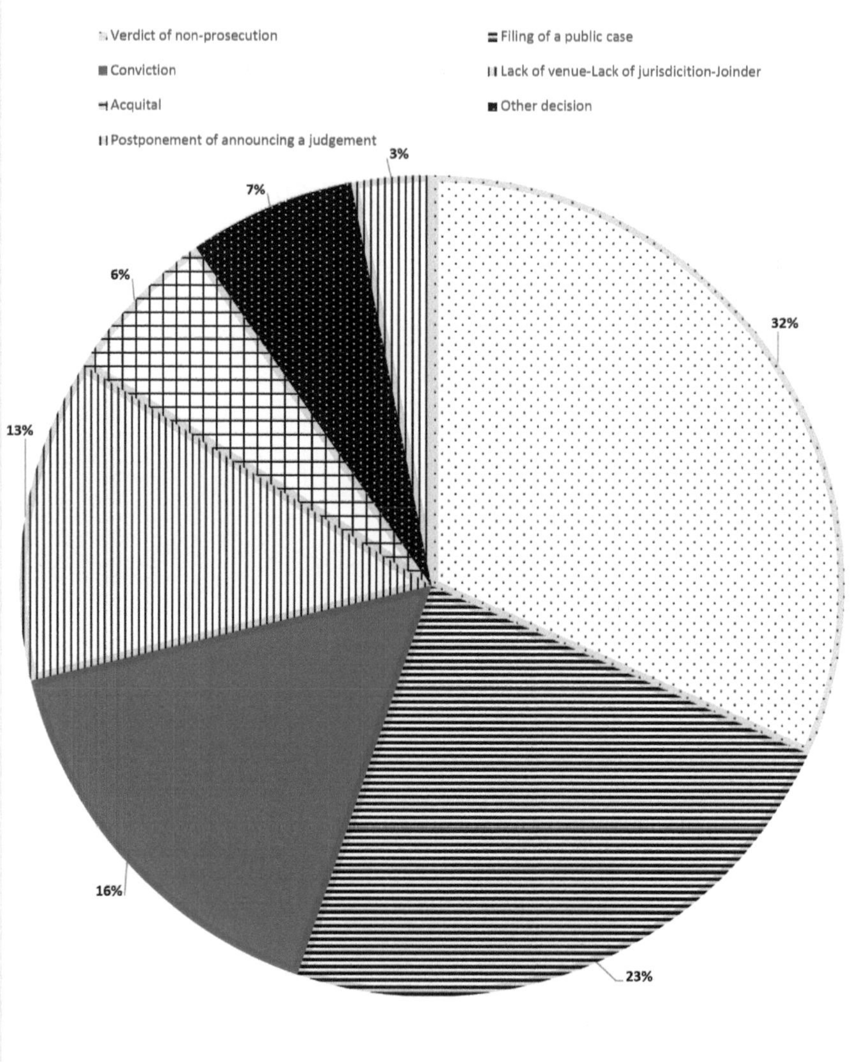

Figure 8.2. Total percentages of various decisions/judgments made for all types of sexual offences, from 2017 to 2021. ***Source*****: Figure 8.2 is created by the Authors, with the data Republic of Turkey, Ministry of Justice, General Directorate of Judicial Record and Statistics, Judicial Statistics (<https://adlisicil.adalet.gov.tr/Home/SayfaDetay/adalet-istatistikleri-yayin-arsivi> accessed December 18, 2022)**

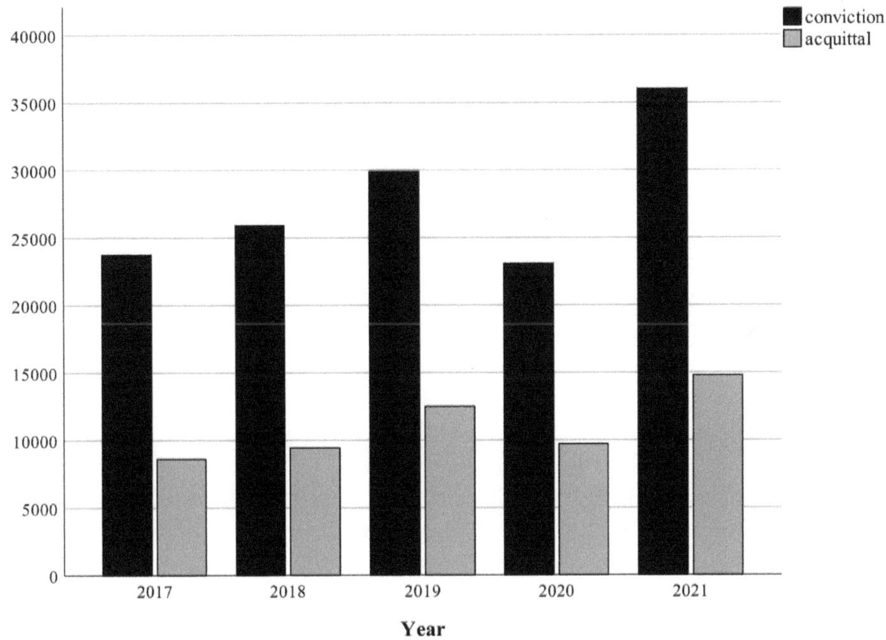

Figure 8.3. Bar graph of rate of conviction and acquittal, by year. *Source*: Figure 8.3 is created by the Authors, with the data from Republic of Turkey, Ministry of Justice, General Directorate of Judicial Record and Statistics, Judicial Statistics (<https://adlisicil.adalet.gov.tr/Home/SayfaDetay/adalet-istatistikleri-yayin-arsivi> accessed December 18, 2022)

Table 8.2 represents that at which stages sexual offenses omitted from the system since the types of decisions and judgments point to the authorized persons as public prosecutor, the court, and the judge in each stage of criminal procedure. It should be noted that the judicial statistics lack the data to demonstrate the area of attrition in sexual offenses, indeed. To illustrate, some questions such as to why the prosecutor made the decision not to prosecute; or as to the reason why some cases were dropped from the system, e.g., due to the withdrawal of the complaint by the victim or the lack of evidence, remain unanswered in the judicial statistics. Further, information on the cases which were reported, but were not even subject of any prosecution is not readily available from the police and public prosecutor office. Even if pointing out the major areas of attrition in sexual offenses in Türkiye is difficult, nevertheless, an inference can be drawn that the conviction rate is low over the last five years considering the period from 2017 to 2021 (see Table 8.2).

Considering the other type of decisions and judgments in terms of all types of sexual offenses throughout 2017 to 2021, the percentage of conviction is

16.3 whereas the acquittal rate is 6.36 percent. As it can be noticed in the Figure 8.2 below, 77.6 percent of judgments are ruled some other decision than conviction and acquittal. This data show that attrition rate in Türkiye from 2017 to 2021 is, indeed, rather high.

However, regarding comparison between the conviction and acquittal over the last five years, every year the number of conviction and acquittal rates are at least twice as different; and the former is higher than the latter. What becomes evident here is that in the case in which the other type of decisions and judgments are not taken into consideration, the last five years' comparison between the conviction and acquittal numbers alone shows the high rate of attrition in Türkiye (see Figure 8.2).

CONCLUSION

This chapter aimed to present the Turkish law approach and solutions on difficulties of proving sexual offenses (sexual assault against adults) through the current Turkish case-law, especially when the only evidence appears is the statement of the victim. That is well known as '"He Said—She Said" situation. That being said, the chapter first showed the necessity of being aware of the influence of rape myths' on proving as an unspoken impediment. In this regard, for Turkish law, an inference can be drawn that the change in wording in provisions on sexual offenses, e.g., avoiding resistance and categorizing these crimes against individual rather than public moral, as a result of the paradigm shift in Turkish law in 2005 led to decrease of the influence of rape myths in sexual offense cases in Türkiye. This can be a baby step improvement when considering rape myths' influence on case-law as a chronic disease of sexual offenses, though.

As a central point, the chapter highlighted the significance of corroborating all evidence. This was a result of the presumption that sexual offense cases, predominantly, have evidence beyond victim statements. Accordingly, corroboration may be found in many ways. These are: modus operandi and time period for filing a complaint (1), whether the victim's statements are consistent throughout the process (2), natural flow of life: no previous hostility between the victim and the defendant (3), and finally, whether there is any reason for the victim to slander the defendant (4). But it has four main examples applied in a cumulative manner by the Turkish case-law. To reach a judgment, the satisfaction of a single element is not sufficient. It cannot be concluded that the court's interpretation is towards victim blaming and the defendant friendly or vice versa. The courts are aware of the difficulties in proving sexual offenses and produce the case-based solutions. They do not offer any "one-size-fits-all" solution for every sexual offense case. This is because of the complexity of sexual offenses. As a matter of fact, even if they are stemming from the idea of corroborating evidence, because sexual offenses are intensely attached to society's value, culture, and many other understandings, we are to be very cautious. Having the perfectly designed legal provision does not suffice alone, rather it requires the criminological data and studies. Therefore, the chapter offers some data collected from judicial statistics over the last five years. Indeed, the comparison between the conviction and acquittal numbers during that period shows the high attrition rates in sexual offenses in Türkiye.

NOTES

1. Yargıtay, 9. CD., Date: 29.03.2021, E. 2021/3657, K. 2021/10428.
2. Ibid.
3. The dissenting opinion of the Judge, *Serdar Coşkun*, in Yargıtay, 9. CD., Date: 29.03.2021, E. 2021/3657, K. 2021/10428. To the dissenting Judge, thus, the defendant was to be acquitted. Because "the allegation that the accused kissed the lips while giving a facial care to the victim is not a proven fact. Even the victim's children, who were in another room at the scene of the incident, did neither see nor hear them. Complaint was not filed immediately, but six days later. Since there is no other evidence, but the victim's statement does, it is lawful for the suspect to be acquitted by interpreting the suspicion in favor of the defendant (*in dubio pro reo*) in cases where there is no other evidence suitable for concluding neither the existence nor the absence of it. There is no reason to favor the statement of the victim over the statement of the accused."
4. Renée L. Binder and Dale E. McNiel, '"He Said—She Said." The role of the forensic evaluator in determining credibility of plaintiffs who allege sexual exploitation and boundary violations' (2007) 35 (2) Journal of the American Academy of Psychiatry and the Law Online 211.
5. What is far worse than this, in some cases, even the victim statement may not exist, since sexual offenses are of an invasive nature, they cause various psychological consequences for victims and they cannot give a statement before the judicial authorities. See Jonathan Doak, Claire McGourlat and Mark Thomas, *Evidence in Context* (4th ed., Routledge 2015) 92.
6. Yargıtay, CGK, Date: 19.11.2013, E. 2013/14–326, K. 2013/461.
7. Jörg-Martin Jehle, 'Attrition and Conviction Rates of Sexual Offenses in Europe: Definitions and Criminal Justice Responses' (2012) 18 Eur J Crim Policy Res 145, 151.
8. Ibid. 145.
9. Ibid. 152.
10. Ibid. 151. See e.g., Andy Kaladelfos, 'Gender, Victimisation and Prosecutorial Discretion in the Attrition of Sexual Offenses' (2018) 5 law& history 86, 91 ff.

11. Doak, McGourlat and Thomas (n 5) 92.

12. Martha R. Burt, 'Cultural Myths and Supports for Rape' (1980) 38 (2) Journal of Personality and Social Psychology 217; Dana A. Weiser, 'Confronting Myths About Sexual Assault: A Feminist Analysis of the False Report Literature' (2017) 66 (1) Family Relations Special Issue on Feminist Framings of Sexual Violence on College Campuses 46, 47.

13. Kimberly A. Lonsway and Louise F. Fitzgerald, 'Rape Myths: In Review' (1994) 18 (1) Psychology of Women Quarterly 133, 135.

14. Ibid. 136.

15. 'Myths and Facts about Sexual Violence' <https://www.law.georgetown.edu/your-life-career/health-fitness/sexual-assault-relationship-violence-services/myths-and-facts-about-sexual-violence/> accessed January 13, 2023.

16. Fiona Leverick, 'What do we know about rape myths and juror decision making?' (2020) 24 (3) The International Journal of Evidence & Proof 255, 257.

17. See e.g., Kaylee Vance, Megan Sutter, Paul B. Perrin and Martin Heesacker, 'The Media's Sexual Objectification of Women, Rape Myth Acceptance, and Interpersonal Violence' (2015) 24(5) Journal of Aggression, Maltreatment & Trauma 569; Kristen C. Elmore, Tracy M. Scull, Christina V. Malik and Janis B. Kupersmidt, 'Rape Myth Acceptance Reflects Perceptions of Media Portrayals as Similar to Others, but Not the Self' (2021) 27(3–4) Violence Against Women, 529.

18. See e.g., Leverick (n 16) 257.

19. Louise Ellison and Vanessa E. Munro, 'Reacting to Rape: Exploring Mock Jurors' Assessments of Complainant Credibility' (2009) 49 (2) The British Journal of Criminology 202, 214.

20. Leverick (n 16) 273.

21. Yargıtay, CGK, Date: 22.11.2018, E. 2017/394, K. 2018/555.

22. Ayla Duygu Nasuhoğlu, 'Cinsel Saldırı Suçuna İlişkin Mitlerin Türk Ceza Hukukunda Yargı Kararlarındaki Olası Tesirlerinin Araştırılması' (Master Thesis, Istanbul University, İstanbul 2023) 119–120.

23. See Rahime Erbaş, 'Challenges in Regulating Sexual Offenses in Turkey' in Rahime Erbaş (ed), *Global Problems in Sexual Offenses* (Lexington Books, 2022) 9.

24. See heading in this chapter below as "Consent as an Object of Prove: Resistance?."

25. Nasuhoğlu (n 22) 104.

26. <https://magdur.adalet.gov.tr/home/TumHaberler/1> accessed January 15, 2023.

27. Biological evidence such a DNA analysis has a *high probative value* in the case-law *of Yargıtay*, the Court of Cassation in Türkiye. *For example,* in a case of 2013, the Court overruled the conviction by holding that a person cannot be convicted by basing only on her statements. In fact, however, there are cigarette butts found in the car used for committing the charged crime. Therefore, the court remarkably held if there is no other evidence except the accused statements, DNA samples of accused is to be analyzed (Yargıtay, 2 CD., Date: 25.02.2013, E. 2012/16734, K. 2013/3690)

28. Doak, McGourlat and Thomas (n 5) 92.

29. Fahri Gökçen Taner, *Türk Ceza Hukukunda Cinsel Özgürlüğe Karşı Suçlar* (2nd edn, Seçkin 2020) 262–263. See e.g., Rahime Erbaş, 'Evidentiary Challenges to an Effective Criminal Investigation for Domestic Violence: An Introduction,' in Valentina Bonini and Rahime Erbaş (eds) The *10th Anniversary of The Istanbul Convention: Italian–Turkish Conference* (Pisa University Press, 2021) 101.

30. Regarding the scope of Art.6 of the ECHR's in terms of this rule see F. Pınar Ölçer, 'Illegally Obtained Evidence in European Treaty of Human Rights (ETHR) Law' (2011) 40 (57) Annales de la Faculté de Droit d'Istanbul 65, 136, n.155.

31. Doak, McGourlat and Thomas (n 5) 252.

32. (Emphasis added). The term "free" necessitates a legal reasoning. Any assessment without reasoning is considered as an absolute ground for legal remedy to the Court of Cassation pursuant to Art. 289. See Metin Feyzioğlu and Fahri Gökçen Taner, *Ceza Muhakemesinde İspatın Ölçüsü Olarak Vicdani Kanaat* (2nd edn, Islık 2015) 324. As for the concept, *"free conscience,"* can be found within the Continental European approach. For example, in Italian, it is called as *"il libero convincimento."*

33. Feyzioğlu and Taner (n 32) 323.

34. Taner (25) 264.

35. Feyzioğlu and Taner (n 32) 344; Taner (25) 264.

36. Büşra Demiral Bakırman, 'Unlawfully Obtained Evidences in Turkish Criminal Procedure Law' (2015) 3 (1) Journal of Penal Law and Criminology 239, 244.

37. Rahime Erbaş, 'Pre-Trial Procedure in Turkey: Post-Salduz,' in Johnston E, Erbas R. and Jasinski D. (eds), *A Comparative Analysis of Pre-Trial Procedure in Europe: The Search for an Ideal Model* (Istanbul University Press, 2020) 201, 210 and 217.

38. Yargıtay 12. CD., Date: 21.11.2018, E. 2018/1722, K. 2018/9484.

39. Ezgi Çetiner, *Mağdur Beyanına Dayalı Hüküm Kurulması Bağlamında Nitelikli Cinsel Saldırı Suçunda İspat* (On İki Levha, 2022) 63.

40. Mahmut Koca and İlhan Üzülmez, *Türk Ceza Hukuku Özel Hükümler* (8th edn, Adalet,2022)372; Erbaş (23) 3.

41. Selman Dursun, 'Türk Ceza Hukuku'nda Cinsel Suçlara Genel Bir Bakış'(2014) 9 (24) Ceza Hukuku Dergisi 5; Erbaş (23) 6–7.

42. Erbaş (23) 7.

43. Ibid. 11–12.

44. See *M. C. v. Bulgaria,* App no 39272/98 (ECtHR, 4 December 2003) para. 156.

45. Ibid. para. 166.

46. Taner (25) 121; Durmuş Tezcan, Mustafa Ruhan Erdem and R. Murat Önok, *Teorik ve Pratik Ceza Hukuku* (18th edn, Seçkin, 2020) 400; Erbaş (23) 11. This way of regulation, "as an offense based on the absence of freely given consent without requiring the use of force," was appraised by The GREVIO report in 2018. See GREVIO's (Baseline) Evaluation Report (GREVIO/Inf(2018)6, 2018) 8 <https://rm.coe.int/eng-grevio-report-turquie/16808e5283> accessed December 22, 2022.

47. Erbaş (23) 12.

48. Taner (25) 117.

49. Yargıtay, 14. CD, Date: 25.3.2021, 2019/5092 E., 2021/2392 K.

50. Ibid.

51. Taner (n 25) 177–178.

52. Julia R. Schwendinger and Herman Schwendinger, 'Rape Myths: In Legal, Theoretical, and Everyday Practice' 1974 (1) Crime and Social Justice 18, 20.

53. This supposition is illustrated in a TV program in the USA with the words "A woman with her skirt up can run faster than a man with his pants down," Schwendinger and Herman Schwendinger (n 52) 19–20.

54. See e.g., Yargıtay, 9. CD., Date: 11.11.2021, E. 2021/1435, K. 2021/9173.

55. Yargıtay, CGK, Date: 29.06.2021, E. 2020/14–93, K. 2021/319.

56. Yargıtay, CGK, Date: 30.06.2015, E. 2014/810, K. 2015/268.

57. Ibid.

58. Steven H. Gifis, *Dictionary of Legal Terms* (5th edn, Barrons 2016) 283.

59. Yener Ünver and Hakan Hakeri, *Ceza Muhakemesi Hukuku* (19th eds, Adalet 2022) 91–92.

60. "According to the victim, on the date of the offense, she met the defendant on a dating site at 13.00 and at 15.00 on the same day, that they went to the defendant's house together with beer and cigarettes from the market after the defendant said that he had to drop by his house. The respondent entered the house upon the insistence of the defendant which then the defendant attacked the respondent by using force and threats inside the house and raped her anally, orally and vaginally for about two hours, that she was photographed against her will and then left and went home, and that the next day the defendant persistently called her on the phone and sent her messages, which she then went to the police station about 23 hours after the incident and filed a complaint. (. . .) According to the occurrence and the scope of the entire case; the fact that no findings of sexual assault were obtained through the medical reports issued against the participant, the defendant's defense that he had consensual sexual intercourse with the respondent at all stages of prosecution, taking into account the level of education and culture of the participant the fact that there was no justifiable and acceptable reason for not applying to the investigating authorities immediately after the incident, the pictures taken of the defendant's relationship and the insisting of the defendant to the respondent to come again, and the filing of complaint in the police station approximately 23 hours after the incident, the absence of conclusive, concrete and convincing evidence, it is free from all reasonable doubt that the accused had forced sexual relations and detained the respondent against her will" (Yargıtay, CGK, Date: 30.06.2015, E. 2014/810, K. 2015/268).

61. Yargıtay, CGK, Date: 30.3.2021.E. 2020/14–185, K. 2021/149.

62. Schwendinger and Herman Schwendinger (n 52) 18.

63. According to the individual application *B.A.* numbered 2016/9123 dated 18.05.2021 before Turkish Constitutional Court, the applicant filed the complaint with prosecutor office that she had been raped by eight men after eight months. After six months later the date alleged rape incident, she applied to the psychiatry department of a university hospital, she has been diagnosed depression and following visits and being applied MMPI and Rorschach tests, it revealed that she traumatized about 6 or 7 months ago, however she could gradually remember what happened because

of traumatic amnesia. For the full text of individual application *see*. Anayasa Mahkemesi, Application of *B.A.*, App no. 2016/9123, Date: 18.05.2021, para. 12.

64. Yargıtay, CGK, Date: 25.03.2003, E. 2002/5–324, K. 2003/55.
65. Yargıtay, 14.CD, Date: 20.06.2012, E. 2012/6645, K. 2012/7000.
66. Yargıtay 14.CD., Date: 02.06.2020, E. 2019/3764, K. 2020/2381; Yargıtay, 14 CD., Date:13.04.2021, E. 2020/3852, K. 2021/2924; Yargıtay, CGK, Date: 23.06.2020, E. 2019/14–357, K. 2020/313.
67. Yargıtay 14. CD, Date: 13.4.2021, E. 2020/3852, K. 2021/2924.
68. Yargıtay, CGK, Date: 01.12.2020, E. 2020/14–218, K. 2020/496.
69. Yargıtay, CGK, Date: 01.06.2021, E. 2019/38, K. 2021/233.
70. Ibid.
71. Ibid.
72. Ibid.
73. Yargıtay, CGK, Date: 23.03.2021, E. 2019/14–637, K. 2021/139.
74. Yargıtay 14.CD., Date: 02.06.2020, E. 2019/3764, K. 2020/2381.
75. Pınar Bacaksız and Tuğba Bayzit, 'Yargıtay'ın Cinsel Dokunulmazlığa Karşı Suçlarda İspata Yaklaşımı' (2019) 21 (2) Dokuz Eylül Üniversitesi Hukuk Fakültesi Dergisi 379, 398.
76. Yargıtay, 14. CD., Date: 23.06.2014, E. 2012/8212, K. 2014/8562. See e.g., Ersan Şen and Buğra Şahin, 'Yargıtay Kararları Işığında Cinsel Dokunulmazlığa Karşı Suçlar' (2022) 185 Terazi Hukuk Dergisi 118, 125.
77. Şen and Şahin (n 70) 125.
78. Yargıtay 14. CD., Date: 17.11.2014, E. 2014/7697, K. 2014/12784. See e.g., Çetiner (n 12) 94–95.
79. Şen and Şahin (n 70) 124–125.
80. Yargıtay, CGK, Date: 26.5.2009, E. 2008/5–187, K. 2009/128. See e.g., Ahmet Bozdağ and Kader Sarıusta, 'Ceza Yargılamasında Mağdurun Beyanı ve Delil Değeri' (2017) 8 (2) İnönü Üniversitesi Hukuk Fakültesi Dergisi 573, 596.
81. For critics see Bozdağ and Sarıusta (n 80) 596.
82. Taner (25) 264; Bozdağ and Sarıusta (n 80) 596.
83. Regarding the approach of the Turkish criminal procedure system see Erbaş (n 37) 209–210.
84. Doak, McGourlat and Thomas (n 5) 39.
85. Yargıtay 14. CD., Date:21.03.2016, E. 2016/2371, K. 2016/2708. See e.g., Şen and Şahin (n 70) 124.
86. Yargıtay 14. CD., Date: 14.01.2020, E. 2019/4645, K. 2020/381. See e.g., Şen and Şahin (n 70) 124.
87. Regarding judicial statistics and other official statistics resources in Türkiye see Galma Akdeniz, 'Homicide Trends in Turkey: A Review of Publicly Available Data' (2019) 7 (1) Ceza Hukuku ve Kriminoloji Dergisi-Journal of Penal Law and Criminology 1, 11.
88. Akdeniz (n 87) 11.
89. See e.g., Akdeniz (n 87) 16.
90. Kaladelfos (n 10) 91.

BIBLIOGRAPHY

Adli Destek ve Mağdur Hizmetleri Dairesi Başkanlığı, <https://magdur.adalet.gov.tr/home/TumHaberler/1> accessed January 15, 2023.

Akdeniz, G., 'Homicide Trends in Turkey: A Review of Publicly Available Data' (2019) 7 (1) Ceza Hukuku ve Kriminoloji Dergisi-Journal of Penal Law and Criminology 1–25.

Bacaksız, P., & Bayzit, T., 'Yargıtay'ın Cinsel Dokunulmazlığa Karşı Suçlarda İspata Yaklaşımı' (2019) 21 (2) Dokuz Eylül Üniversitesi Hukuk Fakültesi Dergisi 379–414.

Binder, R. L., & McNiel, D. E., '"He Said—She Said." The Role of the Forensic Evaluator in Determining Credibility of Plaintiffs who Allege Sexual Exploitation and Boundary Violations' (2007) 35 (2) Journal of the American Academy of Psychiatry and the Law Online 211–218.

Bozdağ, A., & Sarıusta, K., 'Ceza Yargılamasında Mağdurun Beyanı ve Delil Değeri' (2017) 8 (2) İnönü Üniversitesi Hukuk Fakültesi Dergisi 573–602.

Burt, M. R., 'Cultural Myths and Supports for Rape' (1980) 38 (2) Journal of Personality and Social Psychology 217–230.

Çetiner, E., *Mağdur Beyanına Dayalı Hüküm Kurulması Bağlamında Nitelikli Cinsel Saldırı Suçunda İspat* (On İki Levha, 2022).

Demiral Bakırman, B., 'Unlawfully Obtained Evidences in Turkish Criminal Procedure Law' (2015) 3 (1) Journal of Penal Law and Criminology 239–248.

Doak, J., McGourlat, C., & Thomas, M., *Evidence in Context* (4th edn, Routledge 2015).

Ellison, L., & Munro, V. E., 'Reacting to Rape: Exploring Mock Jurors' Assessments of Complainant Credibility' (2009) 49 (2) The British Journal of Criminology 202–219.

Elmore, K. C., Scull, T. M., Malik, C. V., & Kupersmidt, J. B., 'Rape Myth Acceptance Reflects Perceptions of Media Portrayals as Similar to Others, but Not the Self' (2021) 27(3–4) Violence Against Women, 529–551.

Erbaş, R., 'Challenges in Regulating Sexual Offenses in Turkey' in Rahime Erbaş (ed), *Global Problems in Sexual Offenses* (Lexington Books, 2022) 3–24.

Erbaş, R., 'Evidentiary Challenges to an Effective Criminal Investigation for Domestic Violence: An Introduction,' in Valentina Bonini and Rahime Erbaş (eds) *The 10th Anniversary of The Istanbul Convention: Italian – Turkish Conference* (Pisa University Press, 2021) 101–117.

Erbaş, R., 'Pre-Trial Procedure in Turkey: Post-Salduz,' in Johnston E, Erbas R. and Jasinski D. (eds), *A Comparative Analysis of Pre-Trial Procedure in Europe: The Search for an Ideal Model* (Istanbul University Press, 2020) 201–228.

Feyzioğlu, M., & Taner, F. G., *Ceza Muhakemesinde İspatın Ölçüsü Olarak Vicdani Kanaat* (2nd edn, Islık 2015).

Gifis, S. H., *Dictionary of Legal Terms* (5th edn, Barrons 2016).

GREVIO's (Baseline) Evaluation Report (GREVIO/Inf(2018)6, 2018 <https://rm.coe.int/eng-grevio-report-turquie/16808e5283> accessed December 22, 2022.

Jehle, J. M., 'Attrition and Conviction Rates of Sexual Offenses in Europe: Definitions and Criminal Justice Responses' (2012) 18 European Journal on Criminal Policy and Research 145–161.

Kaladelfos, A., 'Gender, Victimisation and Prosecutorial Discretion in the Attrition of Sexual Offenses' (2018) 5 (2) Law& History 86–110.

Koca, M., & Üzülmez, İ., *Türk Ceza Hukuku Özel Hükümler* (8th edn, Adalet 2022).

Leverick, F., 'What do we know about rape myths and juror decision making?' (2020) 24 (3) The International Journal of Evidence & Proof 255–279.

Lonsway, K. A., & Fitzgerald, L. F., 'Rape Myths: In Review' (1994) 18 (1) Psychology of Women Quarterly 133–164.

'Myths and Facts about Sexual Violence,' <https://www.law.georgetown.edu/your-life-career/health-fitness/sexual-assault-relationship-violence-services/myths-and-facts-about-sexual-violence/> accessed January 13, 2023.

Nasuhoğlu, A. D., 'Cinsel Saldırı Suçuna İlişkin Mitlerin Türk Ceza Hukukunda Yargı Kararlarındaki Olası Tesirlerinin Araştırılması' (Master Thesis, Istanbul University, İstanbul 2023).

Ölçer, F. P., 'Illegally Obtained Evidence in European Treaty of Human Rights (ETHR) Law' (2011) 40 (57) Annales de la Faculté de Droit d'Istanbul 65–153.

Schwendinger, J. R., & Schwendinger, H., 'Rape Myths: In Legal, Theoretical, and Everyday Practice' 1974 (1) Crime and Social Justice 18–26.

Şen, E., & Şahin, B., 'Yargıtay Kararları Işığında Cinsel Dokunulmazlığa Karşı Suçlar' (2022) 185 Terazi Hukuk Dergisi 118–128.

Taner, F. G., *Türk Ceza Hukukunda Cinsel Özgürlüğe Karşı Suçlar* (2nd edn, Seçkin 2020).

Tezcan, D., Erdem, M. R., & Önok, R. M., *Teorik ve Pratik Ceza Hukuku* (18th edn, Seçkin 2020).

Ünver, Y., & Hakeri, H., *Ceza Muhakemesi Hukuku* (19th edn, Adalet 2022).

Vance, K., Sutter, M., Perrin, P. B., & Heesacker, M., 'The Media's Sexual Objectification of Women, Rape Myth Acceptance, and Interpersonal Violence' (2015) 24(5) Journal of Aggression, Maltreatment & Trauma 569–587.

Weiser, D. A., 'Confronting Myths About Sexual Assault: A Feminist Analysis of the False Report Literature' (2017) 66 (1) Family Relations Special Issue on Feminist Framings of Sexual Violence on College Campuses 46–60.

Index

About the Editor

Dr. **Rahime Erbaş** is assistant professor of criminal law at Istanbul University. She studied law at Selçuk University and pursued public law master with the topic 'The Mandatory Reporting Duty of Healthcare Providers from a Comparative Law Perspective' at Istanbul University and at Justus Liebig Universität Gießen in Germany (Erasmus Exchange) in 2012. In 2019, she completed her PhD with the title 'Legal Duty to Act in Crimes of the Omission *(delicta commissionis per omissionem)* in the Turkish Penal Code' at Istanbul University. Dr. Erbaş carried out doctoral research at the Osnabrück Universität in Germany between 2016 and 2017 and has been a visiting scholar at the Max Planck Institut in Freiburg (2019), Zürich Universität (2020) and Alma Mater Studiorum– Università di Bologna (2023). She has four edited books: E. Johnston, R. Erbaş and D. Jasinski, A Comparative Analysis of Pre-Trial Procedure in Europe: The Search for an Ideal Model (Istanbul University Press, 2020) and V. Bonini and R. Erbaş, The 10th Anniversary of the Istanbul Convention (Pisa University Press, 2022), the third and fourth books as sole editor, Global Problems in Sexual Offenses (Lexington, 2022) and Combatting Violence against Women from a Criminal Law Perspective (Turkish: Adalet, 2022). She is section editor at *Journal of Penal Law and Criminology*. Further, she serves as an Editorial Board Member of *Women's Studies International Forum*, an Elsevier journal.

Her research interests focus on the substantive part of criminal law, criminal procedure law, medical criminal law, restorative justice, sexual crimes, and violence against women. She speaks Turkish (native language), English, German, and Italian.

Rahime lives in İstanbul and is very passionate about travelling.

About the Contributors

Miguel Lorente Acosta, associated professor in the School of Medicine of the University of Granada (Spain), advisor of the Equality, Sustainability and Inclusion Vice-rectorate of the university, PhD in Medicine and Surgery (graduated with honors), Specialist in Legal Medicine, Master in Bioethics and Law (University of Barcelona), and Forensic Doctor. He works and research on interpersonal violence and, specially, on violence against women and gender-based violence. He also works on masculinity and how men identity and androcentric culture are related with violent and power behaviors. As a consequence of his work, he has collaborated as an expert with the United Nations, WHO, EIGE (EU), EC and other organisms and institutions. He has occupied political positions related to his work, being Delegate of the Government for Gender-based Violence in the national Government from 2008 to 2011. He has published more than eighty scientific papers in national and international journals, and has written nine books, basically on violence against women and masculinities. He also has two blogs, one, "Autopsia" ("Autopsy") related to VAW, equality and social problems related; and the other, "Cardiopatía Poética" ("Poetic Cardiopathy") on poetry, his other passion.

Ahsen Akdemir is a research assistant at Istanbul Medeniyet University in the field of Criminal and Criminal Procedure Law. She graduated from University of Marmara, Faculty of Law with an honors degree in 2020 after a one-year exchange program in Paris V René Descartes University in 2018. Currently studying in Istanbul University for her master's degree in Criminology and Criminal Justice, she focusses on the criminalization of violence against women as a separate offence in her thesis. Relating to research she conducted 2021 on online violence against women, she has one published journal article in Dokuz Eylül University Law Faculty Journal titled "A Phenomenological Study On The Typology Of Violence Actions Performed Against Women In Cyber Environment And Their Perpetrators."

Dr. sci. **Ena Kazić-Çakar** is acting dean and associate professor at the Faculty of Law of the International University of Sarajevo, in the scientific area of Criminal Law where she teaches at both undergraduate and graduate study levels. She completed her undergraduate and graduate legal studies, including her Ph.D., at the Faculty of Law of the University of Sarajevo. She obtained outstanding success during the First and Second Cycle at the Faculty of Law of the University of Sarajevo, as the best student in her cohort for what she received two gold medals. She continued her professional training in various types of seminars, international scientific conferences, and work in practice. Her research currently addresses topics of sexual violence prevention, corruption prevention and restorative justice. She was a coordinator of a national project about the application of restorative justice in Bosnia and Herzegovina and a national consultant/expert for Bosnia and Herzegovina in the same field. She received several prestigious summer scholarships for scientific development abroad. Dr. Kazic Çakar co-authored several books in the criminal law area, including "Sexual Violence in the Contemporary Criminal Law" (2020), "The Application of Educational Recommendations as a form of Restorative Justice in Canton Sarajevo in 2012-2017" (co-author, 2019), and is an author of many scientific papers published in indexed publications.

Selen Çakırhan graduated from Boğaziçi University psychology department in 2021 and is pursuing a criminology and criminal justice master's degree with the topic "Psychopathology and Life History in Sexual Offenses." She aims to examine the psychological factors in sexual crime behaviors and the effects of traumatic life events experienced in childhood and early youth on these factors from the perspectives of criminology, law, and psychology. She has one article published: 'Kadına Yönelik Şiddette Uzlaştırma Mümkün Olabilir mi? Alternatif Bir Uzlaştırma Modeli Olarak Brezilya Örneği' in Rahime Erbaş (ed), Ceza Hukuku Perspektifinden Kadına Yönelmiş Şiddetle Mücadele I (Adalet 2022) 79–104.

Neslihan Can is a research assistant in the Department of Criminal and Criminal Procedure Law at Recep Tayyip Erdoğan University Faculty of Law in the meantime, a PhD candidate in the Istanbul University Institute of Social Sciences Department of Public Law. She graduated from Istanbul University Faculty of Law in 2017 and pursued a public law master's with the topic 'The Protection of Personal Data Processed by Law Enforcement and Judicial

Authorities' at the same university. Her areas of research include medical law and ethics, human rights law, and women's rights. Currently, she works on so-called "criministrative law" where criminal law and administrative law intersect before regulatory agencies on administrative fines' practices.

Lena Gmelin, mag. iur., is a research assistant at the Chair of Criminal Law, Criminal Procedure, Comparative Criminal Law, Medical Criminal Law, and Legal Theory of Prof. Dr. Liane Wörner, LL.M. (UW-Madison) at the University of Konstanz since April 2021. Following her undergraduate law studies at the University of Konstanz, she opted for the criminal law specialization offered there (Criminal Justice: Economic Criminal Law, Criminology, Europeanisation and Practice). In 2020, she completed her studies with the First State Examination in Law. Parallel to her studies, she worked in a Constance law firm with a special focus on criminal defense from 2018 to 2021. In her doctoral studies at the chair of Prof. Dr. Wörner and, as part of her academic work and her dissertation project, she is working on gender-specific issues of criminal law, in particular gender-specific homicide (femicide).

Fiona Leverick is professor of criminal law and criminal justice at the University of Glasgow. She has undertaken a major study of mock jury decision-making for the Scottish Government (with Ipsos MORI Scotland, James Chalmers, and Vanessa Munro), which reported in October 2019. Other recent research projects include Resorting to Crime: The Practice of Criminalization (a project investigating patterns of criminal offence creation from the 1950s to the present day) and Post-Corroboration Safeguards (a project exploring the causes of wrongful conviction and the safeguards that might be necessary to introduce in Scots law following the abolition of the requirement for corroboration in criminal cases). Fiona Leverick has authored three books on criminal law: the fourth edition of Gerald Gordon's The Criminal Law of Scotland (with James Chalmers, SULI/W. Green, 2017); Killing in Self-Defense (Oxford University Press, 2006); and Criminal Defenses and Pleas in Bar of Trial (with James Chalmers, SULI/W. Green, 2006). She has published over thirty papers in peer reviewed journals and has informed policy on the prosecution of sexual offences in the United Kingdom.

Dr. **Elena Martínez García** is full professor in civil and criminal procedural law at Valencia University (Spain).She defended her doctoral thesis on arbitration and mediation in Intellectual Property (2000). She has been a fellow of the German Alexander von Humboldt Foundation (2011-2013) in Germany by Prof. Vogel (München Universität). She has done several research stays at the World Intellectual Property Organization, at New York University, Oxford University, Center for Comparative Law of Lausanne (Switzerland). Dr. Martínez García a specialist in processes for violence against women and also in the illegality of evidence and transnational evidence. These main lines of research are accompanied by numerous publications, national public funding and numerous European collaborations. She has recently completed the task of the position of Vice Chancellor for Equality, Diversity and Sustainability in the Government Team of the University of Valencia.

Dr. **Dennis Martinsson** is an assistant professor in law at Stockholm University. He studied law at University of Auckland, Stockholm University and University of Iceland. In 2016, he completed his LL.D. thesis with the title 'Mistake of Law' (in Swedish: Om straffrättsvillfarelse). His research interests are broad and include, for instance, the general part of criminal law, criminal law and policy and the post-conviction review process.

Dr. **Marta Palmisano** earned a master's degree cum laude in Criminal Law at the University of Palermo in 2013. She attended a Specialization Course in Human Rights in Rome and in 2015 she obtained the diploma at the School of Specialization in Legal Professions (University "La Sapienza," Rome). Since 2017 she is lawyer. She was winner of the Cassini Call for Proposal 2017 and she collaborated with the University of Palermo, the Institut Français and the French Embassy in Italy in order to organize the international conference "Environmental crimes and liability of public and private bodies. Italian and French law system." In the same year she won the Falcone Borsellino Scholarship aimed at conducting research on organized crime. In 2017/2018 she was visiting scholar at the Max Planck Institut für Ausländisches und Internationales Strafrecht in Freiburg (Germany). In 2019 she obtained her Ph.D. in Criminal Law at the University of Palermo. Since 2019 she is nominated "Criminal Law Expert" at the University of Palermo. In 2020/2021 she attended an Internship at the General Secretariat— Presidency of the Sicilian Region. She also worked at the Programming Department—Presidency of the Sicilian Region, dealing with European projects. In 2022 she was selected to work at the Ministry of Ecological Transition in Rome. In 2023, she was selected for a research grant to collaborate on research activities at the University of Turin. Her main research interests include organized crime, gender-based violence, corruption, liability of legal persons and environmental law.

Dr. **Lucia Parlato** is full professor of criminal procedure at the University of Palermo (Italy), Department of Law. Her research interests cover victims' protection; the right of defence; diversions tools; and digital evidence. She has received various fellowships (DAAD, MPI, etc.) and has been spending several research periods at the Max Planck Institute in Freiburg since 2001. Thanks to her international academic upbringing, she has developed a rich comparative approach and a special attention to supranational sources. She is the author of two books, respectively, on La rifusione delle spese legali sostenute dall'assolto (2018, Padova) and Il contributo della vittima tra azione e prova (2012, Palermo). Among the numerous papers she has published, the most recent focus on restorative justice; reopening of criminal trials after convictions by the ECtHR; online investigations; the particular tenuousness of the offence; the probation; victims' vulnerability; migrants' rights in criminal proceedings. Since 2020 she has been teaching in international online courses organized by the University of Berkeley. She has been also collaborating with other foreign universities: among these, the University of West Bohemia and the Universities of Vienna, Munich, Freiburg im Br., Passau, and Bremen.

Dr. **Armando Saponaro** is associate professor of criminology, Department of Educational Sciences, Psychology and Communication, University of Bari Aldo Moro. He studied Law at University of Bari "Aldo Moro" and completed his PhD in the field of Criminology, Criminal Law, and Procedure at same University in conjunction with University of Bologna about the issue of Criminological expertise in the Italian Criminal Procedure Code, doctoral thesis then published as monograph. He studied "English legal methods," at Cambridge University and "Criminal Justice and Criminology," at London School of Economics and Political Science, UK. He was lecturer in Criminal Law at University of Bari and taught many postgraduate courses on "Victimology and Victim Assistance," at Tokiwa University Japan, University of Central Florida, Orlando, Florida, and Interuniversity Centre, Dubrovnik. In 2004, he authored one of the few monographs published in Italy on victimology: Vittimologia. Origini, concetti, temi, (Giuffrè, Milano). He has published many papers in the fields of criminal victimization, the criminal justice system, and the sociology of deviance. Among his main contributions: in the field of theoretical victimology, he has shown how its development reversed main sociological theories about deviance to the victim perspective (2014 Victimology and theoretical development: future horizons through the lens of history) and he has recently elaborated the original construct of counter-stigma or stigma-phobia as feature of late modern societies in the field of sociology of deviance (2023 Stigma and counter-stigma in contemporary society in press).

Dr. **Elisa Simó Soler** is a postdoctoral researcher at the University of Valencia (Spain) currently doing a research stay at the University of Buenos Aires (Argentina). In 2022, she completed her PhD in gender stereotypes in the criminal justice system. Particularly, she studied rape cases and the use of Artificial Intelligence systems to detect stereotypes. She was a member of a research group which carried out a study on violence against women from a legal perspective in collaboration with the Regional Ministry of Justice. She has published papers and book contributions and she has participated in seminars and congresses focused on gender-based violence, artificial intelligence, and recently planetary defense. She was granted to do an online course at the Massachusetts Institute of Technology about Machine Learning: Technology in decision-making. Dr. Simó carried out an online research stay at the University of Pisa, and she did a research stay at the Max Planck Institute for Comparative Public Law and International Law in Heidelberg from July to October 2021. She is a member Knowledge Generation Project "Keys to a digital and algorithmic justice with a gender perspective" (PID2021-123170OB-I00) and Research Project "Building consensus for a sustainable future: Anticipatory governance and administrative foresight (PROFUTURE)" (PID2020-116401GB-I00). She speaks Spanish, English, French, and Catalan.

Hannah Wörner has been studying law at Humboldt University in Berlin since 2019. Starting in the second semester (2020), she works as a student assistant at the chair of Prof. Dr. Luís Greco for criminal law, criminal procedure, international criminal law, and criminal theory. In May 2022, she represented Humboldt University in the Criminal Law Mootcourt with three other students. In September 2022, she completed her major with her student research project on the criminal liability and punishability of verbal sexual harassment. She is now in preparation for the first state law exam.

www.ingramcontent.com/pod-product-compliance
Ingram Content Group UK Ltd.
Pitfield, Milton Keynes, MK11 3LW, UK
UKHW041835031026
15587UKWH00002B/791

9 781666 925135